Rise from the Ashes

The Spiritual Path to a Smoke-Free Life

Gary H. Peck

Rise from the Ashes

ISBN-10:1482060841
ISBN-13:978-1482060843

Table of Contents

Rise from the Ashes

Preface

    My motivation in writing this book is twofold: It comes from being a former smoker, and more importantly it comes from the countless number of good people I have met over the years - and in fact continue to meet on a daily basis - who struggle to break free from the habit and addiction of smoking. My inspiration comes from my precious wife Linda who has spent many years engaged in smoking intervention counseling with patients in the hospital setting. Her tireless work has been under-appreciated and has largely gone unrecognized.

    I myself am a clinical specialist in the pulmonary department of a large metropolitan hospital. I have been a registered respiratory therapist for over thirty years. My days are divided between pulmonary function testing, pulmonary rehabilitation, and smoking intervention. The majority of patients I work with are either active smokers or former smokers. Nearly every day one of my oxygen-dependent patients will make the wistful remark, "If only I had stopped smoking earlier in life!" Back in the 1980's after years of working to treat the effects of smoking, I became interested in prevention. I received training to become a smoking cessation facilitator, and had the opportunity for several years to conduct smoking cessation workshops in hospital and workplace settings. Then in the 1990's my career route took a change. For a couple of years I worked as the associate editor of the journal RESPIRATORY CARE. I then returned to school – Ashland Theological Seminary - to earn a master's degree with an emphasis in spiritual formation. Subsequently, I became an ordained minister and served in the pastorate for eleven years. During the majority of my pastoral ministry years I continued to work bi-vocationally in the field of respiratory care.

    Several years ago, while I was still in ministry, my wife Linda was asked by our district superintendent if she would be willing to put together a continuing education workshop to help pastors understand nicotine addiction and smoking intervention. She in turn encouraged me to dust off my former interest and expertise in smoking intervention and to assist her in putting together the material for the workshop and ultimately in co-facilitating. It is interesting to note that just leading up to this time, I conducted a funeral for a beloved member of my congregation who had succumbed to lung cancer. He had been a long-time smoker, but had always kept his habit on the 'down-low' because he knew it was not condoned by the church. He had recently retired, but still led an active lifestyle. He would voluntarily mow the acres of grass that surrounded the church on a weekly basis; and in the winter he would come early on Sunday mornings to make sure the snow was shoveled from the church walk-ways - so that the elderly parishioners wouldn't slip and fall. But, then came the diagnosis of cancer. Ultimately his active life of service was cut short. During the months of chemotherapy and radiation, I would visit him and I learned to appreciate his deep faith and character. He stoically accepted his fate and acknowledged the role that his own smoking had played in the development of his cancer. Although I had only known him for a few short years before his death, I remember at the time wishing that I had been more forthright in speaking with him about his smoking habit earlier. I wondered to myself what might have happened if a spiritual approach to smoking cessation had been made available to him years earlier – if he had received the appropriate counsel and support, and had discovered for himself the spiritual resources necessary to rise above his addiction and habit.

For years, Linda had lamented over the lack of a spiritual component in the conventional methods of smoking intervention being used. The workshop we ended up giving for the district pastors gave us an opportunity to address the spiritual side of tobacco dependence. The following year I ended up stepping out of the pastoral ministry and assuming the full-time position at the hospital, which I presently hold. I have subsequently received additional in-depth training to become a certified tobacco treatment specialist and have once again actively resumed my role as a smoking cessation facilitator. Linda has unfortunately had to step out of the workplace setting for a while. She was diagnosed with acute myloid leukemia back in the summer of 2010, and as I begin to write is recovering from a bone-marrow transplant which she had in January of this year, 2011.

So, it is on behalf of Linda, my beloved patients, and my former parishioner that I carry the torch of smoking intervention. During an extended family medical leave from work, which I took to care for Linda during the critical 100-day period post-transplant, I was able to devote time to revisit the spiritual side of nicotine addiction and to write this manuscript. It is my prayer that this book will offer new hope to those weary in their unsuccessful attempts to break free from nicotine addiction. May you, the reader, find that it is indeed possible to rise from the ashes of the smoking habit!

Rise from the Ashes

Introduction

In the research literature you will find something referred to as the "Stages of Change Model." With regards to an addictive behavior or habit, people are usually in one of six stages: *Pre-contemplation* (not ready to quit); *Contemplation* (thinking about quitting); *Preparation* (ready to quit); *Action* (quitting); *Maintenance* (staying quit); *Termination* (living quit). The Christian mystical traditions also speak of stages: Awakening, Conversion, Purgation, Illumination, and Union. As a person moves through these stages he/she is growing stronger spiritually, becoming more centered upon the Divine. While it may be true that usually the spiritual stages are representative of a person's life journey as a whole, they may also represent the changes necessary for a person to move from one unique area of brokenness to a place of healing, freedom, and life. I think that as you read on you will find these psychological and spiritual models of change complement one another.

This book, consisting of forty-nine chapters, can be read one chapter a day over the course of seven weeks, or it can be spread out over a longer period of time. The pace you set is up to you; the important thing is not the speed with which you travel, but that you persevere towards the desired destination. A journey of spiritual transformation awaits you - a way of life beckons that can lead to freedom!

Prior to a spiritual awakening a person is in a state of slumber or ignorance; this may be analogous to an addicted person in the pre-contemplation stage, who is in denial – i.e. content in his or her dysfunctional habit. It is probably safe to assume that because you are holding this book in your hands you are already in the contemplation stage with regards to your smoking habit. You have awakened to the fact that smoking is dangerous to your health and wellbeing; you are painfully aware of the rising monetary costs of smoking; and you are finding it increasingly difficult to smoke when and where you want to. If this is true of you then you may certainly skip over the first chapter on pre-contemplation. However, if you are not yet convinced of the need to quit smoking, or if you are in need of bolstering your resolve to quit, then I encourage you to read on. The first chapter is for you.

Rise from the Ashes

Section I:

Pre-Contemplation (Not Ready to Quit)

Rise from the Ashes

Chapter 1

A Nightmare during the Slumber of Pre-Contemplation

What I am about to share with you may be akin to the makings of a nightmare intended to lovingly jolt you awake from your slumber – to move you beyond the pre-contemplation stage with regards to smoking.

Did you know that smoking is considered by the World Health Organization (WHO) and the Centers for Disease Control (CDC) as the single most preventable cause of poor health in the world?[1] An estimated 4.2 million premature deaths per year worldwide are attributed to tobacco?[2] In the United States, cigarette smoking is responsible for about one in five deaths annually, or about 438,000 deaths per year.[3]

Are you aware that cigarettes have not historically been classified as a food, drug, or hazardous substance?[4] This means the tobacco industry has not been required to disclose to the public what is in their products, even though according to the American Lung Association (ALA), "Cigarette smoke contains over 4,800 chemicals, 69 of which are known to cause cancer."[5] What are some of these chemicals, and where are they normally found? How about: Acetone (found in paint stripper); Ammonia (floor cleaner); Arsenic (rat poison); Butane (lighter fluid); Cadmium (car batteries); Carbon Monoxide (car exhaust); DDT (insecticide); Hydrogen Cyanide (gas chambers); Methanol (rocket fuel); Napthalene (moth balls); Toluene (industrial solvent); and Vinyl Chloride (plastics) – to name just a few!

If that isn't nightmarish enough, radioactive elements are thought to be absorbed by tobacco plants from the fertilizer and from the soil, air, and water. Lighting up the cigarette fires these particles into insoluble particles, which in turn are inhaled deep into the lungs. From the lungs they enter the bloodstream and travel throughout the body.

It is no surprise that smoking has increasingly been linked to the development of a wide array of medical disorders. As a smoker you should be aware that chronic obstructive lung disease (COPD), i.e. emphysema and chronic bronchitis; lung cancer; coronary heart disease (CAD); and stroke are not the only ominous villains waiting in ambush for you as you travel down tobacco road. According to the CDC, smoking may also be a contributing factor to the development of the following types of cancer: bladder, cervical, esophageal, renal, laryngeal, oral, pancreatic, pharyngeal, stomach, uterine, and acute myeloid leukemia.[6] The American Cancer Society (ACS) states that "smoking causes an increased risk of macular degeneration, one of the most common causes of blindness in older people."[7] Cigarette smoking has even been linked to hearing loss, and osteoporosis in women.[8] [9] [10]

Perhaps you are someone who has already developed significant smoking-related illnesses. It is not just a threat - it is a present reality! You may rationalize to yourself that it is too late to quit smoking. But, this is not true. Continuing to smoke will just further aggravate your symptoms and hasten the progression of your disease.[11] [12] [13]

You should also be aware that cigarette smoke can interfere with medications that you may be currently taking for a variety of medical conditions. According to the U.S. Department of Health and Human Services, smoking may inhibit or reduce the effect of some of the following medications: analgesics, anti-anxiety agents, heparin, phenothiazines, propranalol, and theophylline.[14]

In addition to the deleterious effect that smoking has upon your own health, you need to consider how your smoking may be adversely affecting the health of those around you (e.g. the loved ones who share your home).[15] Persons regularly exposed to second-hand smoke are at an increased risk of developing smoking related illnesses. In addition to the side-stream smoke coming off of your cigarette which others have to breathe, there is something referred to as third-hand smoke! It is the residue of poisonous chemicals from smoke that settles into the carpets, drapery, and furniture which in turn can be absorbed into the skin. You should also contemplate how your behavior may be influencing the precious children growing up in the shadow of your example.

You should also take stock of the monetary cost of smoking. The price of cigarettes is likely to continue to rise in the future. Have you ever sat down and totaled up how much you spend on cigarettes per month or per year? How about projecting over the course of ten years? You may be surprised! To provide an example, let's just say you smoke 1.5 packs per day. In the near future if not already you could be spending approximately $10/day on your habit. That amounts to $36,500 in ten years going up in smoke. Now tell me there aren't other things you would rather spend your money on! Because of the potential danger that smoking poses to your health and property, your insurance premiums (life, health, and even home) are also likely to be higher than that of non-smokers.

Last but not least, you should also consider the deleterious effect your attachment to a self-destructive, compulsive habit such as smoking is having upon your spiritual life. But, more about that later!

Rise from the Ashes

Section II:

Contemplation (Thinking About Quitting)

Rise from the Ashes

Chapter 2

Awakening to Contemplate the Harsh Light of Day

Okay, so you have awakened to your need to seriously contemplate quitting smoking. Like someone waking from a bad dream you are too haunted and disturbed to fall back asleep. You know you need to quit, but to do so may seem as difficult as getting up out of a warm, secure, comfortable bed on a cold dark morning. Although your tobacco habit may be dysfunctional and destructive, it is nevertheless familiar and has provided you with a certain amount of comfort and security for a long time. You lay there tossing and turning, your mind racing. You begin to contemplate your situation. Your mind may go back to previously unsuccessful attempts to quit smoking. If you are honest with yourself you have to acknowledge that you may be in the grips of a full-fledged addiction. The smoking habit has been likened to a cord consisting of three strands: *psychological*, *physical* and *social*.[1]

From a *psychological* perspective, smoking is a learned behavior. If, for an example, you are a pack-a-day smoker this means you take an average of 200 inhalations per day of cigarette smoke. That's 73,000 inhalations per year! A twenty-year history represents nearly 1.5 million hits off of a cigarette. Smoking has potentially become associated with nearly every activity during the day. Thus, smoking has become both a triggered and automatic behavior.

Once a person has been introduced to tobacco and he or she perseveres through the initial adjustment and learning period of inhaling smoke, the product begins to exert its magic. With the spell effectively cast, tobacco sells itself. The addictive component in tobacco is nicotine, to which a true *physical* dependence quickly develops. In its natural state nicotine serves as a potent, poisonous pesticide that protects the tobacco plant from being devoured. However, once inhaled in small amounts into the human body it is unfortunately a miracle drug. The cigarette is a very efficient means of delivering nicotine. Within 7 seconds after an inhalation of cigarette smoke, nicotine reaches the brain. Once in the brain, nicotine's action resembles that of the neurotransmitter acetylcholine, which stimulates the release of chemical messengers including dopamine, nor-epinephrine, epinephrine, vasopressin, and beta-endorphins.[2] The release of these chemicals form the strong chains of addiction that keep people enslaved in Marlboro Country. The following types of reinforcement provided by nicotine make up the links in the chain of addiction: decreased anxiety; alert relaxation; selective attention; improved memory; enhanced pleasure; management of stress, pain, anger, and weight. The ability to adjust one's level of nicotine through smoking has been referred to as a "mood thermostat."[3] It is easy to understand why you and so many other people continue to smoke when it provides these types of reinforcement.

The majority of smokers begin as adolescents to be accepted by their peers. This rite of passage is very much a *social* thing – a means to identify with the in-group. I can certainly remember doing this myself. I would venture to guess that you can too. Bonds are forged between smokers. Rituals are quickly established between smoking friends and co-workers.   But, times have changed and you are finding it increasingly difficult to smoke when and where you want to. The in-group is no longer smoking - in fact the habit appears to have become politically and socially incorrect.

In addition to the three previously mentioned strands of rope constituting the smoking habit, I would like to suggest there is a fourth strand – i.e. the *spiritual* - which although often overlooked may be of paramount importance. This may not be something you have considered up until now. But, whenever we find ourselves in the grips of a compulsive, addictive behavior – and believe me, I will attest to the fact that there are many of these - we need to step back and look at the situation from a spiritual perspective. Why, you say? An out-of-control behavior may be an indication of a less-than-healthy spiritual life. In the New Testament we are told that one of the fruits of the Holy Spirit in an individual's life is "self-control." In other words, if our day-to-day relationship with God is healthy and growing we should find ourselves more and more capable of controlling our behavior per the dictates of our consciences. To be incapable of refraining from behavior that we know is harmful suggests that something is spiritually out-of-sync.[4]

The literature suggests that someone in the contemplative stage intends to quit within the next 6 months. You may very well intend to quit sooner, but let's not be in too much of a hurry to rush through the contemplation stage. You have spent a long time developing your habit, and you owe it to yourself to take some time to understand your habit before you attempt once again to break free to the non-smoking lifestyle. We will eventually get to the preparation stage where you will set a quit date (usually within 30 days), and then we will move through the action stage of quitting and on into the maintenance and then termination stages. I hope you will come to see me as a traveling companion in the weeks and months ahead as you journey towards freedom from smoking.

Chapter 3

Metamorphosis

When the idea of writing this book first came to me several years ago, I chose the *phoenix* as a metaphor for the person breaking free from the smoking habit. The phoenix is an ancient mythical flying creature that according to legend rose to new life from the ashes of its own self-constructed funeral pyre. Thus, the title 'Rise from the Ashes.' The parallels seemed apropos and the play on words clever. But, as I have contemplated further the process of smoking cessation, the metamorphosis of a caterpillar into a butterfly strikes me as being an even better, real-life metaphor.

The *butterfly* has taken on new significance for my wife Linda and me since her bone marrow transplant for leukemia, owing in large part to the beautiful 'butterfly' cards and balloon given to her during this time by my cousin Kate. We have looked forward to each new card and remember with fondness the balloon that hovered gracefully over Linda's bed during her lengthy hospital stay. The metamorphosis of the caterpillar into the butterfly has become a source of inspiration to us – a metaphor of transformation. After months of chemotherapy to eradicate the leukemia, we anticipate the donor's marrow setting up a new immune system so that Linda will be able to emerge from this illness, healthy and cancer-free.

You have most likely attempted to quit smoking – but without lasting success. Perhaps you have tried quitting numerous times over the years! You may feel like a caterpillar who longs to fly and to rise above the dust, to glide on the breeze, to cavort with the flowers. But all your dreams and attempts to sprout wings and to become smoke-free have failed. You feel doomed to your humiliating fate; you feel like giving up. But, perhaps you are nearer to seeing your dreams fulfilled than you realize. However, for this to occur, a metamorphosis, or transformation, needs to occur in your life. This will require both a death and a rebirth.

The apostle Paul once encouraged the early believers in Christ not to be squeezed into the mold of the idolatrous world around them but rather to be transformed through the renewing of their minds. For transformation to occur, you may need to change your way of thinking – to adopt a spiritual worldview. You may need to awaken to the spiritual nature of your predicament.

Swiss psychiatrist and physician, Paul Tournier, once observed: "When a patient comes to consult us, he tells us the ills he is suffering from, and asks for a remedy. But he is not so ready to tell us of all the things that need to be put right in his way of life, about his vices, the passions that dominate him, the conflicts, rebellions, doubts, and fears that beset him. He knows very well that all this is sapping his powers of resistance, spoiling his pleasure in life, and undermining his health. But he has fought for so long in vain against himself and against circumstances! What he wants from medicine is relief from the consequences of all his faults, and not to be told that he should undertake an impossible reformation of his life."[1]   While shaking the smoking habit may be foremost in your mind, it may never happen until you are willing to do some real soul-searching and until you experience a deeper transformation.

Have you ever noticed that smoking intervention approaches seem 'lite' in comparison to other addiction treatment approaches? For instance, by comparison, Alcoholics Anonymous (AA) requires participants to do an extensive inventory of their lives; making restitution for wrongs committed and rendering forgiveness for wrongs they have been subject to. AA also acknowledges the spiritual nature of men and women and encourages participants to be open to a higher power. Bill Wilson, one of the founders of AA noticed that his New York group had only half the success rate of early groups in Ohio until he began to emphasize the spiritual. He wrote, "We must find some sort of spiritual basis for living, else we die."[2]

It sometimes appears that nicotine addiction has taken a back seat to other more serious addictions; it has perhaps been viewed as the lesser of evils. I can remember in the past being assigned to give breathing treatments to patients in the psychiatric wards of hospitals where I have worked, and noticing how the patient lounge would be filled with smokers. Heavy smoking has also notoriously characterized AA meetings. While it may be true that smoking does not interfere with a person's ability to function responsibly in society, at the work place, or in the family - as much as alcohol, drugs, or serious psychiatric disorders - smoking is nevertheless extremely dangerous both to the health of the smoker and to those exposed to his or her smoke, and it is highly addictive. According to some experts nicotine is more addictive than cocaine or heroin. And, I argue that it has a spiritual component that needs to be addressed in a serious manner. Unfortunately, most conventional smoking cessation programs emphasize behavior modification and pharmacologic treatment to the exclusion of spirituality.

To fail to acknowledge the spiritual side of our nature is perhaps like the owner of an automobile failing to acknowledge that the masterfully crafted vehicle is designed primarily to be used as a means of transportation, not simply a place to listen to music and take an occasional nap. One author suggests "spirituality is a lot like health." He goes on to write: "We all have health; we may have good health or poor health, but it's something we can't avoid having. The same is true of spirituality; every human being is a spiritual being. The question is not whether we 'have spirituality' but whether the spirituality we have is a negative one that leads to isolation and self-destruction or one that is more positive and life-giving."[3] French philosopher, Pierre Teilhard de Chardin suggested that "we are not human beings having a spiritual experience. We are spiritual beings having a human experience."[4]

Perhaps one of the reasons why behavior-modification-type smoking cessation programs fail to acknowledge the spiritual side of our nature is due to the fact that they are designed largely from a psychological perspective, and unfortunately it appears that many psychologists do not believe in God. "A survey of 409 psychologists found that only 40% believed in a personal, transcendent God; and only 18% valued organized religion as a source of spirituality."[5] The renowned Sigmund Freud, father of 'modern psychoanalysis,' referred to religion as being an "illusion," and compared it to a "childhood neurosis" or something to be cured.[6] [7] Freud was born to Jewish parents in the heavily Roman Catholic town of Freiburg, Moravia and later moved to Vienna during a time of extreme, violent anti-Semitism. It has been suggested that this may have contributed to his rejection of religion.[8]

It is interesting to note that the self-reliant Freud had an out-of-control obsession – he was a heavy smoker with a 20-cigar/day habit.[9] Freud believed that smoking enhanced his capacity to work, and believed he could exercise self-discipline in moderating his tobacco-smoking. Eventually he developed a heart condition, and cancer of the jaw and oral cavity - for which he would undergo 33 operations during the final 16 years of his life. Despite being ordered to stop smoking by his personal physician, he continued to smoke until his death. On several occasions he attempted to quit smoking, but eventually resumed - describing the process of withdrawal as a "torture being beyond human power to bear." In his final days, with an artificial jaw in place, he often found it difficult to speak, chew, or swallow, and yet his close friend, Dr. Jones said that he continued smoking "an endless series of cigars."[10]

In contrast, the eminent Carl Jung - a protégé of Freud and the founder of 'analytical psychology' - suggested that the human psyche is "by nature religious." He once stated, "Among my patients in the second half of life – that is over 35 years of age – there has not been a single one whose problem has not been in the last resort that of finding a religious outlook on life. It is safe to say that every one of them fell ill because he had lost that which the living religions of all ages have given to their followers, and none of them have been really healed who did not regain this religious outlook."[11] Perhaps unfortunately, Freud was a case in point. In a letter written by Freud to Marie Bonaparte, he termed "insane" the hope of finding "meaning and value in life."[12] The French philosopher Voltaire once wrote "The burning of a little straw may hide the stars, but the stars outlast the smoke."[13] Freud's life has come and gone, his theories and writings created a lot of attention and will no doubt remain for some time, but the truths of spiritual wisdom are timeless. In the Hebrew psalms and proverbs, a fool is described as someone who spurns the age-old wisdom of the Spirit and refuses to believe there is a God. Though this person may be convinced of his or her atheistic interpretation of reality, the Hebrew Scriptures assert that this train of thought ultimately leads to death. (Psalms 14:1; Proverbs 12:15, 14:12, 19:3)

R. Paul Olson, former Dean of the Minnesota School of Professional Psychology, has perceptively noted: "Clinical psychology has fallen short of providing a description of authentic human experience and what it means to be. It has replaced reverence for the human spirit with a science of human behavior."[14] If we have been created in the image of God, then we must acknowledge and address the spiritual dimension of human nature.

Chapter 4

Metanoia & More

Philosopher and psychologist, William James spent a lifetime interviewing religious people and studying the lives of mystics. In his classic 1902 book *The Varieties of Religious Experience*, this self-professed agnostic concluded that "God is real since he produces real effects." Although he could not fully understand or explain what he observed, as a scientist he could not refute that "contact with the unseen world had produced actual, transforming effects on individual personalities in this world."[1]

When you're sitting in a room and notice the curtains moving you know that there is air movement - perhaps from a fan, heater, or breeze coming in through an open window. You can't see the air movement but you know it exists because of the effect it is having upon the curtains. Jesus compared the workings of the Spirit in people's lives to the wind, which you can't see but know it is present because you feel it.

William Miller, an expert in the treatment of alcoholism, has observed that many addicted people seem to experience 'quantum change' – i.e. epiphanies and sudden insights that transform their lives, which in turn lead to recovery.[2] Referring to this phenomenon, one expert has written, "the value system of such 'quantum changers' is often completely and quickly reversed, and they experience a deep awareness that the addictive behavior cannot continue. Sometimes they also feel as if their desire to drink or use drugs has been removed by a force outside themselves." He goes on to point out that "medical science has no convincing explanation for such overnight transformations. Psychiatrists expect (and usually observe) gradual improvement, achieved by patients who work consciously on their problems. But the world's great religious traditions are full of stories of 'metanoia,' a complete turning about that leads to a renewal of life."[3]

It should be emphasized at this point that embarking upon a disciplined spiritual path is an advisable follow-up to a spiritual conversion or quantum change.   Substantiating this are the findings of a 1991 study in which researchers found that "alcoholics who had achieved long-term sobriety (four to sixteen years) had developed spiritual practices in conjunction with their Alcoholics anonymous participation."[4] Metanoia is but the first step towards freedom.

On a personal note I will tell you that at one point in my adult life, I experienced a life-transforming conversion to Jesus Christ. It was a metanoia that resulted in a quantum change. I had what I believe to be an encounter with the living God. My life turned upside down, or perhaps it would be more correct to say it turned right-side up. Some rather entrenched habits, including smoking, fell away as I pursued my newfound spiritual life. Since that time, as mentioned in the introduction of this book, I have been to Seminary and have served as a parish minister. While over the years I have grown in my respect for the wisdom and spiritual experience of those from other religious traditions, my primary 'religious' language is Judeo-Christian. It is the one I am most familiar with and comfortable in using. It is the path I have trod, from which my personal experience of the Divine comes from. Therefore, as we continue on our spiritual journey you will find that most of the truths and metaphors I share with you will be gleaned from the Judeo-Christian tradition.

Chapter 5

Winnowed Wisdom

An ancient Jewish proverb gives some prudent advice for anyone contemplating making a major life change: "It is not good to have zeal without knowledge, nor to be hasty and miss the way."[1] Attempting to break a long-term, reinforced habit like smoking is just such a life change. Sheer will power and determination have not proven adequate in the past and do not offer much hope for the future. What is needed is not another impulsive stab at quitting. One must prepare! With regards to preparation, we can learn from President Abraham Lincoln who is said to have remarked: "Give me six hours to chop down a tree and I will spend the first four sharpening the axe." To experience true transformation, one needs to take the time to prepare and to gain the necessary knowledge.

We began our journey together stating that the metamorphosis of the caterpillar into the butterfly is a wonderful metaphor for the transformation needed to take place in the life of the person wanting to quit smoking. We will return to this metaphor once again. You may not be aware of an interesting fact. "When a caterpillar nears its transformation time, it begins to eat ravenously; consuming everything in sight . . . the caterpillar body then becomes heavy, outgrowing its own skin many times, until it is too bloated to move."[2] Likewise, you may need to fill your tank with additional "spiritual" knowledge so that you will have the necessary nutrients and fuel to endure the transformation of rising from the ashes of nicotine addiction. That is our task and goal during the stage of contemplation.

One of the premier religious scholars of our age, Huston Smith, has written that in our post-modern age we are suffering from a "loss of religious certainties."[3] While acknowledging that in practice religious individuals have historically exhibited both the best and worst in human nature, he likens religious traditions to "data banks that house the winnowed wisdom of the human race."[4] The winnowing process he is referring to is the age-old technique used to separate the wheat from the chaff – symbolic of removing the good from the bad. Mythologist, Joseph

Campbell, once wrote "one of the problems today is that we are not well acquainted with the literature of the spirit . . . We're interested in the news of the day and the problems of the hour." Thus distracted, we no longer listen to those "who speak of the eternal values that have to do with the centering of our lives."[5]

If these observations are true, then it would seem prudent to become better acquainted with this literature of the spirit in hopes of delving beneath the surface of our addictions, so that our lives can become more centered. As you proceed with this book, you may find yourself launching out into some unchartered waters. But, as Swiss Reformed theologian, Karl Barth wrote, "The way to not grow old and to stay young with advancing years is to continue to learn."[6] In the words of Joseph Campbell again, "The great world traditions are recipes for living . . . tested and winnowed through hundreds of generations."[7] I have found, and I believe you too will find them to be trustworthy and extremely helpful in dealing with the addictive side of our natures.

We're not just looking to fill up our heads with useless, trivial information. Nor, are we looking to gain new spiritual knowledge so that we can come across as being more enlightened or so that we can spout theology out of our mouths. We are looking for a deep inner change of the heart. Woody Allen once remarked "Some drink deeply from the river of Knowledge. Others only gargle." We don't want to merely swish the distilled wisdom of the great religious traditions around in our mouths only to spit it back out, we want to swallow it and digest it and allow it to become a part of our lives. It is only then that we will prove true Sir Francis Bacon's famous assertion: "Knowledge is power."

Russian author, Fyodor Dostoevsky once wrote "Every ant knows the formula of its ant hill; every bee knows the formula of its beehive. They know it in their own way, not in our way . . . Only humankind does not know its formula."[8] So, as we continue on our spiritual sojourn, we are going to look to see what 'formulas for living' or what prescriptions can be found in the data banks of religion and spirituality. Our predecessors may not have been as technologically advanced as us, but spiritually they may have been deeper - at least some of our forefathers and foremothers likely were, and we can surely benefit from standing on their shoulders. In humility we may find the ancient wisdom speaks directly to our unique situations today - to our compulsions and habits.

Although I will be sharing with you some bits of wisdom gleaned from my own experiences, I will be leaning heavily upon the experience and wisdom of others. I have heard it said that "all wisdom is plagiarism; only stupidity is original."[9] I also humbly acknowledge the truth of a passage from the ancient book of Job which states "To God belongs wisdom and power; counsel and understanding are His."[10]

Chapter 6

Symptoms & Diagnoses

If all attempts using conventional methods to quit smoking have been unsuccessful then one must look for a different approach or at the very least a missing component. As discussed in the previous chapters, this is what leads us to religion and spirituality - to gain a different perspective. According to Greek philosopher and mathematician Pythagoras (570-495 B.C.), healing is a Divine art and therefore must address the soul as well as the body.[1] A wise psychiatrist once wrote: "Every bad habit in a man's way of life has its cause in his inmost heart. . . . Man is not just a body and a mind. He is a spiritual being. It is impossible to know him if one disregards his deepest reality."[2]

I recently read a magazine article about an attempted escape from a prison in the Upper Peninsula of Michigan.[3] Rather than attempting to break out of the prison in an above-ground manner, four cell-mates chose to dig a tunnel down through the floor and out past the fences of the prison yard. It was a claustrophobic, painstaking, laborious job that required commitment, patience, and perseverance on the part of the inmates. The process of digging took 3 months (beginning in the dead of winter - ending in early spring). The escape would probably have been successful if a get-away car had been arranged in a timelier fashion to pick the prisoners up on the other side of the tunnel. But alas, it wasn't arranged in time and the prison guards discovered the tunnel before the final execution of the escape could take place.

To some extent the major religious traditions of the world provide us with advice on how to escape the spiritual prisons of the human condition. But this sage advice sends us on a journey within, deep down into our very beings. The process may at times be claustrophobic; at times it may seem never-ending. Things may seem to get worse before they get better, darker before lighter. But the hope of emerging from the dark tunnel is there. The prisoners in the attempted escape used a common metal soup bowl to dig; likewise we can begin this journey with something readily available to us – a simple honest desire for transformation. What is most important is to possess the courage and willingness to dig and descend to the depths of our souls.

I realize that your primary concern may be simply to break free from your smoking habit. Bear with me! Addiction to nicotine is really just a symptom of a larger problem. In order to more fully understand this one specific addiction, I think it is important to step back and gain a wider perspective of the spiritual nature of addiction as a whole. Using the medical model of symptoms, diagnosis, pathogenesis, and prescription, let us see what religion or spirituality has to say about the human condition. As I have already mentioned, my religious orientation, training, and experience is Christian; therefore my discussion of spirituality and religion will be largely from a Judeo-Christian perspective. I will however provide in the endnotes some gleanings of wisdom from other faith traditions - for those readers who may be interested.

Symptoms

Religious traditions across the board agree that suffering, dislocation, and hunger are among the symptoms common to the human condition.[4] [5] [6] The Judeo-Christian tradition speaks of a bondage or slavery to things that do not satisfy the deep inner thirst and hunger of the human soul. One author describes it as "the craving for salt of a man who is dying of thirst."[7] In describing the frustration of the paradoxical human condition, the apostle Paul wrote: "I don't understand myself at all, for I really want to do what is right, but I don't do it. Instead, I do the very thing I hate. I know perfectly well that what I am doing is wrong . . . but I can't help myself . . ."[8]

According to religious scholar Huston Smith, "There is within us – in even the blithest, most light-hearted among us – a fundamental dis-ease. It acts like an unquenchable fire that renders the vast majority of us incapable in this life of ever coming to full peace. This desire lies in the marrow of our bones and deep in the regions of our soul. All great literature, poetry art, philosophy, psychology, and religion tries to name and analyze this longing. We are seldom in direct touch with it, and indeed the modern world seems set on preventing us from getting in touch with it by covering it with an unending phantasmagoria of entertainments, obsessions, and distractions of every sort. But the longing is there, built into us like a jack-in-the-box that presses for release."[9]

Diagnoses

The varied religious traditions suggest that the suffering and hunger that characterize the human condition are largely the result of the expression of selfish desire which has led to narcissism and the feeling of being separated and disconnected from God, others, and one's true self.[10] [11] [12] [13]

One author suggests, "Whether we realize it or not, simply to be human is to long for release from mundane existence with its confining walls of finitude and mortality."[14] In his 'Allegory of the Cave' Plato asked us to imagine that our human existence on planet earth is a bit like that of prisoners chained in a cave, backs turned away from incoming sunlight, only able to see a shadow-play of real objects on the cave's back wall.[15] [16] We long for something more real than the shadows we find in this world – something beyond our normal senses, something eternal. C.S. Lewis "had awakened to the reality of another world through, such pleasures as Nordic myths, nature, and . . . music. He sensed in our longings not just rumors but 'advance echoes' of that world. Flashes of beauty and pangs of aching sweetness, he said, 'are not the thing itself; they are only the scent of a flower we have not found, the echo of a tune we have not heard.'"[17]

Saint Augustine spoke of our hearts being restless until they find their rest in God. Professor of Psychology, David Benner writes: "Stimulation is a readily available diversion from restlessness." He goes on to explain: "Our society provides an almost endless variety of such sources of stimulation. Television, books travel, music, sporting events, alcohol, drugs, food, gambling, consumerism, exercise, and a large number of other activities all serve as sources of stimulation and escape from restlessness. We speak of being able to relax by means of such stimulation and of being able to let go of the pressures of our busy lives. To some extent this is unquestionably true. However, we also tend to become addicted to these stimulants, or more correctly, addicted to the state of being stimulated. The escape is not simply from pressures but from our inner selves. Thus these sources of stimulation can eventually deaden our spirituality."[18]

It has been suggested that "the human person is . . . conditionally free, alienated from God, self, and others. . ."[19] How we became alienated is what we will consider in the next chapter.

Chapter 7

Pathogenesis Part 1: Fall & Flight

In medical terminology pathogenesis is a study of the origin, development and effects of a disease process. While you are still lying there upon your bed of contemplation I would invite you to close your eyes and to allow yourself to slip once again into a dreamlike state. You are going to allow your imagination to travel back through human history to the beginning of time. It seems only fitting that we look to Genesis, the first book of the Hebrew Pentateuch, to begin our study of the pathogenesis of the human spiritual condition. According to this ancient book, once upon a time the archetypical man (Adam) and woman (Eve) were created by God and placed in a beautiful garden called Eden. They were given authority over the natural world of flora and fauna around them; they in fact served as caretakers for the Creator. The human pair was given by God the privilege of naming the animals. God would visit and walk with them in the cool of the day. There was a Divine-human cooperative relationship. The Garden was a haven of 'Shalom,' which in Hebrew connotes peace, harmony, righteousness, love, etc. One imagines God looking forward to hearing how the humans' day had gone, about the newest flower or animal they had discovered and named, or how they enjoyed the sunset or the type of fruit they had eaten.

It would appear that humans and their animal counterparts in the Garden were all herbivores at this time. God was the provider, like a loving parent. But, as with the parent-child relationship there were rules of conduct established – for protection. The man and woman were free to eat the fruit of any tree in the garden with the exception of one tree – the tree of the knowledge of good and evil. It is reminiscent of a parent telling the children that they could eat any type of candy provided by the parent, but they were not to take candy from strangers, especially strangers pulling up in a car while they played in the front yard or were walking to school. But of course we know that a malevolent stranger in the form of a serpent did entice Adam and Eve to partake of the forbidden candy, in the form of fruit from that one restricted tree. The serpent deceived the first man and woman into doubting God's words and into thinking that God had been holding out on them, and that the fruit would enlighten them with special power and wisdom; and after all the fruit was tantalizingly beautiful. (It reminds me of the "Turkish delight" that the evil Snow Queen offered Edmond in C.S. Lewis's beloved *Chronicles of Narnia*.)

Once the fruit was tasted it was all down-hill from there – thus the term "The Fall." The two human protagonists immediately knew they had done wrong and felt guilty and ashamed (i.e. naked). They quickly scurried out of the light into the safety of the shadows - out of the Garden of Shalom into the wilderness of trees. When their Divine parental friend came at the usual time for a visit, they were in hiding. He searched for them and called out their names: Adam, Eve – Where are you? Adam replied confessing the symptoms of fear and shame they were feeling. God of course knew what had transpired but when He confronted Adam, the blame game ensued. Adam blamed Eve, and then Eve blamed the serpent.

They had been warned that death would result if they were to disobey God, and something did die. First God in his mercy provided a covering of animal skins for Adam and Eve so their shame and guilt could be assuaged. But unlike the fig leaves with which they had attempted to cover their nakedness with, the animal skins required the death of one or more of their fellow creatures. But another kind of death ensued. They found themselves on the outside of a one-way door. They were no longer in the Garden of God's intimacy and provision. In a sense they were now on their own, at least for a time – from our finite human vantage point a very long time. It makes me think of disobedient children being sent away from the dinner table to their bedroom. It is usually meant to be a temporary punishment to allow the children time to consider the error of their ways and learn their lesson - so they will not grow up thinking bad behavior is okay and thus become bad adults. Perhaps this was also our Heavenly Father's reasoning in exiling his first human children from the garden – so they would no longer have access to fruit from the tree of eternal life. Divine tough-love would not allow them to live in an eternal state of delinquency. Hearkening back to the butterfly metaphor, in their original state of infancy, perhaps Adam and Eve were like young caterpillars and the framework of God's rules was like a womb of sorts; once they had eaten of the forbidden fruit it was like impatient caterpillars eating through the chrysalis before they had reached maturation. If they had stayed in the Garden and eaten of the tree of eternal life they would have forever remained caterpillars crawling in the dust. But that has never been, or will it ever be God's desires for us. His plan is for us one day to be transformed into butterflies – to soar above this world. But, we're getting ahead of ourselves here.

It is interesting to note that outside of the Abrahamic faith traditions there are also rumors that we humans have fallen from a state of grace or Shalom – i.e. Paradise. There appear to be striking variations of the same theme in both Hinduism[1] [2] and Taoism.[3] [4] Lao Tzu, author of Taoism's premier text the *Tao Te Ching* wrote "The great Tao [Way] is very even, and yet people love the bypaths."[5] The Judeo-Christian tradition would agree that we have left the straight and narrow path intended by our Creator - we have left the Garden and have taken the side-paths of temptation into the woods, where we have subsequently fallen into a myriad of traps.

In the first century A.D. of the Christian era, the apostle Paul reflected upon the Fall of humankind when he wrote: "Since the creation of the world God's invisible qualities – his eternal power and Divine nature – have been clearly seen, being understood from what has been made, so that men are without excuse. For, although they knew God, they neither glorified him as God nor gave thanks to him, but their thinking became futile and their foolish hearts were darkened. Although they claimed to be wise, they became fools and exchanged the glory of the immortal God for images made to look like mortal man and birds and animals and reptiles. Therefore God gave them over in the sinful desires of their hearts . . . to shameful lusts. . . Furthermore since they did not think it worthwhile to retain the knowledge of God he gave them over to a depraved mind, to do what ought not to be done."[6]

At the heart of that first sin in the Garden, and perhaps much subsequent sin, is to look to created things for something they are incapable of providing - things that only the Creator can give (like wisdom, love, peace, security). The term 'substance abuse' seems more than appropriate here. The substances themselves become idols. It has been suggested that "all God's gifts come to us with the potential for abuse."[7] The Apostle Paul's description of the Fall is reminiscent of the way the good father in the Jesus' "Prodigal Son" story allowed his youngest son to take off with his share of the inheritance to the far country, where in time he would learn the error of his ways.

While these accounts provide us with a historical and/or mythical framework (depending upon your point of view) to understand the human predicament, they are perhaps a bit general. The pertinent question is: How can they help us understand how to personally break free from a life-threatening addiction such as smoking?

Back in the 1970's my father, Don Peck, a gifted artist approaching retirement, came up with a new form of art. In all modesty I must say that my late father was ahead of his time. I wish I had appreciated this at the time as much as I do now. What he discovered was that if he placed common objects, like flowers or stars in a specific mathematical pattern the picture would come alive. It would become 3-dimensional. The principles he discovered would later be used with computers to create 'Magic Eye' 3-D art. Every time I came home from college my Dad would want to show me his newest artistic creations, and in fact anytime anyone came over to the house he would pull out some samples to show. He was always interested to see if people could see the 3-D. It was amusing to observe people's reactions. They fell into three categories. One type of person would stare at the picture and would admit that he or she could only see a 2-dimensional flat picture. (Perhaps their eyesight was limited in some way, or perhaps they weren't patient enough, or it may be they thought it all a bunch of hooey!) The second type of person had heard other people's reactions to the amazing 3-D, or bought into my father's description, and he or she would quickly look at the picture and reply "Oh, yes I see it! How nice. And then, nonplussed, would place the picture down, not bothering to look at the other pictures. (One had to question whether this person actually saw the 3-D at all.) Oh well! Then the third type of person would stare long and hard at the picture and then all of a sudden you would see this look of incredibility come across his or her face as the objects in the picture would either come off the page or descend deep into the page. The person would exclaim "This is amazing! I see it!" He or she would of course want to see more. The fruit of patience and of looking differently than he or she was used to (either cross-eyed or as if looking off in the distance) would pay off.

The holy writings and traditions of Religion are perhaps a little like my father's artwork. Let's return to the Biblical account of the Judeo-Christian tradition. We need to patiently meditate upon it and perhaps look at it differently than we have in the past. We just might be surprised – it may come alive! Rather than simply reading it as something that may or may not have happened to two people long, long ago in a far-away land, we need to enter into the story. We may find that "this strange and eccentric Bible story is allover autobiographic of us."[8] One author suggests that "until you can read the story of Adam and Eve, of Abraham and Sarah, of David and Bathsheba, as your own story, you have not really understood it." He goes on to assert that "the Bible is a book finally about ourselves, our won apostasies, our own battles and blessings . . ."[9]

Another author poses a rhetorical question: "Is the greatest truth about Adam and Eve and the fruit that it happened, or that it happens?" He goes on to write: "This story . . . is true for us because it is our story. We have all taken the fruit. We have all crossed boundaries. We have all made decisions to do things our way and then looked back and said to ourselves, 'What was I thinking?' The fruit looked so great to Adam and Eve for those brief moments, but the consequences were with them for the rest of their lives. Their story is our story. We see ourselves in them. The story is true for us because it happened and because it happens. It is an accurate description of how life is."[10]

A renowned psychiatrist from the twentieth-century wrote: "In some form, all of us repeat the experience of Adam and Eve in the Garden of Eden, seeking to eat of the Tree of the Knowledge of Good and Evil in order to find out for ourselves whether what has been 'told' us is the real 'right' and 'wrong' of things. . ."[11] Another well-known psychiatrist observed: "Not a single . . . [adolescent] . . . passes through this period of emancipation from parents without involving himself in a life of secrecy which is always guilt-ridden. . . As proof of his approaching manhood, he will go off to smoke his first cigarette secretly. It is by having secrets that individuality is formed."[12]

Back in 1973, when I was in high school and just beginning to nurture the cigarette habit, I remember delighting in a song by the one-hit wonder Brownsville Station. The song entitled *Smokin' in the Boy's Room* resonated with my adolescent angst and rebellion: "A-checkin' out the halls makin' sure the coast is clear; Lookin' in the stalls, no there ain't nobody here . . . to get caught would surely be the death of us all! Smokin' in the Boys' Room (Yes, indeed I was!) Now teacher, don't you fill me up with your rules . . . everybody knows that smoking ain't allowed in school. Alright!" More recently, in a song entitled *You're Old*, Paul Simon remembers his adolescence with the line "First time that I smoked – paranoia!"

Once we've reached that age of accountability and stepped through that one-way door to taste that stolen fruit, we are on the run – we are in *flight* from the cover of innocence. It reminds me of some vultures I saw one day while driving; they were on up ahead attempting to snack on some road kill; they appeared so anxious, so furtive, so paranoid, looking over their shoulder with one eye out for oncoming traffic and one talon on the flesh of the prey. We learn to live with what psychologists refer to as 'cognitive dissonance' – "a euphemism for guilt, a symptom of the inner battle raging inside a person who believes one way and acts another."[13] Perhaps singer/songwriter Jack Johnson is acknowledging the existence of cognitive dissonance when he sings, "You and your heart shouldn't feel so far apart!" It occurs to me that if smoking that first cigarette represents an example of eating the forbidden fruit in the garden, then the hiding of the cigarettes, the camouflaging of the breath from parents and teachers must be analogous to hiding from God in the garden and covering shameful nakedness with fig leaves.

Chapter 8

Pathogenesis Part 2: Attachment

Once we have reached that nonspecific age of accountability and have crossed that threshold by asserting our independence, we have initiated certain processes in our hearts and minds. A double life is born - the one that would seek to please our parents, other authority figures, or God; and the one that would seek to please the self, or the peer group by coloring outside of the lines.[1] Once that initial threshold to temptation has been crossed, the body begins pulling the mind away from the spirit. Once our moral conscience is violated we begin to live with cognitive dissonance; the whisper of conscience is drowned out by the loud chatter of desire. We then have a tendency to proceed with life in a duplicitous manner, hiding, keeping secrets, darting in and out of the shadows – looking to things of this world for cover, seeking the companionship of others who are also fugitives, on the run from their consciences. As one author suggests "When we disconnect from God, we find ourselves becoming internally disconnected, 'dis-integrated,' hence experiencing shame and fear and duplicity and hypocrisy. Our disconnect from God and ourselves leads inevitably to further fragmentation, disconnection from other people, disconnection from our environment."[2]

In the Garden of Eden, the first sign of the Fall was for Adam and Eve to feel the need to cover the new delinquent self; then they sought to blame someone else for their own complicity in the disobedient act, thus separating themselves from others – valuing their own reputation and self-respect over that of others.

It has been suggested that because we are lonely and separate, "we try hard to fit in, to be the kind of person that will cause others to like us. Craving and needing very much the affirmation of others, we compromise, put on any face, or many faces; we do even those things we do not like to do in order to fit in."[3] We seek to escape the loneliness, disconnect, fear, worry, and guilt of the human condition oftentimes through dysfunctional behavior. A whole new world of temptation opens up to us and we are faced with a quandary of moral and ethical choices. As Thomas a Kempis (1380-1471), author of the devotional classic, *The Imitation of Christ*,

30

wrote: "Just as a ship without a helm is driven to and fro by the waves, so a careless man, who abandons his proper course, is tempted in countless ways."[4] Modern-day mystic, Richard Foster suggests: "Because we lack a Divine Center our need for security has led us into an insane attachment to things. . . We are trapped in a maze of competing attachments . . . we crave things we neither need nor enjoy. . ."[5] We are left hungering and thirsting for we know not what. As singer/songwriter Jackson Browne sings "There's a God-sized hunger underneath the laughing and the rage!"

Vaclav Havel, leader of the revolution in Czechoslovakia has written: "The alien world into which we are thrown beckons to us and tempts us. . . . We are constantly being exposed to the temptation to stop asking questions and adapt ourselves to the world as it presents itself to us, to sink into it, to forget ourselves, to lie our way out of ourselves and our 'otherness' and thus to simplify our existence-in-the-world."[6] When we give in to artificial means of relieving stress (e.g. tobacco, alcohol, and numerous other habits) we are sinking into the world.[7]

While we are pursuing the objects of our desire – that next cigarette, the next drink, the next conquest or achievement - the cognitive dissonance and deep inner longings of our spirits may temporarily fade into the background, but they don't really disappear! They are simply dormant or hidden while the objects of our desire are temporarily in the foreground taking up our whole field of vision. "Existential anxieties are ignored while we are pursuing objects of desire."[8] But, unfortunately, "every act of physical, psychological, or moral disobedience of God's purpose is an act of wrong living, and has its inevitable consequences."[9] Wouldn't you agree that it is plausible to suspect that living with cognitive dissonance over a long period of time might be a contributing factor in the development of anxiety and depression?

We eventually develop habits, and attach ourselves to the objects of our desire. "The word attachment has long been used by spiritual traditions to describe this process.[10] It comes from the old French 'attache,' meaning "nailed to." Attachment "nails" our desire to specific objects and creates addiction."[11] While it may be true that Adam and Eve directly went against God's instructions and ate from the forbidden tree, could part of their sin have been that they were abusing the substance (thus the term 'substance abuse') – looking to the fruit to make them wise, to give them God-like power? Enchanted into allowing the fruit to become an idol? The first sin represents turning away from God as the authority and provider to be trusted. It is a foolish trusting in something/someone else to meet our needs or to satisfy our desires and longings. It is also greed; wanting more than God is providing. It is a self-seeking attempt to grab status and privilege and secret knowledge. It is ultimately deception because in the end it is God alone who wants to give us the best, and who is ultimately capable of doing so!

It has been suggested that "cigarettes, cigars, and pipes are really nothing but adult thumb-sucking, adult pacifiers, pseudo-food, love substitutes."[12] Pulitzer-prize winning author, Annie Dillard "tells of experiments in which entomologists entice male butterflies with a painted cardboard replica larger and more enticing than the females of their species. Excited, the male butterfly mounts the piece of cardboard; again and again he mounts it. 'Nearby, the real, living female butterfly opens and closes her wings in vain.'"[13] In referring to a similar phenomenon among human beings, C.S. Lewis spoke of the lure of the "sweet poison of the false infinite."[14] One pastoral counselor has written: "The objects we attach ourselves to become our gods and compulsive obsession results; we lose the freedom of decision-making and something like a corporate takeover occurs!"[15] He goes on to state: "Psychologically, the obsession uses up energy. It is like a psychic malignancy sucking our life force into specific obsessions and compulsions, leaving less and less for other people and other pursuits."[16] We become less able to really love other people, and God; and obsessions will control us at the expense of our own well-being.

I am reminded of Gollum and his 'precious' ring or even Bilbo Baggins and the same ring. They were under its spell. If you've seen the *Lord of the Rings* movies, or better yet have read the books by J.R.R.Tolkien, you know what I'm talking about. The look on their faces changed when in the presence of the ring; all love and kindness seemed to drain out, being replaced by a rather nasty compulsive air. Oddly enough, I have noticed that writing this book has become a bit of an obsession with me. I don't want to be interrupted when I am working on it, and there are times when I must catch myself. The time I have to spend with my precious wife, who is recovering from a bone-marrow transplant, during this extended medical leave is definitely more important than working on the book, and yet if I am not careful my emotional availability to her will be less than it should be if I get too absorbed in writing.

Psychiatrist Gerald May has suggested: "Virtually all body functions take place as a result of shifting balances among chemicals that have opposing effects."[17] He defined stress as "the body's reaction to disequilibrium. Stress includes both the alarm responses that signal imbalance and the coping mechanisms that seek restoration of equilibrium. Within the nervous system, cells cope with imbalances by means of three basic responses: feedback, habituation, and adaptation. These three mechanisms are also the neurological dynamics of attachment. Progressively, like three stair steps descending into slavery, feedback, habituation and adaptation lead to addiction."[18] Feedback represents the adolescent's first exposure to cigarettes – the natural response is to cough and move away from the smoke; nausea may even be part of the response. Habituation is the body's secondary response to continued exposure to the smoke – to minimize the response to the overwhelming substance. Adaptation is the final response, where the body gives up trying to protect itself or to minimize the effect of the foreign substance, and just accepts the invader as part of its make-up – enthusiastically embracing the dependence. Then one begins to live for the next hit of the substance in order to experience peace.

Danish philosopher and theologian, Soren Kierkegaard once wrote: "Riches and abundance come hypocritically clad in sheep's clothing pretending to be security against anxieties and they become then the object of anxiety . . . They secure a man against anxieties just about as well as the wolf which is put to tending the sheep secures them . . . against the wolf."[19] The same could be said of any idol or object of addiction, including cigarettes. It is common to hear people say they smoke to calm down and to deal with stress. But, once nicotine addiction is established there is a repeating cycle of craving, smoking, withdrawal-induced anxiety, and craving.

Saint Augustine described how at first evil passes our door as a stranger, then enters as a guest, but ultimately becomes master.[20] A quote from the *Tobacco Atlas* sums it up: "Smoking a cigarette for the beginner is a symbolic act. I am no longer my mother's child, I'm tough, I am an adventurer, I'm not square. . . The act of smoking remains a symbolic declaration of personal identity. . . . As the force from the psychological symbolism subsides, the pharmacological effect takes over to sustain the habit."[21]

Chapter 9

Pathogenesis Part 3: Addiction

According to the Biblical account, our original position in creation was to have dominion over the works of God's hands;[1] our role was that of God's steward, representative, friend and caretaker of creation.[2] However, it is interesting to note that the very things of creation over which humans were originally given authority by God, have now gained authority over us. We were to have dominion over the plant world, and animals were our friends - not originally to be eaten. Diabetes, heart disease, obesity, lung diseases are largely due to the control that carbohydrates, animal fats, and tobacco have upon us. Drug addiction and alcoholism are a result of the control that plants/vegetables have upon us (e.g. poppies, cannabis, mushrooms, potatoes, wheat, grapes, etc.) We try to fill ourselves up with these substances, hide behind them, to drown ourselves in them, and then before long we are addicted and our identities become one with the idols we serve.

One author suggests that this side of the Fall, "we are [spiritually and psychologically] bent . . . toward the creature, attempting to find our identity in him. Slowly and compulsively the false self closes it hard, brittle shell around us, and our loneliness remains. . . ." She goes on to add "The un-fallen position was, as it were, a vertical one, one of standing erect, face turned upward to God in a listening-speaking relationship. It was a position of receiving continually one's true identity from God."[3] One wonders if the god of this world (i.e. the devil) does not laugh at our attempts to exert control and authority over creation (now that we have detached from the Creator, and have taken off the robe of authority with which we were created). John Wesley, the founder of Methodism, suggested that as a result of the Fall, humans have "sunk into pride and self-will, the very image of the devil; and into sensual appetites and desires, the image of the beasts."[4] [5]

It has been suggested that "addictions – to drugs, alcohol, tobacco, and other substances – [are] the devastating disorders in which we appear to lose the God-given freedom to control our behavior."[6] Indulging in pleasure apart from the Creator's intent can lead to a form of slavery. "An ever increasing craving for an ever diminishing pleasure is the devil's formula."[7] Our human cravings and desires may be compared to "rivers that tend to overflow their banks."[8]

Aristotle (384-322 B.C.) observed: "It is the nature of desire not to be satisfied, and most human beings live only for the gratification of it."[9] A contemporary author has defined addiction as "a deep-seated form of idolatry." He went on to say "The objects of our addiction become our false gods. These are what we worship, what we attend to, where we give our time and energy, instead of love. Addiction, then, displaces and supplants God's love as the source and object of our deepest desire . . . a counterfeit religious presence."[10]

Lest one think that addiction and passion are restricted to 'bad' things and that only sorry specimens of humanity struggle with it, consider this disarmingly honest quote from Renaissance painter, sculptor, and architect Michelangelo: "So now, from this mad passion which made me take art for an idol and a king I have learnt the burden of error that it bore; And what misfortune springs from man's desire . . . The world's frivolities have robbed me of the time that I was given for reflecting upon God."[11] Addictions, fueled by the fires of passion become lovers who compete with the Divine lover and other humans in our life who are deserving of our love. Addicted persons may know their behavior is wrong and that it is harmful both to themselves and others around them, but the object of their desire – the addictive substance - provides them with an acute happiness or fix that for the moment seems better than anything else they could possibly experience. Addiction defies logic.

I am convinced that the more one gives in to addiction, the more it wants! The more one feeds a pet, the more it grows and the hungrier it gets. A patient once proudly told me that he was down to a few cigarettes per day, and he smoked them only at certain times (e.g. when first waking up, after meals). But a person can't really control a habit anymore than a child can control a lion by grabbing its tail! It is an illusion. The person is still addicted and feeding the habit, keeping it alive as long as they are still smoking. They are still hooked, controlled by it, and it still does them harm. One author warns, "We think we are pushing and we are being pushed. We do not rule, we are ruled." [12]

Like I said earlier, once we give in to temptation we unfortunately find ourselves on the run. I am reminded of a story of three hapless car thieves who were attempting to break into a pick-up truck. "The owner saw them and chased them yelling. He hailed a policeman, and he, too, gave chase. The thieves made a valiant effort to escape. They scrambled over a tall fence with barbed wire ripping their pants and scratching blood out of their shins. But it was worth it. The rotund truck owner and the middle-aged cop could never scale a fence like that. They didn't have to. The cop looked through the wires and said, 'Congratulations, men. You just broke into San Quentin!'"[13] Do we in our flight from God break into our own prisons? Fall into traps of our own making? The Hebrew Scriptures would suggest we do.

Israel's God, Jehovah, warned the people during their sojourn from Egypt to Canaan, that if they should in the future fail to carefully follow His laws and to revere and honor his glorious and awesome name, they would no longer experience prosperity. Rather than experiencing his blessing they would find themselves ruined, destroyed, and uprooted from the Promised Land–scattered among the nations to the ends of the earth, where they would "worship other gods – gods of wood and stone," previously unknown to their fathers. Moses told them: "Among those nations you will find no repose, no resting place . . . There the Lord will give you an anxious mind, eyes weary with longing, and a despairing heart."[14]

What may be the "prisons" or "nations of exile" of popular culture? Addictions to tobacco, drugs, music, sex, food, alcohol, materialism, success, status, rigid-religion, jobs, homes, sports could all be possibilities. Addressing God, one author writes: "When it stands before You and your infallible truthfulness, doesn't my soul look just like a market place where the second-hand dealers from all corners of the globe have assembled to sell the shabby riches of the world?"[15]

As a person in the throes of nicotine addiction, with every unsuccessful attempt to break free, you are reminded how much of a failure you are. With every new method that is tried to break the habit, hope rises and falls – harder each time. The hopelessness of not being able to break free from an addiction like smoking can be overwhelming. It has been said that "the temptation to despair is most lethal."[16] But, let me lovingly assure you that once you have finally reached the point where you quit trying to quit (on your own), and look up, the solution may be near at hand.   A contemporary psychologist points out: "As we attempt to scurry away from this light, exhaustion and heaviness set in. Thus, a heavy heart may be a sure sign that we are trying to flee from Him who would bring healing, if we would but settle ourselves and learn what it is that the pain has to teach us."[17] In the metaphor of the butterfly, the caterpillar reaches a point of exhaustion and heaviness after it has consumed everything in sight. Perhaps this is analogous to an addicted person reaching the end of the rope – where he/she is receptive to hearing the prescription that the rich tradition of religious wisdom has to offer

Chapter 10

Prescription: A Religious Perspective

One contemporary clinical psychologist emphasizes that in counseling it is important for the therapist to look for the "sanity that accompanies all neurosis," because in his own words "most clients have lost sight of their basic sanity."[1] He goes on to say that the first sign of basic sanity is a repulsion over the way one is living, and the second sign of sanity is a longing to transcend the sense of self. When asked, "What, in your opinion, is the essence of neurosis?" the renowned Carl Jung replied "Neurotics are all searching for religion."[2] It is interesting to break down the word religion: The prefix "re" means "again" and the root "lig" (as in ligament) means "connect." One author suggests that religion "is about the reconnection of the creator with creation; it is about reconnecting people with God, people with one another." He goes on to write, "The human predicament, monotheists believe, is that disconnect is possible, and not just possible, that it is actual, that it has happened. We intelligent creations have the capacity to at least partially disconnect from God via willful rebellion, defiance, resistance, indifference, or ignorance – and we have used that capacity with tragic results."[3]

All religious traditions teach the importance and necessity of personal change; they each prescribe unique methods to help one become more spiritually centered and to overcome selfishness and addiction.[4 5 6 7 8 9 10] The common prescription is to begin living in accordance to the dictates of one's conscience, to get in sync with the moral fabric of the universe, to practice the Greatest Commandment – that of loving God, others, and self; this will in turn reduce cognitive dissonance and lead to liberation.

The argument that the Judeo-Christian tradition makes is that on our own – with our human limitations – we are unable to break free from our selfishness, the karma of past actions, the habits and addictions that bind us, the 'sin' that is part of our nature. In the words of Richard Foster, "the ordinary method of dealing with ingrained sin is to launch a frontal attack . . . we rely on willpower and determination . . . [but] the struggle is all in vain, and we find ourselves once again morally bankrupt, or worse yet proud of our external righteousness." Foster goes on to point out that resisting can endow a habit with more power.[11] It has been suggested that "it is in the very nature of addiction to feed on our attempts to master it."[12] Like a person who has fallen into quicksand, the more one struggles the deeper one sinks. What is needed is for someone who is standing on solid ground to reach out and pull the person to safety. I am reminded of a story I read of a TV repairman: "When asked about the worst kind of damage he'd ever seen to a television set, he said, 'the kind that results from people trying to fix their TVs on their own.'"[13]

Self-help formulas, positive thinking, and behavior modification methods may be helpful in overcoming addiction, but ultimately they may not be enough. What we may need is Divine help. Persons addicted to nicotine know the futility of trying to quit; even after seemingly successful attempts they find themselves eventually sliding back into the dysfunctional but comfortable rut. I remember hearing a fable of a cat that was trained to serve as a waiter to the King. All was going well; the cat was bringing the King a cup of hot tea. But, then all of a sudden a bag of mice was opened onto the floor. The frightened mice scurried in different directions. The cat quickly dropped the scalding beverage in the King's lap and began chasing the mice.[14] Training is not enough to change our nature. Something deeper is required.

John Baker, founder of *Celebrate Recovery*, asks us to imagine that we are in a boat whose auto-pilot is set for east. But, we want to go west! So with all our might we turn the wheel and force the boat to go in the direction of our preference. The only problem is we get tired, and as soon as fatigue sets in we let go of the wheel and then we are once again heading east. He makes the point that what is needed is to have the boat's autopilot reprogrammed. The implication for us, or for anyone held captive to an addiction, is that we need to have our inner auto-pilot reprogrammed. We need transformation; sheer will-power alone is not a permanent long-term solution.[15]

It has been suggested that "until we stop running away from ourselves and hiding from God, there is no real possibility of spiritual growth."[16] One author writes "Sometimes . . . we are blinded by our attachments; we are so preoccupied – our attention is so occupied – our attention is so kidnapped by our compulsions – that we tune out the background of God's love. I am convinced that our brain cells do, in fact, habituate to the constant reality of God's love. We may want to notice Divine love, but we ignore it like we ignore our own breathing, in favor of the things that have captured us."[17]

But, the good news according to the Christian gospel is that God is seeking us and desires to help us, like a good physician. Jesus, as the representative of his heavenly father said "It is not the healthy who need a doctor, but the sick. I have not come to call the righteous, but sinners."[18] I once heard the story of a lady who was pulled over at night for speeding. When the policeman stepped up to her window she quickly rolled down the window to explain that someone was following her in another car. She said that she had seen this person quickly approaching her in the parking lot of the mall as she got into her car. She had frantically locked the car and taken off, only to find that he was following her. She had been trying to lose him. As the policeman listened he shined his flashlight into her mini-van only to find someone holding a knife crouching down behind her seat. Just then another car pulled up and a man jumped out saying that he had seen this person break into her vehicle, and that he had been trying to warn her of possible danger. Perhaps, in our flight from God and our God-given consciences we are a bit like this lady. We have locked ourselves into our dysfunctional, but seemingly secure habits and are fleeing from the One who truly understands and loves us – our Creator. Our shame and guilt keep us running from the One we are afraid to face – the One who seeks to forgive and embrace us.

Frederick Buechner has written: "The Bible is hundreds upon hundreds of voices all calling at once out of the past and clamoring for our attention like barkers at a fair, like air-raid sirens, like a whole barnyard of cockcrows as the first long shafts of dawn fan out across the sky. . . And somewhere in the midst of them all one particular voice speaks out that is unlike any other voice because it speaks so directly to the deepest privacy and longing and weariness of each of us that there are times when the centuries are blown away like mist, and it is as if we stand with no shelter of time at all between ourselves and the one who speaks our secret name. Come, the voice says. Unto me. All ye. Every last one."[19] But, even if God is knocking on the door to our hearts, we hold the key. In the words of C.S. Lewis, "the door to hell is locked from the inside." And, as has been suggested, "there is no slavery that can compare to the slavery of ingrained habits of sin."[20] We must open the door and invite God into the areas of our addiction.

If God was an oncologist and your diagnosis was acute myloid leukemia, like my wife Linda's, he or she would tell you that induction chemotherapy needs to be started as soon as possible to get rid of the leukemia cells that are crowding out all of the healthy cells in your blood; the immediate goal would be to put you in remission. But, as in my wife's case it required a lengthy hospital stay in isolation. If God was an orthopedic specialist and you presented with a dislocated bone or worse yet a broken bone that had healed incorrectly, he or she would treat the dislocation by resetting the bone or treat the break by re-breaking the bone and resetting it; then the bone would be immobilized in a cast for a lengthy period of time while it healed. In the case of someone addicted to smoking, the Divine physician may need to break, wound, or humble the person before he/she can be lifted up and restored to health.

The inability to quit smoking may be the chink in the armor of an otherwise well-adjusted person; the opening in which the Holy Spirit can flow to accomplish a deeper work of grace.[21] For those who profess to have a faith, it may be an indication that something is amiss, in need of serious attention; the Divine-human relationship needs work. But, that's a good thing to realize! Alcoholism experts Kurtz and Ketchem write: "God comes through the wound: Our very imperfections – what religion labels our 'sins,' what therapy calls our 'sickness,' what philosophy terms our 'errors' – are precisely what bring us closer to the reality that no matter how hard we try to deny it, we are not the ones in control here. And this realization, inevitably and joyously, brings us closer to God."[22] A touching story goes like this: "God in heaven holds each person by a string. When you sin, you cut the string. Then God ties it up again, making a knot - and thereby bringing you a little closer to him. Again and again your sins cut the string - and with each further knot God keeps drawing you closer and closer."[23]

Brokenness has been compared to a thin place in the ice of a frozen pond, through which you could see sunlight if you were trapped under the ice. There is hope in brokenness that rescue and escape may be near at hand. After interviewing many people claiming to have experienced epiphanies and sudden life-transforming insights referred to as 'quantum changes,' researchers Miller and C'de Baca noted: "If we had to describe in a few words the most common candidates for quantum change, they would be people who were desperately unhappy, had been for some time, and saw no way out through their own willful efforts."[24]

Perhaps we are like a computer; when all else fails it may be time to power down - to disconnect from the power source. After giving up and acknowledging our powerlessness over the addiction, there must be an "awakening of the desire to believe."[25] After 400 years of bondage in Egypt, the Hebrew slaves reached the point of desperation and cried out to God – and He heard their cries and sent a deliverer. The apostle Paul reached a point of personal crisis and desperation when he cried out "who will recue me from this body of death?" after lamenting: "When I want to do good, evil is right there with me. For in my inner being I delight in God's law; but I see another law at work in the members of my body, waging war against the law of my mind and making me a prisoner of the law of sin at work within my members. What a wretched man I am!"[26]

It is interesting to note that the words human, humor, and humility all come from the root 'humus' which is defined as a brown or black substance resulting from the partial decay of plant and animal matter. It would appear that when we acknowledge before the Creator that we are nothing but a collection of dust, carbon-based compounds, we are then finally in a good position to see something good –on the order of miraculous – happen. We are at this point like good receptive soil. Jesus acknowledged this when he said "God blesses those who realize their need for him."[27] He went on to assure his disciples that despite human limitations and past failures, "all things are possible with God."[28]

Listen to a charming story entitled *The Tale of the Sands*, which comes from the Sufi tradition: "A Stream, from its source in far-off mountains, passing through every kind and description of countryside, at last reached the sands of the desert. Just as it had crossed every other barrier, the stream tried to cross this one, but it found that as fast as it ran into the sand, its waters disappeared. It was convinced, however, that its destiny was to cross this desert, and yet there was no way. Now a hidden voice, coming from the desert itself, whispered: 'The Wind crosses the desert, and so can the stream.' The stream objected that it was dashing itself against the sand, and only getting absorbed: that the wind could fly, and this was why it could cross a desert. 'By hurtling in your own accustomed way you cannot get across. You will either disappear or become a marsh. You must allow the wind to carry you over, to your destination.' But how could this happen? 'By allowing yourself to be absorbed in the wind.' This idea was not acceptable to the stream. After all, it had never been absorbed before. It did not want to lose its individuality. . ."[29] It is human nature to want to hold onto what's familiar - even if dysfunctional; we are afraid to let go of our defects, our identity. But, at some point - if freedom is what we truly want - we need to step out in faith and, as they say, "let go, and let God!" We need to allow ourselves to be lifted up by grace and to ride the wind of the Spirit!

Those in AA are known to say something to the effect that it is not until you have hit bottom that you look up. Bill Wilson, co-founder of Alcoholics Anonymous, described his stepping-out-in-faith experience as follows: "My depression deepened unbearably and finally it seemed to me as though I were at the bottom of the pit. I still gagged badly on the notion of a Power greater than myself, but finally, just for a moment, the last vestige of my proud obstinacy was crushed. All at once I found myself crying out, 'If there is a God, let Him show Himself! I am ready to do anything, anything!' Suddenly the room lit up with a great white light. I was caught up into an ecstasy which there are no words to describe. It seemed to me, in the mind's eye, that I was on a mountain and that a wind not of air but of spirit was blowing. And then it burst upon me that I was a free man."[30] After repeated failures to quit smoking, if you have not already begun to look up, perhaps you are more ready than you have ever been. This is what needs to happen if you want to really be free of smoking – this is the prescription!

Chapter 11

A Longing to Return to Eden

A Hopi Indian saying goes, "One finger can't lift a pebble." If you have reached this point in the book, hopefully you have been 'awakened' to your need for help in overcoming your addiction – to quit smoking. You can't do it on your own! Hopefully too you are now willing to acknowledge that this help needs to be of a supernatural kind. But, also if we are honest with ourselves we need more than just a temporary fix - a rescue from this one particular addiction - because we are not static individuals, we are dynamic. To be human is to be engaged in the process of becoming. Like a canoe on a river, the question is not how to start to move but rather where your current course of moving is taking you.[1] To break free of one snare but to continue heading in the wrong direction is not a true solution. The awakening is a "yellow light" on the highway of life; it cautions us to slow down and prepare to stop. But at the "red light" we need to make a choice: do we continue on in the same direction or do we turn? Conversion begins when we make a U-turn.

It has been written: "We are east of Eden. Something is not right. The Germans have a word for this. They call it 'ursprache' . . . the primal, original language of the human family. It's the language of paradise that still echoes in the deepest recesses of our consciousness, telling us that things are out of whack deep in our bones, deep in the soul of humanity. . . Something is not right with the world."[2] The apostle Paul, referring back to the Garden, writes "Meanwhile we groan, longing to be clothed with our heavenly dwelling, because when we are clothed, we will not be found naked."[3] I would suggest that we long to have our guilt forgiven and our right standing with our Creator restored! We long to reclaim our God-given identity and authority.

Again, I am reminded of the magazine article to which I referred in a previous chapter - about the attempted Michigan prison escape. The 42-year old inmate who dug the tunnel with the soup bowl describes the feelings he had as the first chunks of concrete in the prison floor were pried loose to reveal an underlying bed of sand: "Its golden-brown luster brought back childhood memories: a family vacation in Brighton,

44

Michigan. I was five years old . . . running from the car to the beach. . . feeling the warm sand beneath my feet. . . building sand castles . . . the smell of the lake and the sound of the water . . . chasing minnows in the shallows near the shore . . . splashing . . . playing . . . laughing . . . a time of innocence. My mind a clean slate. I could have been anything but wanted to be an astronaut. Big dream for such a small boy. I wondered what happened to him. How did I ever end up in this prison?" This was written by a man serving a 25-50 year sentence for bank robbery; someone who acknowledges that "stealing was a rush, flushed with adrenaline," and recalls how after the first bank job, "he and his girlfriend rolled naked in the money!"[4]

I dare say that the language of paradise was echoing in the inmate's consciousness; he was longing to return to the Garden where Shalom prevailed.[5] Although his story may be an extreme – the choices he made, the actions he took - our stories in essence are probably not that different. In our own ways we have strayed from the innocence of childhood, and may find ourselves wishing we could turn back the hands of time or longing to break out of the prisons of our own making. Both the Old and New Testaments of the Bible attest to this fact: "We all like sheep, have gone astray, each of us has turned to his own way . . ."[6] and "All have sinned and fall short of the glory of God . . ."[7] It has been suggested that "the psychological, neurological, and spiritual dynamics of full-fledged addiction are actively at work within every human being."[8] Nicotine addiction is just one of many addictions that afflict the human soul.

Psychiatrist and spiritual counselor Gerald May, who personally struggled with overcoming the addiction of smoking, wrote: "At the outset, most of us tackle an addiction simply because it is giving us trouble, and our only conscious desire is to be rid of it. We want to change a specific addictive behavior, and that alone is challenge enough. If my primary desire, as best I know it, is simply to change a troublesome addictive behavior, I will hardly be interested in giving my life to God in order to do so. Why should I embark on a spiritual journey that threatens the foundations of all my normalities when the only thing I want is to quit smoking or to . . . lose a few pounds? . . . Every sincere battle with addiction begins with an attempt to change addictive behavior. Literally we try to reform our behavior, substituting constructive actions for destructive ones. In the process, we will have opportunities to notice the spiritual significance of our struggles; we will be invited toward something deeper. If we say yes to that invitation, it means we are willing, at least to some extent, for God to transform our desire."[9]

It has been suggested that the first work of Divine grace is simply to enable us to understand what is wrong – that we are not in control.[10]   I would say that in this context the second work of grace may simply be to enable us to see that there is sin in our lives that needs to be confessed, which will ultimately lead to repentance and conversion. Jesus told his first century disciples "When he [the Holy Spirit] comes, he will convict the world of guilt in regard to sin and righteousness and judgment."[11]

If you go to a physician for help you must honestly give the details of your history, lifestyle, and symptoms. Likewise when dealing with the Divine physician, if you want real deliverance from an addiction, you need to be transparent. If you don't just want surface, cosmetic treatment, then you need to allow the physician to order diagnostic tests such as blood work, x-rays, cat scans and the like, to see what's going on inside of you; you may at some time even need to allow a surgeon's knife to go deep within to really correct an underlying problem. The Hebrew King David learned the necessity of coming clean with the Lord. He wrote, "My strength evaporated like water on a sunny day until I finally admitted all my sins to you and stopped trying to hide them." His heart cry became "Search me, O God, and know my heart. . ." [12] [13]

Chapter 12

Dealing with Guilt & Sin

Guilt has been referred to as the weak spot in the armor of the subconscious.[1] The Kahunas of Hawaii recognized that those guilty of sin were more susceptible to the harmful effects of evil spirits.[2] Christian theologian, Walter Brueggemann asserts: "The poison of guilt is at least as dangerous as nuclear waste. It must be put away where it cannot destroy or contaminate."[3] The Hebrew Teacher in Proverbs offers wise counsel: "You will never succeed in life if you try to hide your sins. Confess them and give them up/ then God will show mercy to you."[4]

According to one Christian counselor, "Psychological guilt is the fear of being found out. It is the recognition that one has violated his standards. It is the pain of not having done as one knows he ought to. . . . Ventilation of feelings must be replaced by confession of wrong doing"[5]

In his classic book, *Whatever Became of Sin?*, Psychologist Karl Menninger wrote: "For me, wrong is basically what my mother and father taught me that one should not do, or at least what I should not do. . . . As I have grown older, I have increasingly confirmed or rejected parts of the code in the light of experience and reason."[6] In the beginning of the Epistle to Romans, in the New Testament, it is mentioned that one of the characteristics of fallen humanity is not only a failure to honor God, but also one's parents! One of the Ten Commandments in the Jewish Torah is to honor our father and mother. Now I realize that some people today do not have a father and/or mother, and I also acknowledge that some individuals grow up with parents who are poor role models. For some children, grandparents may fill in as parental/authority-type figures. But, in an ideal world, one would like to think that even a flawed parent, or authority figure, is someone who for the most part has the child's best interest at heart. Over the years, I have met many smoking adults who will not allow their children to take up the habit. If a person takes up smoking and continues to smoke despite the advice of parents or outcry of other family members, this definitely is a legitimate reason for guilt.

But ultimately guilt is not just the result of violating the correct or incorrect standards passed down to us by parents or other human authority figures in our lives, it may also be that nagging feeling that we are breaking some kind of moral law – that we are going against nature. What is most important as an adult is to ascertain what is truly right and wrong; and when one surveys the winnowed wisdom of the world's religions one finds much agreement on the basics of morality and conduct. At the heart of religion there is a deep reverence and respect for life.[7]

Seminary professor Terry Wardle writes: "It is . . . very important that . . . dysfunctional behaviors be identified for what they are; sinful responses to pain and unmet needs in people's lives. Whenever people kill pain and try to meet needs in unhealthy ways, they are falling short of God's desire for them. And the simple definition of that set of choices is *sin*. Failure to identify this truth takes away the personal responsibility for their actions that people must accept. Even when a person is in pain or facing a genuine need, choosing to address it in a way that is hurtful to themselves or to others is a sinful response. The presence of underlying wounds does not absolve people from responsibility for the unhealthy choices they make. . . Sin must be recognized and dealt with before the Lord as an integral part of the inner healing process. "[8]

One author has written "Surely they [Adam and Eve] are responsible for what they do, but they do not really seem like hostile rebels; instead they seem innocent and gullible, almost like little children."[9] He went on to suggest that their real problem may not have been so much rebelliousness as foolishness. Jesus cried out from the cross "Father forgive them for they know not what they do," suggesting that ignorance of the severity and consequences of our actions may certainly be at the root of the human problem. But, whether sin starts out as rebelliousness or foolishness, or is just a natural part of growing up, it is still a failure to honor the Great Commandment of loving God, neighbor, and self. When we reach adulthood we are largely responsible for our present actions. It is time to stop blaming other people, our environment, or even our genetic make-up. If we had parents or role models that encouraged us to take up smoking, then perhaps we blame them or even God for placing us in such an environment in the first place. But we should not be so quick to exonerate ourselves. Listen to the following Jewish story (a midrash): "When a baby is to be conceived, an angel brings its soul before God. God then decrees what type of life the child will have, rich or poor, easy or hard. God does not decree whether one will or will not live a righteous life, however. This critical part is the person's choice."[10] At some point we need to stop blaming others for our present actions.

If on the other hand we had parents who did not approve of smoking, then we must repent of smoking because it is evidence of disobedience and lack of respect. One author points out that while "the task during adolescence is to search for and to find some sense of personal identity apart from our parent" it is incorrect to assume "that in order to develop our own values and beliefs we must defy and dishonor our parent."[11]

Most importantly we need to repent of smoking because it is sin against God, our Creator; we are not honoring our bodies by cultivating such an unnatural habit. Think about it! - A child sitting by a campfire will naturally move away from smoke. The unnatural act of learning the behavior of directly inhaling smoke leads to the equally unnatural behavior of leaving the workplace to go out into sub-zero weather to sneak a cigarette while hiding out in one's car – as I see fellow hospital employees do. (Now that's an unnatural drive!)

It is interesting to note that when King David of Israel was confronted by the prophet Nathan concerning his adulterous affair with Bathsheba and the subsequent arranged death of her husband Uriah, he confessed "I have sinned against the Lord."[12] Likewise, the prodigal son in Jesus' parable acknowledged that not only had he sinned against his earthly father, but in his wayward actions he had also "sinned against heaven."[13] Both of these biblical characters acknowledged that they had somehow done more than hurt another human being - they had also somehow hurt or failed to honor and love God. In this way that had violated a higher moral law. As Chuck Colson, writes "Sin is not simply the wrong we do our neighbor when we cheat him, or the wrong we do ourselves when we abuse our bodies. Sin –all sin- is a root rebellion and offense against God . . . ."[14] Colson was the former hatchet-man for President Richard Nixon, who served prison time for his involvement in the Watergate scandal.

C.S. Lewis suggested that if we conceive of the Divine as just a great mysterious Life-Force, we may not feel the need to repent of sin like we would if we conceive of God as a Heavenly Father with a personality and a will.[15] He went on to point out that this may be an attraction for some people who want to believe in the Divine but don't want to be accountable for their actions. But, I would suggest that the Divine is more than all of our religious and philosophical conceptions – more than a personality, more than intelligence, more than a life-force. All of our conceptions of the Divine are limited, culturally tainted, and incomplete; but whatever our conception, we are still compelled to live in harmony with what appears to be the Divine will and order. When we stray from or violate this order we must personally acknowledge our error and seek to get back in alignment with the Eternal Way. I believe this is the essence of confession and repentance

Chapter 13

Not Running through the Valley

It appears that we humans, like sheep, have strayed from the Path and have gotten lost in the wilderness, only to have subsequently fallen into a pit or gotten caught in a snare. Our instinctive first response is to cry out for help. That is understandable. But while we are waiting for help, we should reflect on the part we have played in getting into the fix we are in. If we are honest with ourselves this will naturally lead to an acknowledgement of our waywardness - a confession of guilt. Then when and if we are rescued we won't continue to journey deeper into the woods – getting further lost - and we won't just fall into another trap or pit. Instead, in a newfound appreciation of grace and humility, we will allow our rescuer to guide us back through the woods, avoiding snares and pits, to the straight and narrow path of Shalom. Rather than solely wanting to get out of the jam of the addiction, we should be open to allowing our hearts to be changed for the better.[1] Transformation may take awhile - we must not run through the valley.[2]

In the devotional classic, *Streams in the Desert*, L.B. Cowman offered wise counsel: "Beloved, never try to get out of a dark place, except in God's timing and in His way. A time of trouble and darkness is meant to teach you lessons you desperately need. Premature deliverance may circumvent God's work of grace in your life. Commit the entire situation to Him, and be willing to abide in darkness, knowing He is present. . . You may be able to rush the unfolding of some aspects of God's will, but you harm His work in the long run. You can force a rosebud open, but you spoil the flower."[3]

If you think about the children of Israel, they provide a good object lesson here. Have you ever wondered why they spent some 400 years of slavery in Egypt? Was God giving them time to contemplate why and how they ended up there? Originally God had promised their ancestors, the Patriarchs, that they would inhabit the land of Canaan. But, as described in Genesis Ch. 37, when the sons of Israel sold their young brother Joseph to Midianite merchants, things took a turn for the worse. Perhaps little Joseph represented their innocence and idealism. Eventually we know that the innocent, pure, child-like brother rose to prominence in Egypt, and the rest of the delinquent family ended up nearly dying of hunger. Rather than the promised land of Canaan they headed for the false security and eventual bondage of Egypt. But God's Spirit, as it had hovered over the waters during creation, was hovering over the Hebrews while they endured 400 years in the chaos of captivity; and eventually when the time was right, God was moved by their groaning and responded to their cries by sending a deliverer in the person of Moses and orchestrating their exodus from Egypt. The Judeo-Christian scriptures attest to the fact that ultimately, "God does not take away life; instead, He devises ways so that a banished person may not remain estranged from him."[4]

When a person goes back to smoking or falls back into a familiar habit, he/she often attributes it to the stress of living in a messed-up world with other messed-up people. Russian author Leo Tolstoy astutely observed, "Everybody thinks of changing humanity and nobody thinks of changing himself."[5] The following amusing story shows how getting our personal priorities straight might make all the difference: "One Sunday afternoon a father was trying to take a nap, but his little boy kept bugging him with 'Daddy, I'm bored.' So, trying to occupy him with a game, the dad found a picture of the world in the newspaper. He cut it up in about fifty pieces and said, 'Son, see if you can put this puzzle back together.' The dad lay back down to finish his nap, thinking the map would keep his son busy for at least an hour or so. But in about fifteen minutes the little guy woke him up: 'Daddy, I've got it finished. It's all put together.' 'You're kidding.' He knew his son didn't know all the positions of the nations, so he asked him, 'How did you do it?' 'It was easy. There was a picture of a person on the back of the map, so when I got my person put together, the world looked just fine.'"[6]

When I was in college, during a time of personal chaos leading up to my conversion to Christ, a song entitled *Be Yourself* by Graham Nash especially affected me. One of the verses went "We needed a Savior, but by our behavior the one that was worth it is gone; Songbirds are talking and runners are walking, a prodigal son's coming home." And the chorus followed with "Be yourself, you've got to free yourself." One author states that "all of creation is oriented toward God, but the direction of that orientation is one of either rebellion or submissive service.' . . . [and] . . . 'An awareness of who we are before God, and the awful reality of our rebellion against him, is the beginning point of all true psycho-spiritual growth." He goes on to suggest, "When we pursue our selves in the presence of God we are able to find our true and original spiritual selves, which will forever elude us if we pursue self-fulfillment apart from God."[7]

According to the Bible there is also another factor that needs to be taken into account. Whether we like to acknowledge it or not, Scripture indicates, and Jesus himself acknowledged, there is a malevolent 'god' of this world – an adversary – who is also afoot in the forest prowling like a lion looking for someone to devour. And if you think about it, the natural world we live in certainly has real danger lurking around every corner (e.g. carnivores, bacteria and viruses, cancer, earthquakes, tsunamis, poisonous mushrooms). Why should we naively assume that the unseen spiritual world is different? The apostle Paul said that we wrestle not only with our own fallen natures but with spiritual powers and authorities in the high places! We need a powerful spirit-guide to help us get back to the path; a good shepherd to protect and guide us back to the safety of the sheepfold.

It has been suggested that "people caught in an addiction cry out to God in desperation, but not in repentance."[8] While this unfortunately may be too often true, when the addicted person, i.e. smoker, cries out to God with a humble, repentant spirit – acknowledging his or her complicity in the pathogenesis of the problem – God will respond. It may not be immediately, but perhaps when God is convinced that the person has learned his or her lesson and the Spirit-directed transforming work has been accomplished in his or her hearts, the person will then experience deliverance. He or she will then be set free from the snare. The step after acknowledgement of guilt is repentance – which necessitates a forsaking of the wrong behavior, i.e. smoking. After confession and repentance the person may enter what seems like a dark night of the soul. During this time he/she may experience withdrawal from the addictive substance, may feel like he/she is in suspended animation, or even like he/she is dying. It may be analogous to the anesthetization a person undergoes when a broken bone is reset; or when the leukemia patient is hospitalized and put in isolation to receive the chemo; or to use the metaphor of the butterfly, when the tired caterpillar hangs itself upside down on a branch. But in God's good timing the Dawn will break and the sun will appear in glorious colors on the horizon; the person with the broken bone will wake up from the operation sporting a cast, or the person with cancer will finish the course of chemotherapy and be declared to be in remission, or the caterpillar hanging from the branch will no longer be seeing everything upside down but will be enveloped by a womb-like chrysalis and on its way to becoming a winged creature.

Referring to the previously mentioned phenomenon of 'quantum change,' the researchers have observed that dramatic transformation does not typically arrive through the "person's own powers of logic and observation." Rather, it breaks upon them "like a sneaker wave, while their backs were turned to the sea."[9] Although a prolonged incubation process may lead up to the 'metanoia,' when the breakthrough finally comes, it may occur as quickly and dramatically as when ice turns to water or a bubble bursts![10] When the quantum change takes place, most individuals claim that everything changes. The transformations are "usually at the level of personality, of core guiding principles, of the person's way of perceiving and understanding self and reality."[11] The individual will have experienced what the Judeo-Christian tradition refers to as 'grace.'[12] Through no efforts of his or her own other than surrender, he or she will have escaped the snare, and will have experienced both liberation from the besetting sin and forgiveness for guilt. He or she will come to learn that God's healing involves not only release from addiction, but release from moral anarchy.[13]

Section III:

Preparation & Awakening (Ready to Quit Smoking)

Chapter 14

Coming Up with a Game Plan

Although you may have wanted to quit smoking now for quite some time, all of your attempts to quit have been short-lived; your hopes seem nothing more than a dream. But, in the words of one author "the best way to make your dreams come true is to wake up."[1] You have awakened from your second 'spiritual' dream and now as you lay in your bed you begin to rehearse what you are going to be doing once you finally get up. It is time to set a quit date and to begin actively preparing for it. If you are reading this book at a pace of one chapter a day, then you will be on schedule to smoke your last cigarette one week from today. However, you can set your quit date further in the future if you wish to take more time to prepare. It is really up to you. But, don't procrastinate. Come up with a firm quit date and work towards it diligently.

Mark Twain is quoted as having said "Quitting smoking is easy. I've done it a thousand times."[2] It is not uncommon to hear stories from smokers of when they tried to quit abruptly and failed miserably in short order. They had an overwhelming desire to rid themselves of the habit, but no plan formulated to make it possible. It is also not uncommon to hear of other quitting attempts that took place over a period of days or weeks, involving a gradual reduction of cigarettes smoked per day until a seemingly impenetrable barrier was reached. This approach was one Mark Twain himself must have employed, as evidenced by another of his quotes "Habit is habit, and not to be flung out of the window by any man, but coaxed downstairs a step at a time."[3] Tiptoeing down the stairs, secretly hoping that the habit is following, the hopeful quitter reaches the bottom stair only to feel a strong tug on the collar. He/she has discovered two things: how long the leash is that he/she is attached, and how immovable and strong the master is at the top of the stairs. The most important cigarettes smoked during the day, which control the habit, have been uncovered. But, no plan has been formulated as to how the master can be coaxed down the steps (i.e. how the most important, controlling cigarettes can be overcome). Smoking only a few cherished cigarettes per day might even strengthen attachment.[4] In addition to being unable to overthrow the last few tyrannical cigarettes, most people will only be willing to endure the hardship of smoking just a few cigarettes per day for a short period of time. They rationalize, after all, "I am still smoking!" And, if they are still smoking then they might as well climb back up the stairs to a more comfortable level where they feel less of a tug from the leash and can experience less withdrawal discomfort and more calm, stability, and well-being.[5]

Using football as a metaphor, this may resemble the underdog doing well against their better opponent during the first 3 quarters, only to lose in the final quarter or minutes of the game. It may seem as if the better team was merely toying with the lesser-ranked hopeful team, only to crush them in the end when it really matters. It is the ability to close the game out in the final minutes that counts. Reducing the number of cigarettes smoked per day, although encouraging and admirable, is not good enough. What is necessary is to completely kick the habit, to quit smoking, to win the game.

Although God may ultimately inspire you and empower you to become smoke-free, you must play an active role. As the apostle Paul wrote, we need to work out our salvation.[6] If you are going to be successful at quitting you must look at the chains that are binding you and attempt to institute a plan that will weaken them in some way. It has been suggested that "nothing can be changed until it is faced."[7] Many smoking cessation programs or approaches get the participants to look at their smoking habits. The habit needs to be seen as the opponent, and it is best to thoroughly know your enemy. Using the football metaphor again, it would be foolish for a team not to study the game films of their upcoming opponents prior to game day. It is important in formulating a strategy to win, to intimately know the characteristics of the opponent's running and passing games, their special teams, and their defensive attack. By analyzing one's smoking habit moment by moment, day by day, you can learn much valuable information. The "Freedom from Smoking" program of the American Lung Association (ALA) advocates the use of recording and rating sheets (pack tracks). The idea is to discern why one smokes each cigarette throughout the day and week. It is helpful to assign a need level to each cigarette. By doing this you will become better acquainted with your habit. You also want to take notice of the types of things that seem to trigger your desire to light up. Discern which cigarettes you smoke purely out of habit, and which you smoke to meet a specific need (e.g. management of stress, concentration, control of anger, energy boost, pleasure enhancement, relaxation, overcoming boredom, or to do something with their hands or mouth). What are the different moods you are in when you smoke different cigarettes: sad, angry, fearful, blah, happy, and etc? I highly suggest that you begin engaging in this preparatory exercise today, and that you continue with it until you feel confident that you know your habit inside and out!

Once you begin to know the makeup of your habit, you can design and implement alternative coping strategies. An offensive and defensive plan is formulated! These strategies, once employed, may ultimately serve to break down or dissolve the strong chains of addiction.

For those cigarettes smoked purely out of habit, i.e. meeting no apparent need, you may find that changing your routine slightly may be enough to shake up the habit. An example might be getting up immediately from the table, upon finishing a meal, and doing something incompatible with, or not associated with, smoking (e.g. brushing one's teeth, or taking a walk). Another example might be jumping in the shower or doing some light exercise upon waking in the morning, rather than heading to the kitchen for coffee and a smoke. Just keeping busy during the initial days after quitting, and waiting out the urges or cravings, can be an effective strategy. According to the ALA, urges will fade away within 5-6 minutes, even if the person does not smoke a cigarette![8] Finding substitutes for hand-mouth stimulation may also be helpful as you wait out the urges (e.g. stress ball, cinnamon or mint toothpicks, swizzle sticks, sugarless gum, carrot or celery sticks).

For managing stress or relaxing, there are time-proven methods available that can be alternative coping strategies. Among the simplest methods are slow, deep breathing techniques (e.g. diaphragmatic breathing during inhalation, and pursed-lip breathing during exhalation). When smoking a cigarette, you most likely inhale slowly and deeply, and then you exhale slowly without even giving it a second thought. Something about slow, deep breathing tells the rest of the body to slow down and relax. It communicates calm. Just because one no longer smokes, is no reason to refrain from taking opportunities throughout the day to breathe in this fashion, to slow down and to gain a measure of composure. This technique is very practical because it can be employed in almost any situation. Muscle tension/relaxation routines (from head to foot) are also a common means of releasing some of the pent up stress within the body. Imaging (i.e. closing one's eyes and calling forth in the imagination the memory of a peaceful setting), prayer, meditation, and listening to a relaxation tape or peaceful music are other ways to bring stress under control.

Exercise (whether it is conventional exercise or just getting up to stretch, take a stroll, or climb some stairs) can also be a means of temporarily relieving stress, and of providing the body with an energy boost. Exercise also tends to increase the level of catecholamines in the body. This in turn produces mental alertness. Sustained exercise results in the increased production and release of endorphins (naturally produced morphine-like substances) within the brain. Endorphins produce feelings of well-being (euphoria) and relaxation.[9] They also help to relieve pain and control anger to some extent. It has also been demonstrated that endorphins play a significant role in lessening or clearing symptoms of depression and schizophrenia.[10] Exercise, therefore, can provide many of the same rewards that smoking appears to provide for the smoker. But there is a difference! Exercise offers the promise of better health, improved memory and a possible slowing down of the aging process.[11] What does smoking promise? – A downward spiral of worsening health.

Once you have quit smoking you must persevere in reminding yourself that there is no good reason for turning back. Even weight gain is not a valid reason. Some experts have suggested that "to present with the same health hazard as smoking a pack of cigarettes per day, one must be 125 pounds overweight."[12] Smokers tend to weigh less than nonsmokers. Possible reasons for this include:[13]

- Cigarettes often mark the end of a meal instead of dessert;
- Nicotine appears to raise the level of glucose in the blood;
- Nicotine interferes with digestion (food moves through the lower G.I. tract quicker than usual);
- In smokers, food appears to stay in the stomach longer (thus maintaining fullness);
- Smoking decreases the senses of smell and taste;
- Nicotine increases the metabolic rate.

Once you quit smoking, if you attempt to exercise regularly and you don't drastically increase or decrease your daily caloric intake, you should not experience a significant weight gain According to the American Cancer Society (ACS), "even when steps aren't taken to try to prevent [weight gain], the gain is usually less than 10 pounds."[14] It is interesting to note that if someone drastically reduces his or her daily caloric intake (which some people do upon quitting smoking to prevent weight gain), he/she may actually gain weight. This phenomenon has been referred to as the 'Double Whammy.'[15] It is thought that this rather paradoxical phenomenon may occur due to the fact that in the face of a sharp reduction in caloric intake, the body slows down its metabolism. This drop compounded with the natural drop in metabolism resulting from the removal of nicotine from the body can be dramatic.

Acupuncture and laughter also appear to be ways of tapping the treasure store of endorphins within the body.[16] Low-level laser therapy (also called cold laser therapy) is used, like acupuncture needles to stimulate the body's acupoints, which in turn is intended to bring relaxation through the release of endorphins. Unfortunately, according to the ACS, there is little or no scientific evidence that acupuncture or laser therapy help people stop smoking.[17] Hypnosis is yet another tool that may enhance the success of smoking cessation. But, according to the ACS: "Hypnosis methods vary a great deal, which makes it hard to study as a way to stop smoking. For the most part, reviews that looked at studies of hypnosis to help people quit smoking have not supported it as a quitting method that works. Still, some . . find it useful."[18] If you want to try hypnosis, it may be a good idea to ask your physician to recommend a reputable hypnotherapist.

Once appropriate coping strategies have been selected, they should be reviewed and practiced prior to quitting. Borrowing again from the football metaphor, the game plan strategies should be reviewed, practiced, and memorized prior to game day. You will need to feel confident in your plan before attempting to break free. There appears to be some evidence that instituting an exercise regime prior to quitting (as early as 2-3 months ahead of time) might significantly improve the outcome. One expert has been quoted as saying "In treating hundreds of smokers, I saw that the ones who participated in aerobic exercise were most likely to quit."[19] Aerobic exercise specialist, Dr. Kenneth Cooper, has also recognized this phenomenon. He is quoted as having said "I have received hundreds of letters from cigarette smokers telling me how they could never break the habit until they started exercising. Regular aerobic activity seems to have given them an overall discipline and self-control they didn't have before."[20] There appears to be some truth to the idea that in the pursuit of a lofty goal, hindrances seem to fall way almost unnoticed. If you become obsessed with exercising and with better health, smoking will be in your way. You will likely find it easier to discard the habit, under these circumstances, than if you were only trying to rid yourself of a bad, but familiar, habit.

It should also be mentioned at this point that while you certainly can successfully quit smoking by yourself, you may benefit from enrolling in a smoking cessation program. Group support and accountability can be especially helpful during this time. According to the ACS, "Studies suggest that smoking cessation programs can significantly reduce the number of relapses to smoking. Regardless of the type of cessation program, significantly more smokers 'treated' . . . maintain abstinence one year later than those who tried to quit unaided."[21]

Whether you go it solo or as part of a collaborative effort with others, once your plan for escape has been formulated and tested in small simulated trials (i.e. practice attempts), you are at the point where the pains of withdrawal (i.e. the cost of freedom) must be weighed and faced

Chapter 15

Anticipating Withdrawal & Recovery

Two years ago, I reached the stage in my life where I have become a grandfather. Having vicariously gone through two sets of labor with my wife and now one with my eldest daughter Melissa, I am struck by the similarity between giving birth to a child and quitting smoking. For the expectant mother she has nine months to prepare physically, emotionally, and mentally for the labor that will lead to the birth of her new child. Though she knows the labor may be difficult, the anticipation of the new life pulls her on. When she reaches the point of labor there really is no turning back. Labor must be endured, unless a caesarian is planned and performed. The expectant mother has the choice of natural childbirth - which my wife reminds me is the choice she made - or of receiving some form of medication to assist in the process of labor (i.e. to lessen the pain) – the option chosen by my daughter. Likewise, when you quit smoking you have a choice of going through the process with or without pharmacologic help. But, you will still have to endure the process of quitting - to give birth to your new free non-smoking self. Because no one comes into this world with cigarette in hand, you are really returning to your original state. For this reason, withdrawal symptoms might better be referred to as 'recovery' symptoms.

Quitting smoking via the 'cold turkey' method is analogous to natural childbirth. The withdrawal will have to be faced head on. But there are some natural ways of preparing ahead of time to lessen the intensity and duration of withdrawal. 'Nicotine fading' is a gradual-reduction approach, in which one switches slowly and progressively to lower-nicotine brands, thus slowly weaning off of nicotine. Smoking less of each cigarette and inhaling less smoke with each drag commonly accompanies this approach. When coupled with the formulation and employment of a behavioral modification plan for quitting, this approach does show some promise in easing the harshness of cold turkey withdrawal and may enhance the prospect of success.[1] [2] But, one still needs to eventually make a clean break from smoking altogether.

If you attempt to quit smoking cold turkey, i.e. without the use of any nicotine-replacement products, measures should be taken to facilitate the rapid removal of nicotine from your system. Drinking large quantities of water and eating the right types of food will quicken the process of nicotine removal. Nicotine is excreted more quickly when the urine is acidic. Foods that increase the acidity of the urine include: grains, legumes, eggs, meat, cranberries, rhubarb, cocoa, tea, and nuts.[3] These measures should be taken during the first few days after cessation to hasten the withdrawal process.

If you are someone who is highly addicted to nicotine and you have perhaps experienced intense withdrawal symptoms on previous attempts to quit, the cold turkey approach may not be advisable. Just as there is no reason for a woman to be ashamed of receiving an epidural to take the edge off of the pain of labor, there should be no shame in a highly addictive individual utilizing one of the pharmacologic products available to assist in the cessation process. In labor the ultimate goal is the safe delivery of a healthy child; in smoking cessation the paramount goal is becoming smoke-free. Even with the use of a pharmacologic aide you will still need to break the habit of smoking, utilizing your individualized behavioral modification techniques. But, the employed medication can delay and lessen the nicotine withdrawal while you are learning to live again as a nonsmoker. Down the road once the nonsmoking lifestyle feels comfortable and stable, you can wean off of the medication. In the mean time you will no longer be exposing yourself to all of the hazardous chemicals found in cigarette smoke.

A type of product that is currently being marketed heavily is the electronic, or e-cigarette. This is touted as being a safe alternative to smoking the conventional cigarette. The item looks like a cigarette and when the person sucks on it the tip lights up and a nicotine/water vapor mixture is inhaled. But these products have not been thoroughly tested for safety nor are they approved by the Federal Drug Administration (FDA). One of the aims of marketing is to introduce the e-cigarette as a means of 'smoking' in non-smoking environments. The slick marketing may recruit young people to join the ranks of the nicotine addicted; and may also perpetuate nicotine addiction among those who could have been at the point of breaking the smoking/nicotine habit altogether.

The FDA has approved seven medications for use in the aid of smoking cessation. Nicotine patches, nicotine gum and nicotine lozenges are available over-the-counter, and a nicotine nasal spray and inhaler are currently available by prescription; buproprion SR (Zyban) and varenicline (Chantix) are non-nicotine medications available by prescription.[4] There are also, two additional drugs that may offer some promise in helping people quit smoking, but they are not at this time FDA-approved for this purpose: these are nortriptyline (an older anti-depressant drug), and clonidine (an older drug that is FDA approved for the treatment of high blood pressure).[5]

The nicotine replacement products simply continue to provide the ex-smoker with nicotine. It is important for the person to follow the package insert instructions provided by the manufacturer. Each product has its advantages and disadvantages, therefore the individual may want to seek the counsel of a tobacco treatment specialist or his or her physician before deciding which product to use. It is reasonably safe to say that these products are safer than continuing to smoke. He/she will be getting nicotine - but not the tar, carbon monoxide or 4,000-plus chemicals from cigarette smoke. Ideally the person should quit smoking completely and then immediately begin using the nicotine replacement product. It is not generally recommended that the person start using the nicotine product prior to quitting, because he/she may be exposed to too much nicotine. The American Cancer Website (www.cancer.org) provides a good overview of these products.

Both bupropion (Zyban) and varenicline (Chantix) are prescription medications. Neither of them contains nicotine. There are contraindications and potential side effects associated with each of these medications. The person will need to seek the counsel of his or her physician and get a prescription before trying either of these drugs. Bupropion is an anti-depressant drug that also "acts on chemicals in the brain that are related to nicotine craving. It can be used alone or together with nicotine replacement therapy."[6] Varenicline is a newer drug developed specifically to help people quit smoking. "It works by interfering with nicotine receptors in the brain. This means it has two effects: it lessens the pleasurable physical side effects a person gets from smoking, and it reduces the symptoms of nicotine withdrawal."[7] In contrast to the nicotine replacement products, it is recommended for both bupropion and varenciline that the person begins taking the medication prior to quitting smoking (1-2 weeks). If you plan to use either of these medications, make sure you set your quit date far enough down the road so that you can get the prescription filled and begin taking the respective drug far enough in advance.

Borrowing again from the metaphor of pregnancy and childbirth, the expectant parents prepare for the coming infant. In anticipation, the house is cleaned up and child-proofed, a nursery is decorated, items that will be required to care for the baby are procured. Help and well-wishes from friends and family are elicited in the form of baby shower. Likewise, prior to quit day, you should discard any cigarettes or smoking paraphernalia (e.g. lighters, ashtrays) that could tempt you to smoke. It is also recommended that you empty the ashtrays, clean the windows, and install new air fresheners in your car. It may even be appropriate to set up in advance an appointment with the dentist to have your teeth cleaned shortly after quit day. It is also important that you take time daily throughout the quitting process, to visualize yourself as a nonsmoker in the future and to rehearse in your mind how to handle certain difficult situations as a nonsmoker.

As mentioned earlier, group support and interaction during the first few days, weeks, and months after quitting is very helpful. You will be more likely to persevere through withdrawal and maintain a nonsmoking lifestyle if other people, whose friendships are valued, are supportive. You need to remind yourself that you are joining the ranks of approximately 48.1 million Americans who have already successfully kicked the smoking habit.[8] You need to reject the feeling that you are giving up something. In reality, you are gaining freedom and self-mastery – an exercise in self-determination!

If you quit smoking cold turkey, with no pharmacologic support, there will likely be a period of recovery while your body, mind, and emotions readjust to the absence of nicotine and the other components of cigarette smoke. Be assured that what you are going through is not uncommon. Potential symptoms you might experience include: dizziness; depression; feelings of frustration, impatience, and anger; anxiety; irritability; grief and loss; sleep disturbances; trouble concentrating; restlessness or boredom; headaches; fatigue; increased appetite; weight gain; constipation and gas; cough, dry mouth, sore throat, and post-nasal drip; and chest tightness. According to the ACS, "Symptoms usually start within a few hours after nicotine and its by-products are out of the body. Withdrawal symptoms can last for a few days to up to several weeks."[9]

Due to the enormous stress associated with withdrawal, you should be good to yourself during this time. Get plenty of rest and do not expect to be quite as productive or efficient as usual. Reward yourself frequently, on a short-term basis, while going through the recovery process. Buy something nice for yourself or engage in some activity you especially enjoy. After all, by quitting smoking, you are really doing something very important and very difficult. You should feel good about it and be able to celebrate.

Chapter 16

Knowing Our Spiritual Adversary

In *The Art of War: A Treatise on Chinese Military Science* (c. 500 B.C.), General Sun Tzu wrote: "When one has a thorough knowledge of both the enemy and oneself, victory is assured. When one has a thorough knowledge of both heaven and earth, victory will be complete."[1] Another aspect of preparation, in addition to the physical and psychological, that you need to consider when quitting smoking is the aspect of spiritual warfare.

Religious traditions across the board have long acknowledged the presence of real though perhaps invisible dark spiritual realties: In Islam there is the 'adversary'; in Buddhism there is 'Mara'; in Hinduism there are evil spirits; and in the Judeo-Christian tradition there is Lucifer, Satan, the devil. Now I am not suggesting that you have to envision this evil entity as a red being with hooves and horns and tail; you don't need to buy into the Hollywood depiction of the satanic. But you should at least entertain the possibility of a real live malevolent spiritual being or force working behind the scenes, most notably through the tobacco industry – one that has played a role in the development and continuation of your own addiction. In the remainder of this chapter I am going to share with you some disturbing information that should help solidify these suspicions.

It is important to gain an understanding of the true nature and tactics of these spiritual adversaries before attempting to engage them in battle – i.e. to break free from a stronghold of addiction. In the Gospel record Jesus personally addressed the devil and his demons. He certainly appears to have considered their presence to be real and their influence in the lives of human beings something to be reckoned with. He referred to the devil as a thief seeking only to "steal, kill and destroy."[2] But, in addition to referring to him as a "murderer from the beginning," he went on to call him the "father of lies."[3]

A twofold spirit of greed and deception appears to animate the tobacco industry - that billion-dollar industry working tirelessly to keep you addicted to their death-dealing products. According to the World Health Organization (WHO), "Cigarettes are possibly the most marketed product in the world. While there is no reliable estimate of global cigarette marketing expenditures, it is clearly in the tens of billions of U.S. dollars a year."[4] According to the American Lung Association (ALA), "In 2005, the five largest cigarette companies spent $13.11 billion dollars – or almost $36 million dollars per day – advertising and marketing their products [in the U.S.A.]"[5] In 2002, the WHO estimated 1.25 billion smokers worldwide.[6] In 2008, the ALA estimated that in the USA, 46 million, or 20.6 per cent of adults (> age 18) were current smokers.[7] According to the WHO, "Tobacco companies are cranking out cigarettes at the rate of five and a half trillion a year – nearly 1,000 cigarettes for every man, woman, and child on the planet . . . Over 15 billion cigarettes are smoked worldwide every day."[8]

A report by the U.S. Federal Trade Commission states "The dominant themes of cigarette advertising are that smoking is associated with youthful vigor, good health, good looks and personal, social and professional acceptance and success, and that it is compatible with a wide range of athletic and healthful activities."[9] [10] These themes have been exploited down through the years.[11]

Through advertising the tobacco industry has introduced a number of reasons for people to smoke:

- A 1935 ad read "I'm your best friend, I'm your Lucky Strike." In the background of the ad was a young man holding his girlfriend in his arms. Could the advertizing be suggesting that in a world of broken hearts and passing romance, cigarettes could be the one constant, stable companion for life? It is amazing to witness, the grieving process that many people do go through while attempting to quit smoking. It is as if they are truly losing a very dear friend!
- An ad from 1936, read "For digestions' sake – smoke Camels," thus introducing the seemingly wonderful idea of finishing a meal with a smoke. Another popular ad slogan from this year was "Reach for a 'Lucky' instead of a sweet!" Smoking as a means of weight-management has been more recently reinforced through the feminine 'slim' lines of cigarettes, and slim models in the ads.
- A 1942 ad showed a pilot flying a plane, and tied smoking 'Camels' with having "steady nerves." Other ads from the 1940's and 1950's introduced the cigarette as a stress-management tool,

used by physicians who rushed through their busy schedules full of house calls and medical emergencies. Just having that one moment to themselves for a cigarette, in between crises, enabled them to deal with the unavoidable stresses associated with their important lives of service. Smoking became associated with relaxation and treating oneself after a busy day of work, and of course Santa Claus was portrayed relaxing in his easy chair with his favorite brand of tobacco.

- Still other ads contained testimonials of people claiming that cigarettes helped to give them a little energy boost when feeling sluggish. Thus, the smoking public has been given a full house of reasons and occasions to smoke!

The cigarette industry further reinforces the smoking behavior through advertising directed at the health-conscious smoker. The industry has always sought to assuage peoples' concern over the possibly deleterious health effects of smoking.[12] But, new improved versions of cigarettes, from menthol to filter tipped to low-yield, have not proven to be safe.[13] [14]

For those smokers, who are able to quit, but still need the nicotine, the tobacco industry offers an ever-expanding array of lucrative, smokeless tobacco products (e.g. chewing tobacco, snuff, tobacco lozenges and pouches, electronic cigarettes, nicotine lollipops and lip balms, nicotine water, and nicotine wafers). An advertisement for SKOAL, a brand of snuff, stated "We're out to put a pouch in the mouth of America . . . We're introducing a legitimate alternative to smoking." The same line is being used in a very slick chic manner through the internet to lure people to the new "e-cigarettes." The effect of all of the advertising and the strength of nicotine addiction has been to maintain, over the years, a captive audience for the tobacco industry – a populace to inhabit Marlboro Country. Unfortunately these other nicotine products are not without health risks themselves.[15] [16] [17]

As a smoker you need to fully appreciate the extent that you have been, and are currently being victimized by an unscrupulous, profit-motivated industry.[18] With marketing lines such as "Take a pouch instead of a puff," the tobacco industry has heavily promoted and will continue to promote its newest alternative products. They stand to benefit the most if they are able to keep their loyal customers addicted to nicotine, by shuffling them from one tobacco product to another – maintaining a flow of revenue. This is despite the sworn testimony of CEOs of the seven leading tobacco companies in 1994 that they "believe nicotine is not addictive."[19] If one still harbors any illusion that the tobacco industry is looking out for the health of the smoker consider a disturbing quote from a report for the Tobacco Advisory Council, dated 1978: ". . . With a general lengthening of the expectation of life we really need something for people to die of . . ."[20] Tobacco provides this self-centered, profit-motivated industry just that 'something!' The Oxford Medical Companion gets it right in the statement: "Tobacco is the only legally available consumer product which kills people when it is entirely used as intended."[21]

A long overdue breath of fresh air in this stalemate situation occurred in 2009, when President Obama signed into law 'The family Smoking Prevention and Tobacco Control Act, H.R. 1256.' This Act calls for the creation of a tobacco control center within the FDA that will have authority to regulate the content, marketing and sale of tobacco products. In addition, tobacco companies and importers will be required to reveal all product ingredients and to seek FDA approval for any new tobacco products.[22] [23]

But, as encouraging as it is to see this finally occurring in the U.S., it is a different story worldwide. The tobacco industry is continuing to exploit the rest of the world with cold, calculated marketing and reckless abandon. U.S. based multinational Philip Morris, the world's biggest cigarette company, was quoted by the WHO back in 1989 as stating: "U.S. cigarette exports to Asia account for close to 70% of our volume and 97% of our profits . . ."[24] One survey found that 60% of Chinese adults did not know that smoking can cause lung cancer, while 96% were unaware it can cause heart disease.[25] Another startling quote from Philip Morris 'inter-office' communication, back in 1987, reveals the greedy, culturally insensitive strategy of marketing employed by the tobacco industry: "Work to develop a system by which Philip Morris can measure trends on the issue of Smoking and Islam. Identify Islamic religious leaders who oppose interpretations of the Quran which would ban the use of tobacco and encourage support for these leaders."[26]

Certainly a spirit of greed seems to animate this self-centered profit-motivated industry. I think you would have to agree that all through human history dark, evil spirits have at times influenced large groups of respectable people to do self-centered and terrible things. For an example, one only has to look back to the twentieth century at how the citizens of

Germany were swept along in the tide of inhuman Nazi rhetoric to become engulfed in a spirit of hatred and bigotry.

In the final analysis though, we must recognize that in a sense even the most unscrupulous individuals working for the tobacco industry are not our real enemies. Somehow their consciences have become callous and they have succumbed to an unholy spirit of greed. For them, if possible, we should extend the prayer that Jesus prayed as he hung on the cross looking down at his betrayers, accusers, and torturers: "Father forgive them, for they do not know what they are doing."[27] Our real enemies are spiritual. As the apostle Paul would write: "Our struggle is not against flesh and blood, but against the rulers, against the authorities, against the powers of this dark world and against the spiritual forces of evil in the heavenly realms."[28]

The good news is that although the dark spiritual power which animates the smoking habit appears to be exerting a death grip on you, there is a benevolent spiritual power available to you that is even stronger. It has been said that "Satan's power is external and coercive," whereas "God's power, is internal and non-coercive." The Divine Spirit seeks to "transform gently from the inside out" and respects and values human choice.[29] Jesus said that in contrast to the evil one who is intent upon stealing, killing, and destroying, he himself is committed to rescuing us and giving us life.[30] Whereas the adversary seeks to deceive us, Jesus brings us truth. If we follow in Jesus' footsteps, learn His ways, and allow the Holy Spirit to guide and empower us, we can be set free! I therefore encourage you to read on as we focus on life – on rising from the ashes. Let the spiritual journey continue.

Chapter 17

Resisting Temptation - Part 1

Because as we have established that there is a spiritual side to the smoking addiction, I would like to take time now to offer some advice on how best to deal with temptation. I can assure you that subsequent to quitting smoking you will be tempted to light up again. If you view the substances or behaviors you were formerly attached to as enemies, you may have a tendency to aggressively resist temptation – to fight back in your own strength. This approach seems to come naturally, but unfortunately is not often very successful. You are likely to find that the habit or compulsion has more strength and endurance than your own will power. As mentioned earlier, the very act of resisting temptation often seems to fuel it – like trying to put out a fire with lighter fluid. Now, this is not to say that you should just give up in the face of temptation; I am not giving you an excuse to succumb to the habit. Experts warn of the danger of "changing the rules" when we are unsuccessful in changing our behavior: "We attempt to escape our imperfection by redefining or lowering the standards necessary for 'perfection' or by blaming our flaws and errors on someone else."[1] What I am suggesting however is that, while you will need to be fully engaged in the process of overcoming temptation, you are not alone; Divine assistance is available!

Jesus said to his closest disciples, "Pray that you will not fall into temptation."[2] This seems to suggest an attitude of prayer that will keep you from slipping or falling back into habitual behavior. When asked how to pray, Jesus provided his followers with what has become known as the familiar "Lord's Prayer" or what Catholics refer to as the "Our Father." One of the lines of the prayer is "Lead us not into temptation, but deliver us from the evil one."[3] The Apostle Paul exhorted first-century followers of Jesus: ". . . Continue to work out your salvation with fear and trembling, for it is God who works in you to will and to act according to his good purpose."[4] Both human and Divine involvement is necessary in overcoming temptation. It is a cooperative effort.

73

Your part begins by living in a watchful and prayerful manner so that you are less likely to fall into temptation. In pursuing a smoke-free lifestyle, you will need to identify triggers that make you want to smoke. Once identified, these triggers need to be removed, avoided, or minimized. This may require, as mentioned earlier in the book, that you remove all smoking-related items from your home, car, or workplace. It may require changing your routines so that you are not faced with the temptation to buy cigarettes or to bum a cigarette. In other words, rather than driving by the convenient store where you have previously bought tobacco, change your route; rather than stepping out with your smoking co-workers for a break, find an alternative non-smoking coworker to break with or do something entirely different during this time. I think this kind of logic is behind the instructions God gave the Jews when he commanded them to purge all the idols from their land. As long as the idols were there and idolatrous people were engaging in idolatry, they would be tempted to join in. They would regress or become fixated at a static, infantile stage of spirituality rather than participate in a dynamic, ever-growing, ever-deepening relationship with the real, living God.

Demons have been compared to rats. The implication is that if one gets rid of the rats but leave the garbage, the rats will return. But, it is not just the garbage, or the triggers of the habit, that need to be removed - it is also the scent of the garbage.[5] Once a habit is broken and detachment has occurred it is important to refrain from reminiscing on the offending substance or behavior; otherwise the scent will linger. With regards to human relationships, they say that absence makes the heart grow fonder; unfortunately the same is true with addictive relationships. It is not uncommon, given enough distance and time from a habit, to remember the good feelings associated with it rather than the bad. It is a little like returning to an old familiar abusive relationship, or as Scripture graphically describes, "a dog returning to its vomit."[6]

The next aspect of the human role in dealing with temptation is to acknowledge the ever-present help that God offers. The Jews learned that they could overcome even the most powerful enemy as long as they were obediently trusting in God's lead. With the likes of jars, trumpets, and shouts they would send their heavily armed enemies retreating in terror. With a single smooth stone and a slingshot a little shepherd boy would take down a formidable giant. In numerous passages of the Old Testament we see God assuring Israel that if they trusted obediently in him, they would have nothing to fear; he would be with them, in fact he would go before them into battle and fight for them.[7] Jesus, the one believed by Christians to be the incarnate son of God, echoed the assurance given by his heavenly Father: "Do not let your hearts be troubled and do not be afraid . . . In this world you will have trouble. But take heart! I have overcome the world."[8] The implication is that we can "rest" in the strength and protection provided by the Divine Shepherd. The writer of the book of Hebrews in the New Testament suggested that God desires for humanity to re-enter His rest; to return to the secure parent-child relationship of the Garden of Eden.[9] You may remember, when God created the world, he rested from his labor on the seventh day. The rest we are to enter is one in which we humans can exercise our God-given authority over creation, while at the same time submitting to the authority and providence of the Creator; i.e. to responsibly use and enjoy the good substances of earth once again.

The rest suggested here is not a completely passive kind of rest; it is not lethargy or somnolence. Rather it is an alert relaxation. In dealing with temptation, the person is actively involved in the process of resisting, but in a calm and assured manner. Years ago a friend took me out on his boat and gave me an opportunity to try my hand (and legs) at water-skiing. At first I fought with all my might to get up on those skis as the boat took off, but inevitably I would tumble head over heels. But then gradually I learned how to relax and sit down in a position balancing on the skis. This is a good picture of alert relaxation. Another illustration of calm under pressure might be a good quarterback, with an equally good offensive line, hanging in the pocket long enough to spot the open receiver.

James, the leader of the first-century Church in Jerusalem, and also thought to have been the half-brother of Jesus, wrote "Submit yourselves, then to God. Resist the devil, and he will flee from you. Come near to God and he will come near to you."[10] It is important to take notice of the order in James' admonition. In dealing with temptation, i.e. engaging in spiritual warfare, we are first to submit to God – to draw near to God. Then as we "rest" in God, we can "resist" the temptation and our tempter will flee much like the enemies of the Jews did long ago.

In the Jewish tradition, the high priest went before God in the Temple and offered sacrifices on behalf of the people. The Christian tradition suggests that Jesus is the ultimate high priest who offered his own life as the final sacrificial lamb for the sins of humanity. But the good news of the New Testament is that this Jesus is also available to help us in the here and now when we face temptation; he is presented as a high priest who can sympathize with our weaknesses because he was tempted in every way, just as we are. In fact, we are told that although he overcame the common human temptations that we face, he suffered in the process. He is said to be seated at the right hand of the Father in heaven even as we speak, and he is ever praying for us. For this reason, the writer of the book of Hebrews encourages us to "approach the throne of grace with confidence, so that we may receive mercy and find grace to help us in our time of need."[11]

Regardless of how vigilant you are in attempting to remove, avoid, or minimize your triggers, you will inevitably be tempted from time to time to regress and reattach to those old substances and/or behaviors. Something out of the blue will happen, some crisis, or stressor. But just when you begin to think that your struggle with temptation is unique and somehow hopeless, take heart in the words of the Apostle Paul: "No temptation has seized you except what is common to man. And God is faithful; he will not let you be tempted beyond what you can bear. But when you are tempted, he will also provide a way out so that you can stand up under it."[12] Don't get rattled when temptation fans the flame of an old desire or behavior. Remember to draw near to God and enter into that alert relaxation state.

Chapter 18

Resisting Temptation – Part 2

A comedian once said "Whenever I think about exercising, I just sit down and rest until the feeling goes away."[1] Use procrastination to your advantage. Put off giving in to the temptation of picking up a cigarette or returning to some other familiar habit, to a later indefinite time; that time never needs to really come! You don't ever have to get around to it. Remember to live in the moment. Learn to make use of 'delayed gratification.' According to one author, "The problem with many temptations is that they are close and immediate. If you can put them off a while and give your mind a chance to recover from its panic, you will be in better shape to see the bigger picture."[2]

In the New Testament we learn that our real, most formidable enemies are not other people, but rather spiritual forces inside and outside of ourselves. We also learn from Jesus that we are to love and pray for our enemies. This would suggest to me that a nonviolent approach to dealing with temptation may be advisable; it ties in with the concept of resisting through resting in God. In dealing with illness and disease, of which addiction may be categorized, physician Bernie Siegel advocates choosing a loving approach. He writes, "Choose love, because when you love your enemies, they cease to exist."[3] He goes on to write: "I envision the day that science will show us how to stop waging a war against cancer, thus empowering the disease with the focus upon war and conflict and show us how to heal our lives and bodies. Harsh words such as 'kill,' 'blast,' 'poison,' and 'assault' will be dropped from our medical language, stopping the perpetrating of negative hypnotic effects."[4] I am not sure I completely appreciate his strong sentiment, especially in light of my wife Linda's recent experience with leukemia, but he may make a valid point. While it is hard for me to see cancer, or a harmful vise-like addiction such as smoking, as anything other than evil, I can see that treating these things with hatred may be counter-productive. It has been suggested that the danger of fighting things is that we energize the very things we're fighting against by acknowledging them.[5] Carl Jung once wrote, "What you resist persists."[6] Always one to emphasize the positive rather than the negative,

Mother Teresa is quoted as having said, "I will never attend an anti-war rally. If you have a peace rally, invite me."[7]

Siegel cites a case of a lady who envisioned the peaceful image of birds feeding on the crumbs of her cancer. "This peaceful image was not about killing the enemy and fighting a war, but about nourishment and healing." He also refers to another patient "who had no results when she saw her white cells as vicious dogs eating her tumor, but when the tumor became a block of ice in her visualization, God's light melted it away."[8]

The Apostle Paul advised the first-century followers of the Way, who were later to be called Christians, to love their enemies rather to be vengeful. This was at a time when these love-intoxicated people were being martyred for their faith. He wrote: "Do not be overcome by evil, but overcome evil with good."[9] Little did Paul know that by following the lead of the suffering savior, this upstart religion of peace would overcome the enemy – three centuries later Christianity would be proclaimed the official religion of the Roman Empire![10]

The wisdom of the Far East sheds some light on how best to deal with temptation.[11] The Buddhist approach in resisting temptation might be to simply acknowledge the presence of the tempting thoughts – "to feel their texture" – and then to let them go, rather than "falling into the trap of either repressing or fighting them."[12] When tempted, we can also perhaps learn a lesson from martial arts: "In judo, one steps aside when an adversary throws a blow. Forward motion is used only when the opponent is off balance."[13] Likewise, the art of 'playing possum' – i.e. doing nothing – may actually be helpful when assaulted by temptation. The offender may sniff around for a while, then eventually lose interest and move on.

With regards to our spiritual enemies – our addictions – one Christian author suggests: "Each of us has at least one area of special weakness. We may find temptation too strong there and experience repeated failures. Often we become discouraged and are tempted by a much worse sin: hopelessness." But, he goes on to emphasize that God's love and forgiveness is limitless, and that ". . . someday the area you are weakest in will be transformed into a special strength."[14] Just remember that to fall or to stumble, or to give into that temptation to smoke once again is not the end of the road. The best course of action is to quickly pick yourself up and to resume forward progress; do not allow one slip to be an excuse to return to a full-fledged life of bondage. Remember, a slip is not the same as a relapse. Learn from the ice skater or ball-room dancer, who quickly gets up from a fall and finishes the routine. No professional athlete or musician expects absolute perfection; they may shoot for it, but being realistic they know it is unattainable. For purposes of health and sanity, it is best to accept our slip-ups with grace, humility, and humor. As mentioned before we are human, and we come from 'humus' (i.e. dust and dirt). In our pursuit of perfection – an addiction-free life – it is important to love ourselves in the mean time.

Chapter 19

Wielding the Sword of the Spirit

     If you read the Gospel accounts, you will find that when tempted by the devil, Jesus frequently quoted scripture passages.[1] The apostle Paul referred to the word of God as being the sword of the Spirit which we are to wield when engaging in spiritual warfare. A time-honored object of meditation has always been the great wealth of spiritual wisdom available to us through the living religions and faith traditions. As a Christian, the time I have spent meditating upon the Bible has proved invaluable. I can truly say it has changed and continues to change my life. I can personally relate to John Wesley, the founder of Methodism, who it is said "soaked up life from many different sources. He enjoyed reading as many books as he could get his hands on. But he came to see that while his night sky had may stars in it, there was only one North Star – the Bible. It was his fixed point of navigation, on the sea of life."[2] Whereas there is a lot of great inspirational literature out there from a variety of religious traditions, I believe it is important to narrow one's focus. Seventeenth-Century Scottish Presbyterian theologian, Samuel Rutherford astutely pointed out, "There is but a certain quantity of spiritual force in any man. Spread it over a broad surface, the steam is shallow and languid; narrow the channel and it becomes a driving force."[3] The metaphor of digging a well is certainly appropriate here. It has been suggested that "if what you're looking for is water, better to dig one well sixty feet deep than to dig six wells ten feet deep." The implication then is that "by living more deeply into our own tradition as a sacrament of the sacred, we become more centered in the one to whom the tradition points and in whom we live and move and have our being."[4]

     As opposed to casual reading, speed reading, or study, meditation is slow deep reading. The practice of meditation has been compared to a cow chewing its cud. My limited understanding of bovine physiology suggests that after the initial cursory chewing, the cow swallows the hay; then later the partially digested hay is regurgitated and chewed some more at leisure. It is during this second slow, deliberate process of chewing that every bit of nutrient is extracted from the food; then it is swallowed a second time to be digested further. Meditation has been aptly referred to as "holy leisure." It is during meditation that you should roll over in your mind the bits of knowledge you have gleaned from your religious studies, so that every bit of wisdom can be applied to your life. While I worked night shift at a hospital years ago, and then subsequently worked in home care (during which time I spent hours in my care driving hither and yon), I would meditate upon scripture. As I read through my Bible on a regular basis, if a verse jumped out at me I would write it out on an index card. Then I would carry these cards around with me, either in my shirt pocket or in a recipe box. In those moments of solitude in the dead of night or on the open road I would pull out a verse and meditate on it. It has been a very fruitful endeavor. In thinking of you as you attempt to quit smoking, might it not be helpful to write down encouraging affirmations of spiritual wisdom and encouragement – perhaps scriptural promises – and cut them into cards the size of a cigarette pack? These cards can then be carried in the place formerly occupied by the cigarettes, and when the urge to smoke comes, you can just reach and grab a card to meditate slowly upon until the craving dissipates. Not only will something negative have been avoided but positive spiritual nourishment will have been provided.[5] We will make use of this technique during quit week.

Author Philip Yancey relays an interesting story of the Orange Revolution which took place in the Ukraine in 2004. "When the Ukrainian reformer Victor Yushchenko dared to challenge the entrenched party, he nearly died from a mysterious case of dioxin poisoning. . . On Election Day the exit polls showed him with a comfortable 10 percent lead; nevertheless, through outright fraud the government managed to reverse those results. That evening the state-run television station reported, 'Ladies and gentlemen, we announce that the challenger Victor Yushchenko has been decisively defeated.' However, government authorities had not taken into account one feature of Ukrainian television, the translation it provides for the hearing-impaired. On the small screen inset in the lower right-handed corner of the television screen a brave woman raised by deaf-mute parents gave a different message in sign language. 'I am addressing all the deaf citizens of Ukraine. Don't believe what they [authorities] say. They are lying . . . Yushchenko is our President!'"[6] What ended up happening is that deaf viewers began texting-messaging the truth to their friends, and "over the next few weeks as many as a million people wearing orange flooded the capital city of Kiev to demand new elections. The government finally buckled under the pressure, consenting to new elections, and this time Yushchenko emerged as the undisputed winner."

By meditating upon Scripture, spiritual truths will appear in the small-screen inset of our minds, disputing the distorted messages we are constantly being exposed to in a fallen, materialistic, idolatrous world. As one author asserts, "In a culture filled with multiple and conflicting voices, we need to be grounded in revelation."[7] Twentieth-century missionary E. Stanley Jones credits the health of his spiritual life to his "listening post" time. "A rare photograph shows him at his quiet time sitting with his Bible, a notebook, and a pen.[8] Memorized scriptures serve as unique 'anti-bodies' readily available to help us fight off the infection of temptation. Listen to the words of the psalmist, "I have hidden your word in my heart that I might not sin against you."[9] Don't forget, two of Jesus' closest friends succumbed to temptation: Judas betrayed the master, and Peter denied him. One wonders if part of the reason for their weakness under trial was because they had never really allowed Jesus' words to sink fully into their hearts and minds.

According to physician Herbert Benson, "The brain is malleable and changes constantly, mille-second after mille-second, according to our life experiences . . . The brain is its own artist, its own chemist and engineer, constantly remaking and reconstituting itself. . . Scientists call this capacity for change 'plasticity.'"[10] He goes on to state, "We have adaptable wiring that enables us to learn new things and to practice new ways of thinking that can, over time, replace the patterns of thinking the brain was accustomed to inputting, evaluating, and acting upon."[11] We have within us the capacity for change, and although as we have rightly learned that true lasting change results from Divine-human cooperation, our personal motivation for change is also crucial. Abraham Lincoln once wrote "Always bear in mind that your own resolution to succeed, is more important than any other one thing."[12]

Benson also speaks of the concept of 'remembered wellness,' which is an integral part of the relaxation response. I believe for the person trying to maintain a smoke-free lifestyle it may be helpful to take time to remember a time when one enjoyed life without the habit of smoking or the addictive substance of nicotine. But if one cannot do so, then the person must establish new memories of enjoying a substance-free life to look back fondly upon in the future.

As we meditate upon a holy book such as the Bible, we need to approach it with reverence and humility. It has been said in reference to Scripture that "instead of seeking to master the text, we allow the text to master us."[13] Richard Foster writes, "Regarding the Bible, then, perhaps the most basic question is: shall we try to control the Bible, that is, try to make it 'come out right,' or shall we simply seek to release its life into our lives and into our world? Shall we try to 'tilt' it this way or that, or shall we give it complete freedom to 'tilt' us at its will?"[14] Dietrich Bonhoeffer wrote, "The Word of Scripture should never stop sounding in your ears and working in you all day long, just like the words of someone you love. And just as you do not analyze the words of someone you love, but accept them as they are said to you, accept the Word of Scripture and ponder . . . this Word long in your heart until it has gone right into you and taken possession of you."[15] This was written by a German pastor who lost his life because of the courageous stand he took in opposition to the Nazi regime.

With regards to Scripture, John Wesley once said "The Spirit of God not only inspired those who wrote it, but continually inspires, supernaturally assists those that read it with earnest prayer."[16] It has become quite popular today in some circles to de-construct much of what Jesus said and did, to the point where in my opinion Scripture is over-analyzed. While some analysis may be helpful to clarify and bring out truth, ultimately the goal of meditating upon scripture, or any source of spiritual wisdom for that matter, should not be to increase our knowledge and inform our intellects, but rather to change our lives and transform our personalities. I am reminded of the admonition found in the Hebrew Proverbs: "Trust in the Lord with all your heart and lean not on your own understanding. In all your ways acknowledge Him, and He will direct your paths."[17] Meditation upon Scripture will enable us to trust the Divine mystery, even in the presence of unanswered questions.[18]

It has been said that the Holy Spirit can only bring to remembrance what has been stored in the memory. Therefore it is imperative to meditate upon spiritual wisdom so that it sinks down into our memories to be called up in our times of need. When the Holy Spirit brings to mind a scriptural truth that demands a response or change of behavior on our part, we need to learn to act without delay. Meekness is a quality highly prized by God; in fact, Jesus said the meek will inherit the earth. John Baker writes, "The Greek word for meekness actually means 'strength under control.' The word is used to describe a wild stallion that is tamed and taught to be ridden. That stallion still has all its strength, but now its strength is under control, ready for its master's use."[19] In the Psalms the voice of God rings loud and clear: "I will instruct you and teach you in the way you should go;

I will counsel you and watch over you. Do not be like the horse or the mule, which have no understanding but must be controlled by bit and bridle or they will not come to you."[20]

Chapter 20

The Descent & the Ascent

I would like to take some time now to provide you with what I hope is a helpful summary of the ground we have covered as well as a glimpse of where we are headed on our journey towards freedom – a skeletal map of the lay of the land. In subsequent chapters we will enlarge portions of this map to get more intimately acquainted with specific locales. But for now an overview of sorts will suffice.

I have heard it said that at any given moment in the journey of life we may describe ourselves as being in one of four spots: a settled place; an ending; an in-between time; or a new beginning. We tend to move through these phases in a cyclic fashion. I would like to overlay onto this 4-phase model a spiritual template of my own, which consists of a *Descent* – 7 steps into slavery, and an *Ascent* – 7 steps unto freedom. I would suggest that at any given moment in our lives we are positioned on one of these steps.

The Descent

1. Settled Place of Innocence: We are born into this state. It is perhaps a bit like Eden. Especially if we have a good, secure childhood in which our basic needs are met; we anticipate the best in others; we enjoy life day by day without undue worry for the future; we don't need to possess things. We live within the framework of morality and truths set for us by our parents and other authority figures. We are blissful in our ignorance. We are right with God.
2. Awakening to the Lie of Something More: We like Adam and Eve reach a point in our lives when we begin to question authority; we feel like we may be missing out on something; we are impatient to exercise our own free will and to test our wings. We begin to contemplate the possibility of change.

85

3. Temptation: We begin listening to the lies of the spirit of the age and along with our young peers begin to formulate a plan of escape from the garden of innocence. We rehearse the possibilities in our imaginations and prepare our minds.

4. The End of Innocence: We muster the courage to take action. We go against our conscience and partake of some forbidden fruit. Smoking that first cigarette is just one example of such an action. We look to this new experience as a rite of passage into a new world of freedom and adulthood.

5. The Flight of the In-Between Time: Our wayward actions fill us with a rush of exhilarating adrenaline mixed with a certain amount of fear, apprehension, guilt, and perhaps shame. We grow accustomed to the unsettling feeling of cognitive dissonance. But because we can't go back, we continue our flight of independence under the cover of secrecy and hiding from our parents and other authority figures. We find ourselves detaching more and more from the truth claims of our childhood and the moral chains that once bound us in the obedient ignorance of our youth. We continue dying to our former self – to the intimacy of relationship we once had with our parents and with God.

6. The Attachment of New Beginning: We begin to attach ourselves more and more to our chosen course of action and the new objects of our desire, fired by the peer pressure and fads of our generation. We continue to be influenced by the spirit of our age. We look to the things of the world to fulfill us.

7. Settled Place of Addiction: We eventually reach a settled place of dysfunction – the point where we have bought into the lies of our culture and our generation; we identify more and more with our pursuits and possessions to the point where we are consumed by them and held hostage. We begin to be convinced that this is all life has to offer; we are forever thirsty and find ourselves captive to activities that only temporarily provide relief. Our lives are out of control; we struggle with anxiety and depression. We become preoccupied with self; though outwardly we may possess much in the way of health and wealth, inwardly we are poor and empty – and we know it.

The Ascent

1. Settled Place of Addiction: This represents both the final step of the 'Descent into slavery' and the first step of the 'Ascent unto freedom.

2. Awakening to the Truth of Something Better: We begin to suspect and hear rumors that there is indeed a better way to live and that there may be hope for us to escape the captivity and fruitlessness of life.

3. Temptation: We are tempted to believe that we can change; indeed we begin to imagine, plan, and prepare for our escape.

4. The Action of Ending: We turn around and take that step of faith letting go of that which binds us. This is the essence of repentance. We are longing to return to Eden.

5. The In-Between Time of Flight: We continue to detach ourselves from our false idols and addictions, and leave behind the lies that we have believed in for so long. We continue to die to our old self and our old spiritual master. We no longer look to the world to fulfill us.

6. The New Beginning: We continue to attach ourselves to a lifestyle of health and goodness. We are open and responsive to the leading of the Divine Spirit.

7. The Settled Place of Contentment: We have reached a point of maturity and wisdom where our actions are in concert with our consciences; we sense that our hearts and lives are in harmony with the Divine; we find ourselves more and more concerned with the welfare of others. We are living in the fullness of the fruit of the Spirit – which includes self-control among other things like peace, joy, love. Though outwardly we may possess little in the way of health and wealth, inwardly we are rich and full.

The Christian mystical stages of the spiritual life are descriptive of the ascent mentioned in the previous model. *Awakening* is just that – realizing the need and possibility for change. Smoking may be the one out-of-control unhealthy habit that awakens us to the need for conversion. It may be what convinces us that our lives our out-of-sync spiritually. *Conversion* is acknowledging through action of the need to do an about-face. *Purgation* is the slow painful process of detachment - leaving behind the old life of bondage and individual isolation. *Illumination* is the ongoing process of following the lead of the Holy Spirit – of attachment to a life of holy purpose. Purgation and Illumination are most likely coexistent phases that we experience on the journey towards freedom. *Union* is reaching a point of stability, maturity, and fruitfulness and fullness of Spirit – a dynamic lifestyle rather than a static endpoint.

While these stages and models are descriptive of a person's life journey as a whole, they may also represent the very process that one needs to go through when dealing with a behavioral snag along the way. We all struggle with certain things that can weigh us down or keep us from progressing spiritually, things that trap us in a settled place of dysfunction. We may be well on our way back to Eden and yet find ourselves temporarily caught in a thicket of idolatry and sin. Or we may be dealing with one of the last outposts of the enemy – a habit we have developed, nurtured, and protected for ever so long: One that just needs to be vanquished and forsaken in the light. Smoking may be a perfect example of this. We must own up to the truth of the situation and awaken to our need for repentance and conversion, and then proceed on the purgative/illuminative way.

As I have already suggested, when we first exert our impatient independence through some action that goes against our conscience we may be like a caterpillar prematurely breaking out of the chrysalis. According to the book of Genesis, Adam and Eve willfully partaking of the forbidden fruit started the process. The wonderful news of the Gospel is that a Second Adam has appeared to provide us with an example to follow – of dying to sin, and selfishness; of not allowing the things of this earthly existence as good as they are to captivate us. It is through repentance, surrender and crucifixion of our wills that we can be transformed and can return to Eden – where innocence is regained and intimacy with God is restored. We are no longer separated from God, others, or ourselves. The authority over creation is once again ours. We are once again free to enjoy the good things of creation in the manner in which our Good Creator intended without being controlled by them. Our twisted desires are straightened. As described in the first Hebrew Psalm, like a tree planted by the streams of water, we are fruitful in every season; our thirst is slaked for good.

Section IV:

Action & Conversion (Quitting Smoking)

Chapter 21

Conversion

One day while watching a butterfly, the desire for flight begins to rise in the caterpillar's bosom. And then one day it stumbles upon another caterpillar spinning a chrysalis, and sometime later it witnesses a butterfly emerge from this same cocoon. Then the thought dawns on it that it will never be able to fly in its own strength no matter how much it tries. It must prepare to surrender this life of caterpillar-ness by spinning a chrysalis itself. To experience metamorphosis it must die. Eventually with the spinning of the final thread of the chrysalis it makes a clean break from its caterpillar existence and says a good-bye to the familiar outside world.

This is your last day as a smoker. You will smoke your last cigarette. You will dispose of all your smoking paraphernalia. You will write out a personalized good-bye letter to your abusive lover, i.e. your nicotine habit. I encourage you to pour out your heart on paper. In smoking cessation programs I have facilitated, we encourage our participants to read their letters in front of the group if they are so willing, and it is often a very moving experience. It appears to be a very cathartic experience, especially for the person reading the letter.

If you plan to use the nicotine patch, it may be advisable to initiate its use prior to going to bed tonight. If you are planning to use a different nicotine replacement product then you should have it readily available at the bedside to begin using first thing in the morning. Tomorrow you will wake up and it will be a new chapter in your life – a smoke-free one! In cooperation with the Divine Spirit you will rise from the ashes. But, before you lay your head down on your pillow tonight, if you have not already done so, you need to once and for all commit yourself to the Divine lover of your soul. I will guide you through this process in the remaining pages of this chapter.

1. A Cry for Help
By now you have awakened to the realization that you need supernatural help to break free from this addiction, and you cry out to God to be rescued. But, as you wait for a response, the thought dawns on you

that maybe God will expect something of you; maybe God will see right through your selfish surface request and want to shine his spotlight deeper into your heart. Perhaps the Divine physician will want to probe a bit to reveal what deeper issues are driving this dysfunctional behavior. But you feel vulnerable and are afraid of what else might have to change in your life, what else you might have to give up – of losing your identity. One author suggests, "It's human nature to want to hold onto what's familiar, even when that familiar thing is causing us pain. . . they're comfortable like an old pair of shoes. . . Since we've had them for so long we have a hard time letting them go. . . Sometimes we so closely identify ourselves by our defects that we worry, 'If I let go of this defect, will I still be me?'"[1] It has rightly been noted, "Awakening poses both a comfort and a threat; sometimes we fall back asleep and aren't ready to get up yet.[2]

But the longer you lay there and delay, the more you realize that you've hit bottom, and you can't live with the cognitive dissonance any longer. You realize it is now or never and you must step out in faith. The time for contemplation and preparation has passed. You are ripe for action.

You've also heard something to the effect that "life's tribulations need to be examined rather than avoided."[3] Perhaps you feel as if the 'hound of heaven,' God's spirit, has been tracking you for years and has finally backed you into a corner. And as you examine your life you begin to consider the possibility that maybe God has allowed you to become ensnared to get your attention – to get you to do a 180. The apostle Paul recognized this as a possible strategy that God uses. Listen to two translations of a verse from one of Paul's letters:

- "God has all men penned together in the prison of disobedience, that he may have mercy upon them all."[4]
- "In one way or another, God makes sure that we all experience what it means to be outside so that he can personally open the door and welcome us back in."[5]

Once God has our full attention we may be on the cusp of a miraculous deliverance from the things that hold us hostage, i.e. addiction.[6] The Hebrew psalmist recognized this when he cried out: "My eyes are ever on the Lord, for only he will release my feet from the snare."[7] Like the Jews in Egypt, God may want to set you free so that you can more fully worship Him. You may remember that numerous times, prior to the Exodus, God sent Moses to Pharaoh and He instructed him to say "This is what the

LORD says: Let my people go, so that they may worship me."[8] Remember, worship is not simply the singing and praying that you and I may do while in church. Worship in its fullest sense is how we conduct our lives on a moment-by moment, daily basis. It involves our minds, bodies, and hearts. Addictions and compulsions prevent our full devotion to God; they render us less able to be sensitive to the whisper of the Holy Spirit and thus inhibit our spiritual growth.

2. Repentance

So, you know you need God's help and you want to establish, restore, or deepen your relationship with God, but you don't feel at ease. Perhaps you feel like someone who is contemplating calling up an old estranged friend to ask for a favor; but maybe there are unresolved issues between the two of you, and you are carrying some guilt or a grudge. You realize that if you make the call you must first make amends – clear the air - before moving onto the request. A religious term for this is 'repentance.' In describing repentance, C.S. Lewis wrote, "It is not something God demands of you before He will take you back and which He could let you off if He chose; it is simply a description of what going back is like."[9] Another author writes of meeting a former crack addict who when asked her opinion of Alcoholics Anonymous, replied "Ah, that's a waste of time. All those 12-steps are a waste of time without repentance. You gotta repent to God first."[10] Obviously, Alcoholics Anonymous has a proven track record, but she may make a valid point.

a) Confession of Guilt

It has been suggested by one author that "the starting place for experiencing His [God's] matchless grace is recognizing why we need His mercy in the first place." He goes on to state: "We are like straying sheep, wandering away from God's best, feeding in places that ultimately lead to our own destruction. Many times this happens because we do not know better. At other times we make bad choices consciously, either unconcerned or unconvinced that the consequences are really that serious or sinful. But they are, and there is no responsible way to detour around that reality on the path to inner healing."[11]

So you ask, "What exactly do I need to repent of?" As we have already alluded to you may need to begin by repenting of starting to smoke in the first place and then of continuing to smoke against your better judgment. It has been suggested that "for a good confession three things are necessary: an examination of conscience, sorrow, and a determination to avoid sin."[12] Therefore it is appropriate to invite God to shine his searchlight on your conscience. Are there other obvious wrongs in your life that need to be acknowledged? It is time to do so. But, don't get caught up in doing an exhaustive inventory – God will reveal to you in good time what needs to be confessed and dealt with.

It has been written that "nothing squelches the spiritual life more quickly and completely than un-confessed sin."[13] To confess one's sins is to speak out in agreement with God on the matter of one's spiritual condition.[14] [15] In her classic book, *The Healing Light*, Agnes Sanford wrote, "Through the confessional my heart caught on fire. Its dullness and boredom was burned away, its coldness was turned to warmth, its pride was melted into humility."[16]

   b) Surrender

In addition to confession, you must also firmly resolve not to do smoke anymore – to quit! It will mean dying to your identity as a smoker, but the hope is to rise as a free nonsmoker. This dying to self involves surrendering to God. Jesus spoke of a type of surrender when he sounded the invitation: "Come to me, all you who are weary and burdened, and I will give you rest."[17] And, there is no burden quite so heavy as the guilt of un-confessed sin. The need for repentance and surrender is also recognized in other religious traditions.[18] [19] [20]

I realize that you may have a fear of failure. A recent CD of Paul McCartney is entitled *Memory Almost Full*. Likewise, your memory may be 'almost full' of failed attempts to quit smoking. But you must remind yourself that you are surrendering to the Creator, the Divine physician, and therefore all things are possible. The Bible is full of accounts of healing. It has been noted that "healing is so much a part of God's nature that the Hebrew word 'rapha,' which means 'to cure, to heal, to restore health,' is one of the words used to describe God in Scripture; Yahweh-Rapha is a name for God as healer."[21] Physician Herbert Benson believes humans are 'hard-wired for God.' In other words we are meant to believe in God and to have an interactive relationship with the Divine Spirit. He also suggests that we humans foster an internal healing power.[22] [23] The healing of a longstanding addiction such as smoking is every bit as miraculous as the healing of disease; and both types of healing entail Divine-human cooperation.

A priest who reviewed the faith healings at Lourdes, the famous Roman Catholic Shrine in France, once said that "people are mistaken if they think that 'miracles produce faith.' Quite the opposite, he says, 'faith produces miracles.'"[24] At some point in your brokenness you have to step out in faith and surrender yourself to God's care, believing that you will be healed. Like young little eagles being nudged out of the nest, you must believe that you will be able to fly.

Counselor Leanne Payne writes of her own 'surrender' experience: "The pain of having arrived at the utter end of any confidence in myself had brought me into the haven of God's love and care. There, in His Presence, as one would spread an extremely valuable but shattered vase before a master craftsman, I could dare to lay out the broken pieces of my mind and heart. There, in fullest confidence in His healing love, my eyes fixed on Him in obedience, I watched as He not only mended my broken heart, but united it with His."[25]

When we confess our sins and surrender ourselves into God's care, we are indeed a bit like the mythic Phoenix laying itself down on its own funeral pyre, only to rise again from the ashes - a new creature! In smoking cessation programs, on quit day, participants will often be encouraged to bring whatever cigarettes or smoking paraphernalia (e.g. lighters or ashtrays) to the class. The participants then come up in front of the class to dispose publicly of their smoking items and to read their 'goodbye letter' or to proclaim their decision to quit. You should consider doing this also, even if you are quitting in the privacy of your own home. In addition to writing that letter as I have already encouraged you to do, completely part with all remnants of your smoking persona!

3. *Redemption*

   a) Forgiveness
   When you cry out to God for deliverance from your nicotine addiction, confess your sin in the cultivation and perpetuation of the habit, resolve once and for all to quit, and surrender yourself into Divine care, you are setting yourself up to experience forgiveness and release – to be rescued! A.W. Tozer asserted that "the essence of idolatry is the entertainment of thoughts about God that are unworthy of Him."[26] If you have entertained a picture of God as being a harsh, cruel judge or a distant, aloof potentate in heaven then you will be pleasantly surprised to be embraced by the Heavenly Father, portrayed so well in Jesus' parable of

the prodigal son. In those days in Hebrew culture it would have been undignified for a father to run, let alone to welcome home a wayward son who had disgraced him, but that is just what the father in the parable did.

In speaking of the crucifixion of Jesus, one author suggests that "Golgotha came as a result of God's great desire to forgive, not his reluctance."[27] He goes on to assert, "We do not have to make God willing to forgive. In fact, it is God who is working to make us willing to seek His forgiveness.[28] From the Hebrew scroll of Isaiah, long before the coming of Christ, we read of God proclaiming to his wayward but repentant people: "I have swept away your sins like the morning mists. I have scattered your offenses like the clouds. Oh, return to me for I have paid the price to set you free."[29] An appreciation of Divine mercy and forgiveness is also evident in religious traditions outside of Judeo-Christian faith.[30] [31]

I've heard it said whether we believe in God or not, God believes in us. So, even if you've never considered yourself a person of faith or you consider yourself beyond forgiveness, if you have an earnest desire to know God and you cry out in humility and contrition for forgiveness and help, God will certainly respond. Theologian, Paul Tillich described the kind of reception one can expect to receive from God: "It is as though a voice were saying 'You are accepted, you are accepted, accepted by that which is greater than you , and the name of which you do not know; perhaps you will find it later. Do not try to do anything now; perhaps later you will do much. Do not seek for anything; do not intend anything. Simply accept the fact that you are accepted.[32] It is also imperative that while one is experiencing the forgiveness and acceptance of God, one also learns to forgive and accept oneself.

b) Release

One individual who had experienced a metanoia, or quantum change, wrote: "Before this, my Catholic faith was a veil of tears. You can seek absolution for your sins, but you don't expect a life change; you just expect to be forgiven for your sins and go on about your way in your own compulsive destructive behavior. That's how I was."[33] This probably is not unique only to the Catholic experience. What should a true confession result in? According to Richard Foster, "Confession begins in sorrow, but ends in joy. There is celebration in the forgiveness of sins because it results in a genuinely changed life."[34] In describing the differences between behavioral therapy and spirituality, one group of experts wrote: "Spirituality offers forgiveness and releases the person for life, rather than just releasing them from addiction."[35]

It is interesting to note that most people fall into two categories: either they are in need of being set free from some sort of bondage so that they can enter into a new living relationship with God (like the Jews journeying from Egypt to Canaan); or they are in need of being forgiven of something so they can return to a life of restored intimacy with God (like the Jewish exiles returning to Canaan from Persia). At the inauguration of Jesus' ministry he stood up in the Synagogue and read from the scroll of Isaiah proclaiming that he had come "to set the captives free," and as John the Baptist proclaimed, Jesus also came to be the "lamb of God who takes away the sin of the world."[36] On a grand cosmic scale the assertion of Christianity is that all of humanity has been set free from the prison house – given our walking papers – because someone greater than us agreed to serve the rest of our life sentence. Or we the kidnapped ones have been released because our Savior has paid the ransom; i.e. the Shepherd has laid down his life for the sheep.

Now, I realize some people object to the idea that a loving God would require his son to die for the sins of others; they consider it a barbaric concept. But all through the Hebrew scriptures runs the thread of a substitutionary atonement for sin: from the animals sacrificed in the Garden of Eden to provide covering for Adam and Eve's sin; to the sacrificial ram provided for Abraham on Mt. Moriah; to the Passover lamb sacrificed in each Hebrew home prior to the Exodus from Egypt; to the whole priestly/sacrificial system instituted by God through the Law. Rather than viewing this concept as a relic of a bygone barbaric era, and rather than questioning its relevance, it may be good to reframe it. It may be that it is not so much God's justice that demands a sacrifice as much as it is a human need for guilt to be truly dealt with once and for all. To me, the important take away message is that God will do anything to rescue us, would pay the highest price. When the Romans destroyed the Jerusalem Temple in 70 A.D., the practice of the Jewish priestly sacrificial system ended. But, according to the New Testament, this sacrificial system was rendered obsolete when the God-incarnate Jesus provided the ultimate sacrifice through his crucifixion to absolve the guilt of human sin for all time. The other part of the passage from Isaiah that Jesus read at his inauguration was that he had come to "proclaim the Year of the Lord's favor!" This is in reference to the 'Year of Jubilee,' which was instituted by God back in the days of Moses.[37] It reveals the true heart of God to forgive, pardon, rescue, and give second chances to people. In essence every 50 years in Israel, all debts were to be cancelled and people were to return home to have their familial inheritance restored – even if they had they had gone astray and mismanaged their lives and their assets.

One expert in 'healing prayer' writes: "I am now convinced that the most effective prayers of deliverance are those spoken by the person needing help."[38] Starting tomorrow morning and continuing on through quit week you will be provided with key verses and thoughts for this very purpose. They will become the basis of prayers or affirmations that you can use as you continue on your journey as a smoke-free individual, pursuing God's best for your life.

Introduction to Quit Week

At last, 'quit week' has arrived. You have smoked your last cigarette. You are now a non-smoker. You have made an about-face in your orientation. You are headed into the light, leaving the shadows behind. You are rising from the ashes of your smoking addiction. But, although you may have been set free you have not reached the place of freedom. You must weather the cravings of withdrawal and establish the pattern of a smoke-free lifestyle. This, as you know will take some time and require perseverance.

As we have already mentioned what you are seeking is transformation; and as we have seen in Scripture, this can only occur through the renewing of your mind. What better way of allowing your minds to be renewed than meditating upon the truth. When the cravings to smoke come during this recovery phase of withdrawal and beyond, I would like to suggest as one of your primary smoking cessation tactics that you stop and take the time to write down one of the following passages (whether it be hazards of smoking, benefits of quitting, scripture verses, or inspirational thoughts). I would encourage you to buy several packs of index cards for this purpose. After you have written out the passage on the card, take some time to meditate upon its meaning and to allow the Divine Spirit to open your mind so that the truth becomes relevant and personal to you. Take a few moments to breathe in and out slowly and deeply, picturing yourself receiving life from the Spirit as you inhale and casting your cares and anxiety upon Him as you exhale. Learn how to rest in God's presence. If you have time, perhaps you might even want to get up and take a little walk while you continue to reflect on the truth. Remember, according to the American Lung Association, urges will fade away within 5-6 minutes, even if you do not smoke a cigarette![1]

This Divine stall tactic I am suggesting you engage in during quit week will serve multiple purposes: you will avoid giving in to the immediate craving for a cigarette; you will be developing a habit of looking to your Creator to meet the needs of the hour or minute rather than giving in to the natural but painful emotions that produce stress; and you will be stocking the library of your mind with truth. Borrowing from the metaphor of my wife Linda's bone marrow transplant, you will be allowing a new spiritual immune system to be implanted and set up by God within your inner being. In the future, once you have written down all the passages provided during quit week, you can carry these cards with you and pull them out for the purpose of meditation when the urges to smoke come in the weeks to come. Down the road, when the cravings to smoke come, you may even get to the point where you sense the Spirit drawing appropriate truths from your memory to the surface of your consciousness; you may then be able to leave the index cards behind. But they will always be there for you to refer to if the need arises.

The most tempting time to pick up a cigarette and return to your old familiar but dysfunctional habit will be when you face a stressful situation. Experts agree that whereas there may be numerous stressful situations a person may face, common to all are three basic feelings: anger, sadness, and fear.[2] Anger may be associated with feelings of aggressiveness, rage, hatred, or guilt. Fear may be associated with feelings of inadequacy, helplessness, nervousness, anxiety, or pressure. Sadness may be associated with feelings of disappointment, hopelessness, emptiness, fatigue, or exhaustion. It has been suggested that the painful emotions we feel are the true source of stress, rather than the situations we face. The situations are the stressors or triggers. How we respond to the emotions evoked by these situations will determine the stress. Therefore it is important for us to learn how to deal with these emotions in a healthy manner – to manage them effectively. Happiness is the feeling that one experiences when the stressful situation is weathered and the stress-producing emotions are properly dealt with. Happiness may be characterized by feelings of gladness, gratitude, determination, and excitement.

When we observe an animal, e.g. a cat, which is exposed to a stressor such as a dog, we will notice evidence of the instinctive 'fight or flight' response. The cat's hair stands on end, the back is arched, the nails come out, the teeth are barred, and a hissing sound can be heard. The cat is ready to pounce and fight for its life or make a mad dash in the other direction in full retreat. Built into our human nature is also the 'fight or flight' response. But most of the stressors we face do not warrant fighting or fleeing in a physical sense. We must manage the powerful emotions elicited by the stressor while at the same time refraining from lashing out aggressively in anger, or passively running away in fear or withdrawing into our shell. Learning to be able to stand our ground assertively can be quite a challenge. Often times we rely on those things which we have become addicted, such as cigarettes, to enable us to temporarily manage our stress-producing emotions and to withstand the stressor. But, when the means to manage the stress are harmful in themselves, then we must find healthier means.

Each day of quit week I have provided you with a pack of twenty quotations to write out and meditate upon (in place of smoking one pack of cigarettes per day). Each pack consists of a combination of fifteen scriptural passages and five thoughts to ponder. (All scriptural passages are from Today's New International Version of the Bible unless otherwise noted.) Because cigarette packs today come with warning labels, I have also provided you each day with something analogous to these: three reasons to stay the course of quitting -one negative and two positive. During the course of 'Quit Week' you will build a library of thoughts to meditate upon to counteract the different stress-producing emotions that you are likely to face in your ongoing journey to freedom from smoking. On a daily basis I encourage you to remind yourself that eight out of ten Americans *do not* smoke, and over 48 million Americans have successfully quit smoking.[3][4] You can certainly be one of them, especially with the Divine Spirit working in and through you.

Hazards of Smoking

According to the World Health Organization, "No other consumer product is as dangerous, or kills as many people. Tobacco kills more than AIDs, legal drugs, illegal drugs, road accidents, murder, and suicide combined."[5]

Benefits of Quitting

- 12 hours after quitting, the carbon monoxide level in the blood drops to normal[6] (increased oxygen-carrying capacity of the blood may improve exercise tolerance)
- Fresher, cleaner breath, teeth, fingers, clothes, home, and car

Verses for the Day

1 Peter 2:25

For "you were like sheep going astray," but now you have returned to the Shepherd and Overseer of your souls.

Psalm 25:15

My eyes are ever on the LORD, for only he will release my feet from the snare.

Psalm 40:1-3

I waited patiently for the LORD; he turned to me and heard my cry. He lifted me out of the slimy pit, out of the mud and mire; he set my feet on a rock and gave me a firm place to stand. He put a new song in my mouth, a hymn of praise to our God. Many will see and fear the LORD and put their trust in him.

Psalm 118:5

When hard pressed, I cried to the LORD; he brought me into a spacious place.

Psalm 124:7-8

We have escaped like a bird from the fowler's snare; the snare has been broken, and we have escaped. Our help is in the name of the LORD, the Maker of heaven and earth.

Ezekiel 36:25-26

I will cleanse you from all your impurities and from all your idols. I will give you a new heart and put a new spirit in you . . .

Zechariah 4:6

'You will not succeed by your own strength or by your own power, but by my Spirit,' says the LORD All-Powerful.   (New Century Version)

Matthew 5:3

You're blessed when you're at the end of your rope. With less of you there is more of God and his rule. (The Message)

Matthew 19:26

With God all things are possible.

Romans 8:28

In all things God works for the good of those who love him, who have been called according to his purpose.

1 Corinthians 4:20

 God's Way is not a matter of mere talk; it's an empowered life. (The Message)

2 Corinthians 4:16

We're not giving up. How could we! Even though on the outside it often looks like things are falling apart on us, on the inside, where God is making new life, not a day goes by without his unfolding grace. (The Message)

2 Corinthians 5:17

If anyone is in Christ, the new creation has come: The old has gone, the new is here!

Philippians 1:5

He who began a good work in you will carry it on to completion . . . .

Hebrews 13:6

Since God assured us, "I'll never let you down, never walk off and leave you," we can boldly quote, God is there, ready to help; I'm fearless no matter what. Who or what can get to me? (The Message)

Thoughts for the Day

- "Every act of physical, psychological, or moral disobedience of God's purpose is an act of wrong living, and has its . . . consequences."[7]
- "Addictions – to drugs, alcohol, tobacco, and other substances – [are] the devastating disorders in which we appear to lose the God-given freedom to control our behavior."[8]
- "An ever increasing craving for an ever diminishing pleasure is the devil's formula."[9]
- "We crave things we do not need until we are enslaved by them."[10]
- "It is the nature of desire not to be satisfied, and most human beings live only for the gratification of it."[11] - Aristotle

Chapter 23

Quit Week: Day 2

Hazards of Smoking

Some experts have suggested that "to present with the same health hazard as smoking a pack of cigarettes per day, one must be 125 pounds overweight."[1]

Benefits of Quitting

- 2 weeks to 3 months after quitting, circulation improves and lung function increases[2]
- Improved senses of taste, smell, and vision

Verses for the Day

Psalm 9:10

GOD's a safe-house for the battered, a sanctuary during bad times. The moment you arrive, you relax; you're never sorry you knocked. (The Message)

Psalm 32:8-9

I will instruct you and teach you in the way you should go; I will counsel you with my loving eye on you. Do not be like the horse or the mule, which have no understanding but must be controlled by bit and bridle or they will not come to you.

Psalm 34:7

The angel of the LORD encamps around those who fear him, and he delivers them.

Psalm 55:22

Cast your cares on the LORD and he will sustain you . . .

Proverbs 3:5-6

Trust in the LORD with all your heart and lean not on your own understanding; in all your ways submit to him, and he will make your paths straight.

Isaiah 26:3

You will keep in perfect peace those whose minds are steadfast, because they trust in you.

Isaiah 30:15

This is what the Sovereign LORD . . . says: "In repentance and rest is your salvation, in quietness and trust is your strength . . ."

Isaiah 40:31

Those who hope in the LORD will renew their strength. They will soar on wings like eagles; they will run and not grow weary, they will walk and not be faint.

Matthew 6:34

Give your entire attention to what God is doing right now, and don't get worked up about what may or may not happen tomorrow. God will help you deal with whatever hard things come up when the time comes. (The Message)

Matthew 11:28

Are you tired? Worn out? . . . Come to me. Get away with me and you'll recover your life. I'll show you how to take a real rest. Walk with me and work with me—watch how I do it. Learn the unforced rhythms of grace. I won't lay anything heavy or ill-fitting on you. Keep company with me and you'll learn to live freely and lightly." (The Message)

John 14:27

Peace I leave with you; my peace I give you. I do not give to you as the world gives. Do not let your hearts be troubled and do not be afraid.

John 16:33

I have told you these things, so that in me you may have peace. In this world you will have trouble. But take heart! I have overcome the world.

2 Corinthians 3:17

Where the Spirit of the Lord is, there is freedom.

Philippians 4:6-7

 Don't fret or worry. Instead of worrying, pray. Let petitions and praises shape your worries into prayers, letting God know your concerns. Before you know it, a sense of God's wholeness, everything coming together for good, will come and settle you down. It's wonderful what happens when Christ displaces worry at the center of your life. (The Message)

Hebrews 4:9-11

 The promise of "arrival" and "rest" is still there for God's people. God himself is at rest. . . . So let's keep at it and eventually arrive at the place of rest, not drop out through some sort of disobedience. (The Message)

Thoughts for the Day

- "The habit of smoking . . . appears to psychiatrists to be an oral neurosis, an attempt to recapture the pleasure and warmth of nursing. Cigarettes, cigars, and pipes are really nothing but adult thumb-sucking, adult pacifiers, pseudo-food, love substitutes."[3]
- "Whenever people kill pain and try to meet needs in unhealthy ways, they are falling short of God's desire for them. And the simple definition of that set of choices is *sin*. . . The presence of underlying wounds does not absolve people from responsibility for the unhealthy choices they make."[4]
- "Our addictions are our own worst enemies. They enslave us with chains that are of our own making and yet that, paradoxically, are virtually beyond our control. . . . Addiction breeds willfulness within us yet, again paradoxically, it erodes our free will and eats away at our dignity. . . . Yet, in still another paradox, our addictions can lead us to a deep appreciation of grace. They can bring us to our knees. . ."[5]
- Hardiness is "the ability to view challenges as opportunities to grow."[6]
- Chinese pictogram for "crisis" is the character for danger juxtaposed with the Chinese symbol for opportunity. In medical terminology when a patient is pronounced "critical" the implication is that he or she can either move towards life or death

Hazards of Smoking

"No chemical or industrial by-product comes close to equaling tobacco smoke as a health hazard. One group of researchers estimates that smoking 1.4 cigarettes produces a risk of loss-of-life comparable to consuming 100 charcoal-broiled steaks or living near to a polyvinylchloride (PVC) plant for twenty years."[1]

Benefits of Quitting

- 1 to 9 months after quitting; coughing and shortness of breath may decrease[2] (fewer colds and infections – especially respiratory)
- Improved self-image and feeling of self-control

Verses for the Day

Matthew 5:8

You're blessed when you get your inside world—your mind and heart—put right. Then you can see God in the outside world. (The Message)

Matthew 5:44-46

Love your enemies and pray for those who persecute you, that you may be children of your Father in heaven. He causes his sun to rise on the evil and the good, and sends rain on the righteous and the unrighteous.

Matthew 6:12-14

Forgive us our debts, as we also have forgiven our debtors. . . . If you forgive others when they sin against you, your heavenly Father will also forgive you.

Mark 12:28-31

 One of the teachers of the law . . . asked him, "Of all the commandments, which is the most important?" "The most important one," answered Jesus, "is this: . . . Love the Lord your God with all your heart and with all your soul and with all your mind and with all your strength.' The second is this: 'Love your neighbor as yourself.' There is no commandment greater than these."

Romans 12:21

Do not be overcome by evil, but overcome evil with good.

1 Corinthians 13:11

When I was a child, I talked like a child, I thought like a child, I reasoned like a child. When I became a man, I put the ways of childhood behind me.

2 Corinthians 1:3-4

All praise to the . . . Father of all mercy! God of all healing counsel! He comes alongside us when we go through hard times, and before you know it, he brings us alongside someone else who is going through hard times so that we can be there for that person just as God was there for us. (The Message)

Philippians 2:13

Be energetic in your life of salvation, reverent and sensitive before God. That energy is God's energy, an energy deep within you, God himself willing and working at what will give him the most pleasure. (The Message)

Colossians 3:12-13

So, chosen by God for this new life of love, dress in the wardrobe God picked out for you: compassion, kindness, humility, quiet strength, discipline. Be even-tempered, content with second place, quick to forgive an offense. Forgive as quickly and completely as the Master forgave you. And regardless of what else you put on, wear love. It's your basic, all-purpose garment. Never be without it. (The Message)

Colossians 3:23

Whatever you do, work at it with all your heart, as working for the Lord . . . .

1 Timothy 6:6

A devout life does bring wealth, but it's the rich simplicity of being yourself before God. (The Message)

2 Timothy 2:22

Run away from infantile indulgence. Run after mature righteousness—faith, love, peace—joining those who are in honest and serious prayer before God. (The Message)

Hebrews 12:10-11

. . . God is doing what is best for us, training us to live God's holy best. At the time, discipline isn't much fun. It always feels like it's going against the grain. Later, of course, it pays off handsomely, for it's the well-trained who find themselves mature in their relationship with God. (The Message)

James 1:2-4

Consider it a sheer gift, friends, when tests and challenges come at you from all sides. You know that under pressure, your faith-life is forced into the open and shows its true colors. So don't try to get out of anything prematurely. Let it do its work so you become mature and well-developed, not deficient in any way. (The Message)

1 Peter 1:14-16

Don't lazily slip back into those old grooves of evil, doing just what you feel like doing. You didn't know any better then; you do now. As obedient children, let yourselves be pulled into a way of life shaped by God's life, a life energetic and blazing with holiness. God said, "I am holy; you be holy." (The Message)

Thoughts for the Day

- "The Holy Spirit creates spiritual crises in our lives. We respond to His call by coming as rebels in surrender to God's love . . . we reach the end of our rope . . ."[3]
- "It is by going down into the abyss that we recover the treasures of life. Where you stumble, there lies your treasure." – Joseph Campbell
- "Under each of life's burdens, behind each painful obstacle, past each trial and test lies the pearl of great price."[4]
- "From the standpoint of the addicted person, all the mind tricks and self-deceptions have one dedicated purpose: to continue the addictive behavior. Likewise, there is only one dedicated action that really counteracts addiction, and that is to stop the addictive behavior."[5]
- "Always bear in mind that your own resolution to succeed, is more important than any other one thing."[6] - Abraham Lincoln

Hazards of Smoking

"A pack-and-a-half-per-day smoker gets a yearly dose of radiation in parts of his or her lungs equal to what his or her skin would be exposed to in about 300 chest x-rays."[1]

Benefits of Quitting

- 1 year after quitting, the excess risk of coronary heart disease is half that of a smoker's[2]
- More money to spend on other things (in addition to money saved from the purchase of cigarettes and paying 'sin' tax, nonsmokers can expect to pay less for many types of insurance: life, health, disability, automobile, and home). *Stop and calculate how much you spend on cigarettes per day, per month, per year, and over a 10-year span!*

Verses for the Day

Genesis 4:7

If you do not do what is right, sin is crouching at your door; it desires to have you, but you must rule over it.

Exodus 14:13

Do not be afraid. Stand firm and you will see the deliverance the LORD will bring you today.

Proverbs 25:28

Like a city whose walls are broken through is a person who lacks self-control.

Isaiah 41:10

Do not fear, for I am with you; do not be dismayed, for I am your God. I will strengthen you and help you; I will uphold you with my righteous right hand.

Matthew 16:24

"Anyone who intends to come with me has to let me lead. You're not in the driver's seat; I am. Don't run from suffering; embrace it. Follow me and I'll show you how. Self-help is no help at all. Self-sacrifice is the way, my way, to finding yourself, your true self." (The Message)

Mark 8:34

 Then he called the crowd to him along with his disciples and said: "Whoever wants to be my disciple must deny themselves and take up their cross and follow me.

Romans 8:13; 13:12-14

If you live according to the sinful nature, you will die; but if by the Spirit you put to death the misdeeds of the body, you will live. . . . Let us put aside the deeds of darkness and put on the armor of light. . . . Clothe yourselves with the Lord Jesus Christ, and do not think about how to gratify the desires of the sinful nature.

2 Corinthians 10:3-5

Though we live in the world, we do not wage war as the world does. The weapons we fight with are not the weapons of the world. On the contrary, they have divine power to demolish strongholds. We demolish arguments and every pretension that sets itself up against the knowledge of God, and we take captive every thought to make it obedient to Christ.

Galatians 2:20

I have been crucified with Christ and I no longer live, but Christ lives in me.

Ephesians 6:10-12

Be strong in the Lord and in his mighty power. Put on the full armor of God, so that you can take your stand against the devil's schemes. For our struggle is not against flesh and blood, but against the rulers, against the authorities, against the powers of this dark world and against the spiritual forces of evil in the heavenly realms.

Philippians 4:13

I can do all this through him who gives me strength.

Colossians 1:29

I strenuously contend with all the energy Christ so powerfully works in me.

Colossians 3:1-3,5

Since, then, you have been raised with Christ, set your hearts on things above, where Christ is seated at the right hand of God. Set your minds on things above, not on earthly things. For you died, and your life is now hidden with Christ in God. . . . Put to death, therefore, whatever belongs to your earthly nature . . . .

2 Thessalonians 3:3

The Lord is faithful, and he will strengthen you and protect you from the evil one.

1 John 4:6

. . . The Spirit in you is far stronger than anything in the world. (The Message)

Thoughts for the Day

- "At each of life's major developmental stages, we are free to choose to ignore the demands of maturity, quit growing, or even regress to a more childish level."[3]
- Trappist monk Thomas Merton, a former smoker himself, recognized that habits such as smoking impede a life of prayer and intimacy with God.[4]
- "It is part of the cure to wish to be cured."[5]
- "God can empower the soul only to the degree of personal availability to Him. Partial availability renders partial strength. Total yieldedness causes a saturation of the soul with Divine empowering."[6]
- "Act yourself into a new way of thinking."[7]

Chapter 26

Quit Week: Day 5

Hazards of Smoking

It has been estimated that "an hour a day in a room with a smoker is nearly a hundred times more likely to cause lung cancer in a non-smoker than 20 years spent in a building containing asbestos."[1]

Benefits of Quitting

- 5 to 15 years after quitting, the risk of stroke is reduced to that of a non-smoker[2]
- Reduced risk of fires (or even burn marks on clothing and furnishings)

Verses for the Day

1 Corinthians 6:19-20

Do you not know that your bodies are temples of the Holy Spirit, who is in you, whom you have received from God? You are not your own; [20] you were bought at a price. Therefore honor God with your bodies.

2 Corinthians 7:1

Dear friends, let's make a clean break with everything that defiles or distracts us, both within and without. Let's make our entire lives fit and holy temples for the worship of God. (The Message)

117

Psalm 119:37

Turn my eyes away from worthless things; preserve my life according to your word.

John 14:23

Anyone who loves me will obey my teaching. My Father will love them, and we will come to them and make our home with them.

John 15:5-8

I am the vine; you are the branches. If you remain in me and I in you, you will bear much fruit; apart from me you can do nothing. If you do not remain in me, you are like a branch that is thrown away and withers; such branches are picked up, thrown into the fire and burned. If you remain in me and my words remain in you, ask whatever you wish, and it will be done for you. This is to my Father's glory, that you bear much fruit, showing yourselves to be my disciples.

Romans 12:1-2

With eyes wide open to the mercies of God, I beg you, my brothers, as an act of intelligent worship, to give him your bodies, as a living sacrifice, consecrated to him and acceptable by him. Don't let the world around you squeeze you into its own mould, but let God re-mould your minds from within, so that you may prove in practice that the plan of God for you is good, meets all his demands and moves towards the goal of true maturity. (J.B. Phillips New Testament)

Galatians 5:16-18

Live freely, animated and motivated by God's Spirit. Then you won't feed the compulsions of selfishness. For there is a root of sinful self-interest in us that is at odds with a free spirit, just as the free spirit is incompatible with selfishness. . . . Choose to be led by the Spirit and so escape . . . erratic compulsions . . . . (The Message)

Galatians 5:22-23

The fruit of the Spirit is love, joy, peace, patience, kindness, goodness, faithfulness, gentleness and self-control.

Galatians 5:25

Since we live by the Spirit, let us keep in step with the Spirit.

Galatians 5:25

Since this is the kind of life we have chosen, the life of the Spirit, let us make sure that we do not just hold it as an idea in our heads or a sentiment in our hearts, but work out its implications in every detail of our lives. (The Message)

Ephesians 3:16-17

I pray that out of his glorious riches he may strengthen you with power through his Spirit in your inner being, so that Christ may dwell in your hearts through faith.

Ephesians 4:22-24

Everything—and I do mean everything—connected with that old way of life has to go. It's rotten through and through. Get rid of it! And then take on an entirely new way of life—a God-fashioned life, a life renewed from the inside and working itself into your conduct as God accurately reproduces his character in you. (The Message)

1 Thessalonians 5:16-19

Rejoice always, pray continually, give thanks in all circumstances; for this is God's will for you . . . Do not put out the Spirit's fire.

James 4:8-10

Quit dabbling in sin. Purify your inner life. Quit playing the field. Hit bottom, and cry your eyes out. The fun and games are over. Get serious, really serious. Get down on your knees before the Master; it's the only way you'll get on your feet. (The Message)

1 Peter 4:7

Be alert and of sober mind so that you may pray.

Thoughts for the Day

- "Just as a ship without a helm is driven to and fro by the waves, so a careless man, who abandons his proper course, is tempted in countless ways."[3]
- "When a [tempting] thought enters our awareness, imagine that it is a floating log, just coming into view upstream. Observe the log floating nearer, without becoming attached or involved with it in any way, and finally let it float away and out of sight downstream. . . The goal in this technique is not to fight the images or try to banish them entirely, but simply not to be pushed around and dominated by them."[4]
- Self-denial sets us free to love others, releases us from self-pity, and saves us from self-indulgence. "The way to self-fulfillment is through self-denial."[5]
- "Reject anything that is producing an addiction in you . . . Refuse to be a slave to anything but God. Remember an addiction, by its very nature, is something that is beyond your control. Resolves of the will alone are useless in defeating a true addiction. You cannot decide to be free of it. But you can decide to open this corner of your life to the forgiving grace and healing power of God."[6]
- The fourth-century monk Macarius said that all spiritual progress is "a matter of falling and getting up again, building, something up and then being knocked down again."[7]

Hazards of Smoking

Eye irritation, headaches, nasal irritation, cough, and elevated carbon monoxide levels are common in non-smokers who are chronically exposed to second-hand smoke.[1]

Benefits of Quitting

- 10 years after quitting, the lung cancer death rate is about half that of a person who continues smoking[2] (and the risk of other types of cancer also decrease)
- Social acceptance (smokers are increasingly finding themselves in the politically incorrect minority)

Verses for the Day

Luke 4:17-21

"The Spirit of the Lord is on me . . . He has sent me to proclaim freedom for the prisoners and . . . to set the oppressed free . . ." - Jesus

John 3:17

God did not send his Son into the world to condemn the world, but to save the world through him.

John 8:44

The devil . . . was a murderer from the beginning, not holding to the truth, for there is no truth in him. When he lies, he speaks his native language, for he is a liar and the father of lies.

John 10:10

The thief comes only to steal and kill and destroy; I have come that they may have life, and have it to the full.

John 14:6

"I am the way and the truth and the life." - Jesus

Romans 8:34

Who then can condemn? No one. Christ Jesus who died—more than that, who was raised to life—is at the right hand of God and is also interceding for us.

1 Corinthians 15:45

We follow this sequence in Scripture: The First Adam received life, the Last Adam [Jesus] is a life-giving Spirit. Physical life comes first, then spiritual—a firm base shaped from the earth, a final completion coming out of heaven. The First Man was made out of earth, and people since then are earthy; the Second Man was made out of heaven, and people now can be heavenly. In the same way that we've worked from our earthy origins, let's embrace our heavenly ends. (The Message)

Hebrews 2:18

Because he himself suffered when he was tempted, he is able to help those who are being tempted.

Hebrews 3:1

Holy brothers and sisters, who share in the heavenly calling, fix your thoughts on Jesus, whom we acknowledge as our apostle and high priest.

Hebrews 4:14-16

Since we have a great high priest who has ascended into heaven, Jesus the Son of God, let us hold firmly to the faith we profess. For we do not have a high priest who is unable to empathize with our weaknesses, but we have one who has been tempted in every way, just as we are—yet he did not sin. Let us then approach God's throne of grace with confidence, so that we may receive mercy and find grace to help us in our time of need.

Hebrews 5:8-9

Son though he was, he learned obedience from what he suffered and, once made perfect, he became the source of eternal salvation for all who obey him.

Hebrews 12:1-2

Therefore, since we are surrounded by such a great cloud of witnesses, let us throw off everything that hinders and the sin that so easily entangles. And let us run with perseverance the race marked out for us, fixing our eyes on Jesus, the pioneer and perfecter of faith.

Hebrews 12:2-3

Keep your eyes on Jesus, who both began and finished this race we're in. Study how he did it. Because he never lost sight of where he was headed—that exhilarating finish in and with God—he could put up with anything along the way: Cross, shame, whatever. And now he's there, in the place of honor, right alongside God. When you find yourselves flagging in your faith, go over that story again, item by item, that long litany of hostility he plowed through. That will shoot adrenaline into your souls! (The Message)

1 Peter 2:21-24

This is the kind of life you've been invited into, the kind of life Christ lived. He suffered everything that came his way so you would know that it could be done, and also know how to do it, step-by-step. He never did one thing wrong, not once said anything amiss. They called him every name in the book and he said nothing back. He suffered in silence, content to let God set things right. He used his servant body to carry our sins to the Cross so we could be rid of sin, free to live the right way. His wounds became your healing. (The Message)

1 Peter 4:1-3

Since Christ suffered in his body, arm yourselves also with the same attitude, because those who have suffered in their bodies are done with sin. As a result, they do not live the rest of their earthly lives for evil human desires, but rather for the will of God. For you have spent enough time in the past doing what pagans choose to do . . . .

Thoughts for the Day

- "Let us never forget that deserts are gardens of courtship as well as fields of battle. Struggle with attachment can be seen as warfare with an insidious enemy, or it can be seen as a romance in which the soul seeks the beloved one for whom it thirsts."[3]
- "There is a strange sadness in this growing freedom. Our souls may have been scarred by the chains with which our addictions have bound us, but at least they were familiar chains. We were used to them. And as they loosen, we are likely to feel a vague sense of loss. . . We are like caged animals beginning to experience freedom, and there is something we miss about the cage."[4]
- "The Holy Spirit is present deep within the inner places of the [person's] soul, much as an artesian well flows deep within the earth. He is there in all His power and truth. Being filled with the Spirit means surrendering to the full flow of His presence already within the [person's] life."[5]

- "Whether you think you can or think you can't, either way you are right."[6] - Henry Ford
- "Be the change you wish to see!" – Gandhi

Chapter 28

Quit Week: Day 7

Hazards of Smoking

Passive smoking is associated with a greater incidence of low birth-weight babies, Sudden Infant Death Syndrome (SIDS), and bronchitis or pneumonia in infants, and higher incidence of middle-ear infections and asthma in children.[1]

Benefits of Quitting

- 15 years after quitting, the risk of coronary heart disease is the same as a non-smoker's[2]
- You will no longer expose yourself and others to the over 4,800 chemicals that have been detected in cigarette smoke, 69 of which are known to cause cancer[3]

Verses for the Day

Psalm 42:1-2

As the deer pants for streams of water, so my soul pants for you, my God. My soul thirsts for God, for the living God.

Jeremiah 2:13

My people have committed two sins: They have forsaken me, the spring of living water, and have dug their own cisterns, broken cisterns that cannot hold water.

John 4:13-14

Everyone who drinks this water will be thirsty again, but those who drink the water I give them will never thirst. Indeed, the water I give them will become in them a spring of water welling up to eternal life.

1 Corinthians 9:26-27

I don't know about you, but I'm running hard for the finish line. I'm giving it everything I've got. No sloppy living for me! I'm staying alert and in top condition. I'm not going to get caught napping, telling everyone else all about it and then missing out myself. (The Message)

1 Corinthians 6:12

"I have the right to do anything," you say—but not everything is beneficial. "I have the right to do anything"—but I will not be mastered by anything.

1 Timothy 4:7-8

Train yourself to be godly. For physical training is of some value, but godliness has value for all things, holding promise for both the present life and the life to come.

Psalm 119:11

I have hidden your word in my heart that I might not sin against you.

1 Corinthians 10:12-13

If you think you are standing firm, be careful that you don't fall! No temptation has overtaken you except what is common to us all. And God is faithful; he will not let you be tempted beyond what you can bear. But when you are tempted, he will also provide a way out so that you can endure it.

Proverbs 16:18

Pride goes before destruction, a haughty spirit before a fall.

Proverbs 24:16

Though the righteous fall seven times, they rise again . . . .

Proverbs 26:11

As a dog returns to its vomit, so fools repeat their folly.

James 1:13-15

When tempted, no one should say, "God is tempting me." For God cannot be tempted by evil, nor does he tempt anyone; but each of you is tempted when you are dragged away by your own evil desire and enticed. Then, after desire has conceived, it gives birth to sin; and sin, when it is full-grown, gives birth to death.

James 4:7-8, 10

 Submit yourselves, then, to God. Resist the devil, and he will flee from you. Come near to God and he will come near to you. Wash your hands, you sinners, and purify your hearts, you double-minded. . . . Humble yourselves before the Lord, and he will lift you up.

1 Peter 5:6-10

Humble yourselves, therefore, under God's mighty hand, that he may lift you up in due time. Cast all your anxiety on him because he cares for you. Be alert and of sober mind. Your enemy the devil prowls around like a roaring lion looking for someone to devour. Resist him, standing firm in the faith, because you know that your fellow believers throughout the world are undergoing the same kind of sufferings. The God of all grace, who called you to his eternal glory in Christ, after you have suffered a little while, will himself restore you and make you strong, firm and steadfast.

Romans 16:20

The God of peace will soon crush Satan under your feet. The grace of our Lord Jesus be with you.

Thoughts for the Day

- ". . . No step forward is maintained unless it is followed by further steps. He who does not go forward, goes back. Physical, psychical, and spiritual health is not a haven in which we can take refuge in a sort of final security, but a daily battle in which our destiny is constantly at stake."[4]
- "Freedom is never given, it is won." – A. Philip Randolph[5]
- "No matter how long the night, the day is sure to come." – Congolese Proverb[6]
- "Success doesn't come to you – you go to it." – Marva Collins[7]
- "If there is no struggle, there is no progress." – Frederick Douglass[8]

Rise from the Ashes

Section V:

Maintenance & Purgation (Staying Quit – Part 1)

Chapter 29

Introduction to Purgation

The exhausted, bloated caterpillar has surrendered. It is hanging upside down on a branch. It is enveloped in darkness – surrounded by a restrictive, coffin-like chrysalis (i.e. cocoon), which it has carefully and painstakingly spun. It now enters a second phase in the journey of metamorphosis where its caterpillar body begins to dissolve into a nutritive soup of elements for what is to come. The first step was an external dying to its caterpillar existence; this second step is an internal dying to its caterpillar identity.

At this point in your transformational journey you have surrendered in faith a specific area of weakness and willfulness to God, as best you know how. The evidence of your earnestness is that you have indeed quit smoking and have weathered the initial period of withdrawal, better termed 'recovery.' Technically, today at this moment, you are no longer a smoker! In the language of Christian conversion, you have experienced a 'new birth.' In this instance you have indeed given birth to a new smoke-free you! But, infants need to grow up to become strong, healthy, well-adjusted adults. Likewise, as a new nonsmoker you need to move through the stages of childhood and adolescence to reach the point of stability, maturity, and freedom.

While it is wonderful that you have quit smoking and are on the other side of the early intense period of withdrawal, your journey to freedom has only just begun. Using the metaphor of a garden, the visible weeds may be gone, but some of the roots are still there and the weeds will resurface unless you remain vigilant and continue to tend the garden of your heart. Freud suggested that we have a "destructive drive within us which we try constantly to control or conceal . . ."[1] He also spoke of the "dynamic of the return of the repressed: that which is denied or repressed is not eliminated; it is merely displaced from consciousness." He went on to write, "such repressed unconscious contents seldom remain unconscious. They have a way of pressing for expression and consciousness."[2] Speaking in terms of Christian conversion, one author writes: "Though you have been born anew, though you have walked away from the acts of sin that plagued your former life, you are now forced to admit that though sin does not reign in your heart it does *remain*."[3] To be set free may have been a gift of grace from God, but to achieve true lasting freedom is going to require a co-operative human-Divine effort. As has been suggested, "Deliverance does not remove a person's responsibility; it does empower the person to exercise responsibility simply, gently, and effectively."[4]

We have spoken some about the concept of 'attachment.' I would like to revisit this concept. Looking back to the story of the Garden of Eden, we remember that part of the allure of that tempting piece of fruit was that it appeared to be capable of making Adam and Eve wise, and that somehow by tasting it they would get something more than what God had been willing to give them. But unfortunately, what they desired of the fruit was more than it was capable of providing. As mentioned earlier it may have been the first instance of substance abuse.

One author describes an incident that happened to him while visiting Tibet: "I remember a Tibetan saying to me as I whined about how small the dinner portions were in this one particular restaurant, that one should not eat to feel satisfied but instead, one should eat to nourish the body."[5] The essence of substance abuse is to look to things to provide us with more than they were originally designed to by the Creator. Food is intended to be a pleasurable means of nourishing our bodies, but not to meet the deeper cravings of the human heart. When we become obsessed with it, food can easily become an idol we get attached to. Likewise many other pleasures are meant to be enjoyed up to a point, but once we attach ourselves to them and look to them for meeting deeper needs, they become our master. However, some things were probably never meant to be enjoyed in the way we are using them, and thus the term substance abuse is even more appropriate. I would suggest that tobacco, especially smoking it, falls into this category. It is poisonous, and the act of smoking is unnatural. Early on we may be tempted to smoke to fit into the crowd, or because it seems to be a short-cut to adulthood. Before long we are attached to it.

Returning to our discussion of the Garden of Eden, the next thing the couple did after they went against God's authority was to hide among the trees; then they attempted to cover their perceived nakedness with the leaves of the trees. It is natural to attempt to hide from God and other authority figures when we have violated our conscience. We seek to escape or get lost in the shadows; we prefer darkness to light. I remember when we moved to Texas, we had a detached garage. At night if we were to pull into our garage we would see literally hundreds of 'palmetto bugs' scurrying away from our headlights into the corners of the garage. It was like something out of a horror film to us newly relocated Ohioans.

Once we have left the Garden of intimacy with God and are no longer centered upon the perfect Divine will for our lives, we naturally seek the refuge of our pursuits, pastimes, and careers. We attach ourselves to these as with our substances of choice and soon our identities become defined by them. We begin to see ourselves as smokers, lovers of one specific type of music, fans of one specific sports team, a person of style with certain tastes and standards. Our career begins to define who we are. The things we own, the places we go, the crowd we run with begin to determine our worth. But through attachment we find we have merely constructed a false self that may be as confining as a suit of armor.

The Divine Spirit can flow into a chink in our armor and begin the work of dismantling the false self that is enclosing us and preventing us from breathing and moving about freely. By allowing God to help us detach from one idol, like smoking, we are starting a potential chain reaction where we may be able to see further detachment. We have taken the first step homeward, back from the far country, from exile, from our lost condition in the wilderness. Jesus told those who wished to follow him that they would need to take up their cross daily, which symbolizes the need to be prepared to die to ourselves moment by moment; to be crucified to the things of this world. This means to detach from those substances, pursuits, roles, and relationships that are preventing us from being properly attached to God; those things that prevent us from enjoying this life as it was truly meant to be enjoyed. This does not mean we will no longer be able to enjoy the things of the world around us, but rather that we will no longer be controlled by them and we will find ourselves using them in the way they were originally intended to be enjoyed by our Creator.

By repenting and surrendering to God in the area of smoking, we have begun a process of deconstruction - of detachment. We need to die to the false selves we have created through our attachment to things; and thus we need to give birth to a new self that does not arise from our mothers and fathers, our peers, or ourselves, but rather is called forth by God.[6][7]

In Christian mysticism there is a special term for this process: "purgation." During purgation we are allowing the Holy Spirit to act as a wind clearing away the unnecessary things in our lives, toppling the idols we have erected, loosening the grip that things have upon us – ultimately the 'Spring cleaning' of our hearts and lives. The Holy Spirit has also been depicted as a fire burning away the impurities in our hearts, like the dross is separated from the precious metal. The period of purgation is a step-by-step, Spirit-directed process where the person thoroughly surrenders and lets go of everything to the Divine lover. This process has also been termed 'consecration.'

You might stop me here by saying that while it is true you did want God's help in overcoming smoking, you are not sure you are ready for all this talk of purgation and full surrender. But what you must realize is that if you abort the project now or turn back at this point in the journey, you may as well rip the cast off and start hobbling on the fragile, unhealed bone; or you may as well rip open the chrysalis before the metamorphosis of the caterpillar into the butterfly has occurred.

I have spent my adulthood studying the Bible; it has been the compass and map on my personal journey. It is through the Scriptures that I have been able to calibrate my wayward, earthbound heart to the eternal priorities of the kingdom of heaven. I applaud physician Dale Matthews who, when he feels it is appropriate and the patient is receptive, prescribes prayer and Scripture along with the likes of Prozac. In his words, "The Bible helps people get better because it helps them reframe their problems in a more helpful and spiritually healthy way." He goes on to write, "The Bible's principles of healing are encoded in its stories and sayings . . . we must experience a living encounter with the Word of God."[8] There are several excellent metaphors for detachment (i.e. purgation) found in the Judeo-Christian Scriptures, and we will begin to explore these in the next chapter.

Chapter 30

Purgation in the Old Testament: Exodus & Sojourn

A macro-story of the Hebrew Scriptures is that of the Exodus of the Jews from Egypt. One of the predominant themes of the Exodus and the subsequent 40-year journey through the Sinai Peninsula is 'purgation.' To begin with, prior to the parting of the Red Sea and the glorious Exodus, the Jews were instructed to purge their households of yeast and then to eat only unleavened bread leading up to the Passover. Yeast was a metaphor for sin in the lives of the people. (This may be analogous to you as a smoker getting rid of all your cigarettes, lighters, and ashtrays, and getting the inside of your car cleaned and the windows and drapes of your home cleaned prior to quit day.) Then for the Jews, passing through the waters of the Red Sea symbolized a purging or dying of their life of bondage. The Egyptian army that pursued them and drowned in the waters represented the death of the old master. The Jews then woke up on the other shore and found themselves miraculously delivered. Although they had been set free from bondage in Egypt, they still needed to be purged of the Egyptian slave mentality. Instead of what could have been a 40-day journey to the 'Promised Land' of Canaan, a 40-year journey of purgation ensued. The process of letting go required the dying off of the entire generation of adults who had emerged from Egypt.

While the Jews may have been outwardly set free from the oppressive rule of the Egyptians, they were still inwardly in bondage – thus would begin the long process of becoming truly free. For 400 years, the Hebrews had been shaped into thinking they were only slaves – only fit to serve a superior, more powerful people. Their purpose was to make bricks and to help construct the magnificent edifices of Egypt. This is really all they knew; the promises that Jehovah had made to their forefathers were likely a distant memory, as distant as the memory of the Pilgrims and Plymouth Rock is to modern-day Americans. As far as we know the history and faith of the Hebrews was at that time only being passed on by mouth from generation to generation. Moses had not yet set down to write the Pentateuch (first 5 books of the Old Testament).

This people had been beaten into submission and made to feel worthless. But, as oppressive as the conditions in Egypt may have been, they were at least familiar: there was structure in their routines, and the types of food were predictable. Their daily existence and their relationship with their Egyptian masters may have been as dysfunctional as that of an abusive marriage, but it was nevertheless familiar. Nicotine addiction is a bit like this, isn't it? With each pack of cigarettes bought, one is in essence providing the tobacco industry with one more brick to build and maintain their billion-dollar empire. As you know, life as a smoker becomes routine; there is never any rest for the weary. One can't go to sleep at night unless one has made sure extra cigarettes are available for the next morning. Everywhere one goes, in the back of the mind, one is planning on when the next cigarette can be smoked. It is a 24/7, seven-days-a-week kind of thing.

Now that you've quit smoking you have a feeling of exhilaration mixed with loss. One former smoker has noted that one of hardest things for the new ex-smoker is to get used to the profound emptiness. What is the person to do with his/her hands? What about all those moments during the daily routine that used to be occupied with smoking? One must become accustomed to the unfamiliar 'freedom' of not having to do anything with your hands, or during your work breaks. The Jews had to learn how to be bond-servants rather than slaves. Their new Master, Jehovah God, whom Moses was a representative, was different from their abusive master, Pharaoh. God was calling them to be his servants out of love rather than cruel force. One of the first things God did was to establish the Sabbath – one day out of seven that would simply be a day of rest and leisure. This was strikingly different from the Egyptian taskmasters who demanded tireless unceasing work out of them. It was meant to be a day to be thankful and to celebrate the freedom God had given them. It was also a time to build up their own self-esteem and sense of identity as a unique God-chosen people. They were to retell the stories of how God had rescued them from the Egyptians, and they were to reflect upon the Laws he had given them.

The Ten Commandments which God gave the Jews were reminiscent of marriage vows. The Jews were at times referred to collectively as God's 'beloved.' (In other places in Scripture, Israel was referred to as God's 'son.') It was as if this Jehovah God had risen from the pantheon of Middle Eastern gods and rather than choosing a female goddess as was customary for the time, Jehovah was calling this insignificant group of people to be his bride. In a sense, the wilderness journey was like a honeymoon; it was a time for the Jews and Jehovah to really get to know one another and to bond together in love. They were on their way to the home that the groom had prepared for his bride – i.e. the 'Promised Land' of Canaan.

As a new ex-smoker, you may have a tendency to worry about how long you are going to be able to maintain a smoke-free lifestyle. The Jews were wondering how long they were going to be able to survive out in the desert following Moses before they would run out of food and water. But, God taught them an important lesson that I think applies to someone who has recently broken a habit. It may sound trite, but the thing to do is to learn to 'live one day at a time;' or as someone has said 'if you live life by the inch, it is a cinch, but if you live by the yard, it is hard!' Don't get caught up in worrying about tomorrow. Don't fall into the trap of thinking that there is no way you can remain a nonsmoker for the rest of your life. In the wilderness God taught the Jews that He would provide for them food and water miraculously – but on a daily basis. Food came every morning on the ground with the dew in the form of 'manna,' and fell from the sky every evening in the form of 'quail.' Water gushed from rocks at the appropriate times and the people were directed to springs. If you are looking to God to help you maintain a nonsmoking lifestyle, you will not be disappointed. Remember, it is God who has set you free and it is God who desires to lead you to a place of freedom. In the New Testament we read that Jesus reinforced this approach to life when he told his followers to look at how the Heavenly Father feeds the little insignificant birds and arrays in beautiful colors the wild flowers of the field; the inference is clear – if we seek God first in our lives today, we needn't worry about tomorrow.

There is another important lesson in the dealings between Jehovah and the Jews. If they sought to store up the manna for more than a day it would spoil. It was good only on the day it arrived. As someone who has successfully quit smoking, you must not rest on your laurels. Don't think that you can get a little careless today. You still can easily fall back if you're not careful. One patient who has been smoke-free for several years recently remarked to me "I realize that I am just a puff away from a pack-a-day!" Be vigilant as if you are quitting every day; if you do so, then Divine grace will be there for you every step of the way.

If you have unsuccessfully tried to quit smoking numerous times, it is understandable that you may lack confidence in yourself; it is likely that you suffer a bit from low self-esteem. This is part of the slave mentality. At the time of Moses' birth, the Jewish slave population in Egypt was increasing at a frighteningly rapid rate. Pharaoh's solution was to decree that every male Jew child was to be thrown in the river. But, even though the Jews were large in number they had been beaten into submission. They lacked confidence in themselves, and had learned to cow-tow to their masters. When Moses, who had been miraculously saved in infancy and adopted by Pharaoh's daughter, grew up, he saw how badly his own native people were being treated by the Egyptians. He single-handedly sought to stand up for his people; but, did his people rally around his efforts? No! They were too afraid of what might be the repercussions if they were to rise up against their captors. Forty years later when Moses returned to confront Pharaoh with the request to set his people free to worship God, Pharaoh made the Jews' lives harder. He gave orders not to give the Jews straw for making bricks, but he still required the same daily quota of bricks to be made. Did the Jews rise up at this time against their slave-drivers? No! They were still too afraid. They blamed Moses. They were like a giant beaten into submission by mice. They had no sense of identity, of self-worth, or of their innate capabilities – and more importantly they were clueless of the power that could be unleashed on their behalf if they called upon God.

An Indian fable tells of a tiger cub raised by goats.[1] The cub bleated like a goat, and grazed like a goat, and thought it was a goat. But one day the King of the Tigers stumbled upon the goats and spied the tiger cub. The cub was struck by the majesty of the royal feline, but still had no idea that he too was of this same species. It was not until the King Tiger picked the cub up by the scruff of the neck and carried him to a nearby pond where he saw his reflection, that the cub understood his true nature. Analogously, God had to carry the Jews, his chosen people, out into the wilderness to reveal to them their true nature. But, it would be slow-going because their inferiority complex had been forged over 400 years of slavery. You and I are not meant to be slaves to addiction. We were born to be free – to enjoy the good things in this world rather than to be controlled by them. The longer you continue on this spiritual journey the more God will reveal your true identity and authority.

Early in the Jews' Sinai sojourn they approached the promised land of Canaan and several Jewish spies were sent into the Land to scout it out.

They came back, for the most part terrified. The majority report was that the inhabitants of the land were enormous and the cities invincible. Compared to the giants in the Land, the Jewish spies saw themselves as grasshoppers. The minority report from two of the spies, Joshua and Caleb, was that the Jews had nothing to fear as long as they trusted in God. But it would take nearly 40 more years of wandering in the wilderness, and the passing of a generation, before the Jews would be ready to follow Joshua and Caleb, under God's lead, into the Promised Land. It is interesting to note that the conquest of Canaan was largely accomplished in Divine power. The walls of Jericho collapsed simply with the blowing of trumpets on the part of the Jews. In other battles the Spirit of God put fear and confusion into the hearts of Israel's enemies, who would literally kill themselves; the Jews simply had the privilege of cleaning up afterwards. But, prior to this, in the wilderness the Jew's slave mentality and inferiority complex had to be purged. They had to bond with and gain confidence in their Divine lover, protector, and provider. Likewise as a former smoker, you need to let go of past failures and realize that you are more than capable, with God's help, to maintain a healthy smoke-free life.

Another characteristic of people who are constantly put down and controlled is to complain and gripe and murmur, especially behind the backs of their superiors. I have seen this in the workplace. When employees are treated as contributing adults, with respect and trust, they tend to act like responsible well-adjusted adults. On the other hand when employees don't receive the respect and trust they deserve from their bosses and other coworkers, they begin to act like children whose feelings have been hurt. The Egyptians had to be purged of this tendency. They would murmur and complain at the drop of a hat. Their glorious leader Moses would quickly be demonized by the people once things did not seem to be going the way anticipated. The people would quickly start questioning Moses' authority, and start wishing they were back in Egypt eating leeks and onions by the Nile rather than manna and quail day after day. Quickly forgotten were the 400 years of back-breaking, sun-sweltering labor in the brickyards. God had to purge them of their tendency to wallow in self pity and resentment and their propensity of longing for the security of the dysfunctional familiarity of Egypt. God did so by instituting feasts and festivals to be observed throughout the year to remind them of how far they had come and how much they had to be thankful for, despite the ongoing difficulties of their journey. Although as a new ex-smoker you will have times when the stresses of life make you wish you could crawl back into the smoking lifestyle, you need to pause to reflect on how thankful you are to now be healthier, smoke-free, and growing in your spiritual life. Your need to remind yourself of the money you are saving and of the positive influence you may now be having on those around you. Be intentional to take the time regularly to recalibrate your heart and your resolve to the valid reasons you have for quitting smoking, rather than allowing your fickle emotions to get you out of focus and off course.

There may have also been a quick-fix mentality among the Jews. Their life in Egypt, although less than desirable, was probably at least predictable. They were living in one of the most prosperous civilizations of the world, and when they were hungry they had food to eat; their meager paychecks – if they received them - were at least on time. They had a modicum of control over their lives. And they could visibly see their masters. Out in the desert there was a lack of control, a lack of predictability. They had no permanent home; they lived in tents. When the pillar of fire moved at night or the cloud moved during the day they had to be ready to pack up camp and move on out. They were following the invisible God. When Moses spent too long up on the mountain top meeting with God, the Jews grew restless and fashioned a golden calf to worship. They had to learn patience and trust. But the transition from 'instant satisfaction' to 'delayed gratification' was not easy. Nor will it be easy for you as a new ex-smoker. Within seconds of taking a hit off of a cigarette, as a smoker you felt the click of reinforcement in your brain. The nicotine could be depended upon to provide that quick, instant fix – calming down your nerves, providing alertness, boosting energy. You were able to buy the cigarettes at a nearby convenient store 24/7. The life of faith, on the other hand requires patience and trust which must be learned. Prayers are not always answered immediately. Sometimes temptation must be resisted and hardships endured. But, learning to relinquish control and to settle into the Heavenly Father's lap for solace and strength is priceless. In time you will gain true self control. You will trade 'itchy desire' for 'settled contentment!'

In a letter written to the First-Century Christians living in the city of Corinth, the apostle Paul reflected on the importance of taking to heart the lessons learned from the Jews' exodus and sojourn:[2] "Remember our history, friends, and be warned. All our ancestors were led by the providential Cloud and taken miraculously through the Sea. They went through the waters, in a baptism like ours, as Moses led them from enslaving death to salvation life. They all ate and drank identical food and drink, meals provided daily by God. They drank from the Rock, God's fountain for them that stayed with them wherever they were. And the Rock was Christ. But just experiencing God's wonder and grace didn't seem to mean much—most of them were defeated by temptation during the hard times in the desert, and God was not pleased. The same thing could happen to us. We must be on guard so that we never get caught up in wanting our own way as they did. . . . These are all warning markers—danger!—in our history books, written down so that we don't repeat their mistakes. Our positions in the story are parallel—they at the beginning, we at the end—and we are just as capable of messing it up as they were. Don't be so naive and self-confident. You're not exempt. You could fall flat on your face as easily as anyone else. Forget about self-confidence; it's useless. Cultivate God-confidence."

Chapter 31

Purgation in the Old Testament: The Promised Land

Purging the Land

The majority of the Old Testament consists of God dealing with his chosen people the Jews. As we read through the Hebrew Scriptures, our 21st-Century sensibilities may be shocked at some of the things that are described – and rightly so! An example would be the ethnic cleansing that the Jews were commanded by God to perform as they moved into the promised land of Canaan. But, if we step back and view much of what we read in the Old Testament as we might read such great, rich works of mythical wisdom as Tolkien's *Lord of the Rings* or C.S. Lewis' *Chronicles of Narnia*, we just might find great object lessons opening up for us – ones that provide spiritual insights.

The majority of the New Testament consists of God dealing more with individuals, treating each one of us as if we were adopted sons and daughters; and there is not the exclusivity that there was in the Old Testament. The whole world is being addressed. In contrast with the Old Testament, the emphasis in the New Testament is upon engaging in spiritual rather than physical warfare.[1] Rather than fight with our physical enemies, we are called to pray for them and to love them – even to view them as neighbors. Perhaps such examples as the ethnic cleansing and battles for the Lord described in the Old Testament were meant to give us insight into how we are to engage in spiritual warfare. When we are in the place where God wants us to be (i.e. the Promised Land), we must be merciless in protecting our hearts from enemies within and without - malevolent spiritual forces and desires that would tempt us to turn away from God and to submit to idolatry, ones that would encourage us to attach ourselves to 'false infinites.' The Jews were instructed by God to refrain from worshiping either the idols of their fathers or the idols of the heathen tribes in the Promised Land of Canaan. Neither was acceptable. Likewise, we are not to excuse our idolatrous lifestyle or addictive behaviors on the basis of our upbringing or our environment. At some point we need to take personal responsibility for our actions. As the Apostle Paul urged believers, we are not to be conformed to the pattern (i.e., squeezed into the mold) of the world around us, but we are to be transformed by the Holy Spirit through the renewing of our minds.[2]

The Walled City

Another good metaphor found in the Hebrew Scriptures is that of the "walled city." In the Middle East during the Biblical times, cities were built on hills called "tells." Strong, high walls were built around the cities to protect the inhabitants from villains or other marauding hostile tribes – much like a sheepfold is designed to protect the sheep from wolves and other predators. The first thing the Jews had to do upon returning to Jerusalem from Persian/Babylonian exile was to rebuild the city wall. The once glorious holy city had been razed and the wall was in shambles.

A Hebrew proverb compares a person who lacks self-control to a city whose walls are broken down.[3] The implication is that if we lack self-control in even one area of our life we are as vulnerable and unprotected as a city with a break in the wall. I would suggest that if there is a break in the wall, it is probable that it is due to neglect, and there may be other breaks in the wall as well; the task of trying to repair the entire wall while also fending off the attacks of an enemy would be daunting to say the least. In one's own strength it may be an overwhelming and fruitless task to gain control of all the areas of weakness in our lives.

John Baker describes a game at Chuck E. Cheese's: "They have this game called Wacka Wacka. You use a big mallet to beat down these little moles that keep popping up. But when you whack one, three more pop up. You whack those and five more pop up. That machine is a parable of life. We whack down one relational conflict and another pops up. We whack down one addiction or compulsion and another one pops up. It's frustrating because we can't get them all knocked down at the same time. We walk around pretending we're God: 'I'm powerful; I can handle it.'" Baker goes on to pose a simple and yet profound question: "If we're really in control, why don't we just unplug the machine?"[4]

At this point in your journey you have exerted your free will in a responsible and humble fashion by calling out to God for help. You have invited God in through the break in your city wall which represents your smoking addiction. But, what you may not have fully realized at the time is that God wants to supervise the wall-repair project, and this will require a broad-scale renovation of the wall to bring it up to code! The Apostle Paul wrote that one of the fruits of the Spirit in a person's life is 'self-control' - in other words it is a result of allowing the Holy Spirit to take up residence in one's heart. Unlike the god of this world who tempts, cajoles and attacks, the God of Heaven knocks, whispers and responds to invitation only. God desires to be invited in, but also to be given the respect of a conquering King; God desires to sit on the throne of our hearts. To surrender, as you have already done, is to raise the white flag - to allow oneself to be conquered. If you have allowed this to happen, you have perhaps unwittingly begun a clean-up and repair project of great magnitude to make the city fit for a King, and the Divine Spirit will guide you every step of the way. The end result will be peace, and your city wall will be impregnable. Once the Jews, returning from exile, completed the formidable task of rebuilding the city wall of Jerusalem they set out to rebuild the Temple; but, unfortunately not before they rebuilt homes for themselves to live in. Once a person has overcome a habit such as smoking, with the help of God, the temptation is just to go back to living essentially the way one has in the past, only without this one vice. But, one must not forget that to be cured of one vice is not to be truly healed. And, what one should desire is to be spiritually healed so that one becomes strong and mature in faith.

Cisterns vs. Wells

Another excellent metaphor found in the Hebrew Scriptures is that of the cistern versus the well. God reprimanded his people because they were not depending upon Him to meet their deepest needs – to quench their spiritual thirst. The Hebrew prophet Jeremiah portrayed God as saying: "My people have committed two sins: they have forsaken me, the spring of living water, and have dug their own cisterns, broken cisterns that cannot hold water."[5] God has always wanted to provide for us as He did for the prototypical humans in the Garden. To look for fulfillment in the things that God has created (i.e. the creation) rather than in the Creator is like depending upon a cracked cistern rather than a well. Cisterns were large man-made pits in the ground designed to collect and store rain water. If they had cracks in them obviously the water would eventually leak out; if the water was not used up quickly enough it could become warm, stagnant and thus disease-producing. Wells were man-made tunnels dug down into the earth to tap an underground spring of cool, running water. Once the well was dug it just needed to be maintained and there would be an endless supply of fresh water even in the worst of draughts. The water supply from wells was not affected by changes in the weather or climate, as was that of cisterns. It was as if God was emphasizing to his people the importance of expending their energy in the best manner. Both cisterns and wells required work to establish and to maintain, but one was far the more dependable.

In the New Testament there is a story of the 'Jewish' Jesus meeting a 'Samaritan' woman at a well on a hot, dry day.[6] Though they had never met before, he intuitively saw the thirst in the depths of her soul. He knew that she had been married numerous times and was presently living in an adulterous relationship. He offered to give her something to truly quench her thirsty soul. He compared what he was offering her to "living water." The Holy Spirit has been compared to living water. Using this metaphor, the way of purgation involves letting go of the tendency to look for water in the familiar but undependable cisterns, and simultaneously getting busy clearing away the debris that has clogged up the neglected well. You have witnessed a trickle of this Holy water from the well as you have quit smoking and weathered the withdrawal. There is more water where that came from and the promise of a constant dependable supply if you persevere in the job of unstopping the well and of learning how to maintain it. The temptation while getting the well up and running is to revert back to the cistern; this will be especially so when you're tired and hot, and a sudden unpredictable cloud burst fills up the cistern. But you must persist in the more sure way. Likewise, the temptation to revert back to the familiar habit of smoking will be especially strong during times of stress. The acronym HALT, mentioned by the ALA in their *Freedom from* Smoking program, also reminds us of times when the lure will be strong to return to smoking: when one is hungry, angry, lonely, or tired.

Like filling up the cistern with rocks, I encourage you to close the chapter of your life that included smoking, so that you can get about the business of clearing away the debris from the well of your heart and establishing the new channel for God's Spirit.[7]

Chapter 32

Purgation in the New Testament

The Journey of Jesus

The Lenten season is a time of reflection for the Christian believer, leading up to the observance of Holy Week. Analogously, you went through a period of reflection and preparation leading up to your quit day. Good Friday, when Jesus was crucified, corresponds to the day you died to your smoking habit. The three days during which time Jesus descended in spirit to Hell, while he was dead and buried in the Garden tomb, corresponds to the withdrawal period from nicotine that you endured. Resurrection morning, when Jesus rose from the grave corresponds to you emerging from the intense period of withdrawal to where you are now. But, what you may not realize is that the resurrected Jesus is said to have spent 40 days saying good bye to his followers before ascending to heaven to be with his Father. This 40-day period might correspond to the purgation phase of 'letting go' that you are entering. Of course your period of saying good-bye to addiction may be longer than forty days; remember the Jews' good-bye to Egyptian bondage lasted forty years!

The Secure Home

Jesus told a story that could serve as a metaphor for someone who has just kicked some sort of habit. The person in the story had kicked out some unwelcome guests (whom Jesus referred to as demons), and then proceeded to sweep and clean up the house. But then later the unwelcome guests, having missed their former abode, came back in greater numbers and stormed down the front door. He said the situation for the homeowner was now worse than it had been originally. The implication could be that a person is vulnerable to succumbing once again to an addiction after the habit as been broken if his or her home is unoccupied or left unguarded. What needs to happen is a new stronger guest needs to be invited to occupy the house so that when the unwelcome guests return they will not be able to force their way in.[1]

148

The surrendering of your smoking habit to God is a good and appropriate first step in your journey, but if true freedom and stability are your goals then what you need to do now is surrender your whole self. In the words of the 19th-Century British evangelist, Charles H. Spurgeon, If you desire God to be a perpetual guest, then you must "give him all the keys of your heart; let not one cabinet be locked up from Him; give Him the range of every room and the key of every chamber."[2] And, as contemporary author Max Lucado has written "God loves to decorate." He goes on to assert, "God has to decorate. Let Him live long enough in a heart, and that heart will begin to change. . . It's not enough for Him to own you; He wants to change you."[3] For your home and your life to be secure, the new Master needs to be free to move about and to fully inhabit and guard it.

New Life/New Clothes

In his New Testament epistles, the Apostle Paul spoke of letting go of our old ways so that we can become the new person God intends. This is certainly analogous to shedding our old 'smoking' persona to become a free non-smoker. He uses graphic terms like 'putting to death' or the 'changing of clothes to describe the process of purgation required.[4] [5]

Now that you have quit smoking you need to cease to see yourself as a smoker; i.e. let go of the slave mentality. Like the caterpillar in the cocoon that is no longer living as a caterpillar, you are no longer engaging in the addictive behavior of smoking. But like the caterpillar, your task now is to allow your addictive nature or identity to dissolve. As you look around you may notice there are other aspects of your character or components of your lifestyle that may need to change if you are to move further along toward freedom. (Perhaps you were already on this spiritual journey toward freedom prior to picking up this book, and quitting smoking represents just another break in the wall being attended to or one more attachment you are relinquishing at the prompting of the Divine spirit.) It is important to remind yourself that your ultimate goal is not just to be cured of smoking or some other specific addiction, but to be transformed into someone who knows freedom through self-control and balance – one who is able to live in peace and harmony with the Creator of this world and with all the good things in it! One author has rightly noted: "Detachment is the word used in spiritual traditions to describe the freedom of desire. Not freedom *from* desire, but freedom *of* desire."[6]

Chapter 33

Mastering Your Passions in the Power of the Spirit

Mastering Your Passions

The world's religious traditions all tell us that we must detach ourselves from the things to which we are addicted - in fact it is our responsibility to do so! But the encouraging thing about these spiritual traditions is that they assure us it can indeed be accomplished.[1] [2] [3] [4] [5] In the first book of the Hebrew Pentateuch, God proclaims "sin is crouching at your door; it desires to have you, but you must master it."[6] King David, who certainly struggled unsuccessfully at times with passion, displayed an optimistic determination at some point in his life, as evidenced in one of his psalms: "I will be careful to lead a blameless life . . . I will set before my eyes no vile thing . . . I will have nothing to do with evil."[7] The Christian New Testament Scriptures announce "a powerful and complete victory over sin and its domination. The texts include decisive verbs such as 'destroy,' 'purge,' 'cleanse,' and 'abolish.'"[8] A contemporary author asserts "Our task is to remove the self-imposed blocks or character defects that stand between God and us."[9]

Learning to be Open, Honest, and Sensitive to the Divine Spirit

One psychiatrist and spiritual counselor has written: "Each of our major addictions consists not only of the primary attachment itself; it also includes the involvement of multiple other systems that have been affected by it. To put it quite simply, addictions are never single problems. As soon as we try to break a real addiction, we discover that in many respects it has become a way of life. Because of multi-system involvement, breaking an addiction usually requires changes in many different areas of life."[10] Another author writes, "The healing work of Christ happens at every level of our lives. By helping people identify sin and choose into Christ, the way is opened for the broken to experience a powerful encounter with the Lord. It is in many ways the unlocking of the first door leading into the deepest places of pain and heartache. Dysfunctional behaviors have stood guard, keeping individuals locked away from the places where Christ has wanted to meet and free them."[11]

Using the metaphor of the walled city, it is not good enough to fix one break in the wall, if other breaks are left untended. You have begun a Spirit-directed project of wall restoration. The wall is that which guards your heart and your life. The breaks are any areas where you lack self-control. You must trust your new master, the Divine Spirit, as you would a trustworthy inspector or contractor. You must walk along the wall and allow the Spirit to point out obvious breaks that need repair, and also not-so-obvious hidden evidence of underlying weakness and deterioration that needs attention. You must be honest and open at this point, allowing the Holy Spirit free access to your whole self.

Using the metaphor of the house, you must not hide things from your new master. Remember you have invited him to renovate, protect and to take up residence. Hiding things under the rug or away in locked closets or secret rooms will not do. As one author asserts, "Denial serves only to keep spiritual and emotional toxins hidden away."[12] You must give your new master every key to every door. It has been pointed out that in the Gospel accounts, "Jesus emphasizes freedom, throwing responsibility back on the individual. 'Do you want to be healed?' he asks, and only when a person answers yes does healing take place."[13] God does not force his will upon humans, but instead gives us the privilege of choosing and making our own decisions.[14]

On T.V. there is a show in which the host is invited to a home to help the occupants sort through all the junk they have accumulated – to help the pack rats de-pack! The host attempts to help the occupants prioritize – to differentiate between what is worth keeping and what needs to be parted with. Often the people have a hard time letting go of things. But, unless the clutter is removed, the renovation of the space cannot take place. We may be as blind to our attachments, as pack rats are to their stuff. We may have lost sight of the fact that some of our routines have become ruts. As one author suggests, "Old but familiar and well-worn lifestyles may no longer be in keeping with spiritual liberation."[15] In your life, when the Holy Spirit whispers to let go of something, be assured it is for your good in the long run. So, learn to recognize and be sensitive to this spiritual intuition. Don't resist, but rather comply!

19th-Century Scottish author and poet George MacDonald is said to have inspired the likes of C.S. Lewis, J.R.R. Tolkien, and Madeleine L'Engle. He wrote: "We must refuse, abandon, and deny self altogether as a ruling, or determining, or originating element in us. It is to be no longer the regent of our action. We are no more to think 'What should I like to do?' but 'What would the Living One have me to do?"[16] But as one contemporary Catholic author notes: "Unfortunately most people who are drawn to the spiritual life, pursue it half-heartedly or inconsistently. We organize life around the call of God but with an all-too-familiar pattern of distraction and conflicting goals . . ."[17] He goes on to suggest that "we seek Heaven, but we play with things which will ultimately lead us either downward and way from our eternal destiny, or at best leave us suspended between Heaven and Hell."[18] To resist the Divine promptings of detachment during purgation, can stall forward spiritual progress and result in arrested development.[19]

It has been suggested that "at each of life's major developmental stages, we are free to choose to ignore the demands of maturity, quit growing, or even regress to a more childish level."[20] English poet, William Wordsworth once wrote "the child, or at least the adolescent really is the father of man."[21] My take on this statement is that often the habits and tastes that we develop in these immature stages of life have a tendency to dominate and control future development. Another author notes that "the fading dream of adolescence may challenge every possible fiber of choice for the individual."[22] The smoking habit, which may have begun in adolescence, represents "a fixation at a level of development which one should have passed."[23] In writing to Timothy, his young protégé in ministry, the Apostle Paul offered wise counsel: "Flee the evil desires of youth . . ."[24] In another of his letters, Paul wrote, "When I became a man, I put childish ways behind me."[25]

Before we proceed with the Spirit-led detachment process, I would like to clarify something. Just as our thoughts and actions have consequences, so also do our attachments. The things we are attached to affect God, others, and ourselves. Our abuse of substances, people, and ourselves dishonors and grieves the Creator and adversely affects ourselves and others. When asked by a teacher of the Jewish Law, which of the commandments was most important, Jesus replied, "Love the Lord your God with all your heart and with all your soul and with all your mind and with all your strength.' The second is this: 'Love your neighbor as yourself.' There is no commandment greater than these."[26]

It goes without saying that as the Holy Spirit begins to shine a spotlight on our life, the first things we will be expected to let go of are those which we know deep down in our consciences to be immoral. For instance we will need to let go of any attachments that are injurious to other people, if for no other reason than because the laws of our country also require us to do so. In other words, if we are engaging in some kind of activity that violates someone else's rights or well-being, we must stop. It is sad to say, but I imagine that some people's compulsions lie in these areas. Fortunately, rather than abusing others, most people find themselves abusing either substances and/or themselves.

Chapter 34

Aspects of Purgation: Outward Detachment

Compulsions have been defined as habits that have become "choice-less." One author has suggested that "regardless of how a compulsion appears externally, underneath it is always robbing us of our freedom."[1] Sixteenth-Century Spanish mystic, St. John of the Cross recommended "that one consciously attempt to refrain from any kind of overindulgence."[2] A modern mystic recommends shunning "anything that distracts you from seeking first the Kingdom of God."[3] This is very similar to the advice that the Apostle Paul gave to First-Century followers of the "Way." He wrote, "Everything is permissible for me – but not everything is beneficial. . . I will not be mastered by anything."[4] He compared the life of faith to that of an athlete in strict training: "Therefore I do not run like a man running aimlessly; I do not fight like a man beating the air. No, I beat my body and make it my slave. . ."[5] He suggested that this life is like a marathon, "Therefore . . . let us throw off everything that hinders and the sin that so easily entangles, and let us run with perseverance the race marked out for us."[6]

On the surface, some of the objects of our compulsions may not be bad in themselves. It is our treatment of them that might be wrong. It has been said that good things can be "twisted . . . and used in the wrong way."[7] Think about it: food is not bad, nor is sex, work, sports, music, art, etc. The problem arises when we use them in a manner not intended by the Creator, or when our desire for these things or the attention we give to them grows out of control like a stream overflowing its banks. F.B. Meyer, a member of the 'Higher Life Movement' in Nineteenth-Century England, suggested that the "doorway [to the chamber of a surrendered will] is very narrow, and entrance is only possible for those who will lay aside *weights* as well as sins." Meyer defined a *weight* as "anything which, without being essentially wrong or hurtful to others, is yet a hindrance to ourselves." He went on to state "We may always know a weight by three signs: 1) We are uneasy about it; 2) We argue for it against our conscience; 3) We go about asking people's advice, whether we may not keep it without harm." In conclusion, Meyers made an earnest appeal to his readers: "All these things must be laid aside in the strength which Jesus waits to give. Ask Him to deal with them for you, that you may be set in joint in every good work to do His will (Hebrews 8:21)."[8] The removal of seemingly innocuous, but energy-draining things from our life is analogous to the pruning of superfluous branches and leaves that a vine-dresser does to make the vine more fruitful – to produce more grapes.

It has been suggested that "each sense and faculty of the soul is an 'appetite for God.'"[9] But, as one author points out "All god's gifts, whether a natural aptitude or an everyday pleasure, come to us with raw power to elbow their way out of their intended order and to usurp the Giver who created them. I must have that, no matter the cost, no matter the morality."[10] The real danger of attachment may be that it "binds the energy of the human spirit to something other than love."[11] Could the following suggestion be correct? "Perhaps what we've been after all along have been only appetizers, 'messengers.' Maybe we've been grasping for good things when what we've really desired is the Creator of all good things."[12]

I am reminded of the story of a bag lady who was well known in her neighborhood for her daily walks, during which time she would pick up stray paper, cans, and bottles and put them in her large paper sack. She never spoke with her neighbors and always kept her window shades pulled down. One week her neighbors noticed that they had not seen her perform her routine, so they reported it to the police. When the authorities broke down her door they were shocked to discover, in addition to the lady's dead body, wall-to-wall, floor-to-ceiling junk with narrow tunnels leading from room to room. The kicker of the story is what they discovered after a lifetime's worth of collected junk was finally removed from the house. Buried in the pillows, cushions, and mattress was nearly $2 million in cash; and surprisingly this little old lady lived at the level of poverty.[13] Could our addictive preoccupations prevent us from appreciating and enjoying the truly good, satisfying things of life that go unnoticed by us – that may be right under our noses?

There is a consensus of wisdom among religions across the board that there is danger in pinning our hopes of satisfaction on the temporal, illusive material things of this world.[14] [15] We may have to relinquish our hold of some seemingly good innocuous things for an indefinite time so that the Divine Spirit can correct through spiritual surgery what is wrong in our hearts. In time we then may be able to return to some of these activities or pursuits in a balanced healthy manner, but our relinquishment must be "without loopholes or escape clauses."[16] [17]

Things that are inherently wrong, or harmful (e.g. tobacco use) must simply be forsaken for good. After we have surrendered to God and are awaiting transformation we are much like the caterpillar in the chrysalis; this phase can rightly be referred to as a 'Dark Night of the Soul.' This is a term made famous by St. John of the Cross. Referring to this mysterious work of God in our lives, one modern-day mystic writes, "Every distraction of the body, mind, and spirit must be put into a kind of suspended animation before this deep work of God upon the soul can occur. It is like an operation in which the anesthetic must take effect before the surgery can be performed. There comes inner silence, peace, stillness."[18] It has been suggested that ". . . detachment from externals . . . leaves the soul unencumbered to experience the presence of God."[19]

But, alas this Spirit-guided purgation is like the peeling of an onion, moving deeper into the interior of our lives. The process of detachment moves from external to internal, and uncovers the underlying drives of dysfunctional behavior and the unmet needs in our life.

Chapter 35

Aspects of Purgation: Internal Detachment

It has been suggested that "attachment to habitual ways of thinking and seeing interferes with our ability to think and see clearly."[1] I would go further by proposing that we also may be attached to habitual ways of feeling and reacting to situations, and of managing life.

Our attachment to the past and/or future can be healthy or unhealthy. One author writes, "There are two ways to be confined by the past – replaying it and forgetting it." He goes on to say, "We do not want to be the traumatized amnesia victim who can't remember from where we came, nor do we want to be the former high school star who can't live beyond the 'glory days.'"[2] I would suggest that we also don't want our past failures, offenses, or victimization to determine our future. As another author points out: "We replay all the things we wish we could change. It's like driving a car by always looking in the rearview mirror. A rearview mirror is helpful, because it gives us perspective. Looking at our past gives us perspective, too, but if we look only at our past, we never get to see the present or look forward to the future. Some people focus on the past to the extent that their rearview mirror gets bigger than their windshield. With this kind of driving, forward progress is nearly impossible. In fact, a crash is likely in the near future."[3]

We may have trouble letting go of past memories. Perhaps someone hurt us, and we just can't forgive. We just keep uncovering that old wound and nursing that grudge. If for no other reason than our own health and well-being, we need to forgive. Perhaps on the other hand we are the offender; we have done things for which we are remorseful and ashamed of. Obviously if we have not asked the offended person or God to forgive us, we need to do so. But perhaps we have, and yet we still haven't accepted the forgiveness deep in our hearts. Just like the offended person needs to release the grudge, the offender needs to release the guilt. A remarkable woman, Corrie Ten Boom, who along with her family was instrumental in saving many Jewish lives in Holland, during World War II, has written, "When God throws our confessed sins into the sea of His forgetfulness, He puts a sign on the shore: NO Fishing Allowed!"[4] I also remember reading of a Holocaust survivor who said after the war ended and prior to immigrating to the United States, he made the hard decision to forgive the Nazis. When asked why, he stated that he did not want to bring Hitler with him to America. We need to detach from the tendency to rehash or dredge up past wounds or offenses; it is an addictive process of its own.[5]

A characteristic of the addictive nature is that the person has a tendency to seek a repeat performance, i.e. attempts to recapture the ecstasy of a past experience. A wise pastoral counselor I know tells a story of a young girl who begged her father to pull her around the block in a wagon. The little girl thoroughly enjoyed the first leg of the journey, but unfortunately spent the last three-quarters of the trip begging her busy father to pull her around the block again. She missed the pleasure of the real live present while she was begging for a repeat performance in the future. Eastern philosophy would recommend approaching life with a mixture of attachment and detachment: "A total involvement with each moment and enjoyment of it combine with a detachment from the moment once it passes and a lack of desire that it return."[6]

Some wise experts in the treatment of alcoholism acknowledge that "all spiritual traditions emphasize detachment, but that emphasis does not imply that material reality should be held in contempt."[7] They point out that it is not so much the object, or activity that is the problem, but rather out relationship to these things. Their definition of misery is enlightening: "Misery is the mind-set that we must get and get and get; it is the yearning for more, the push to acquire more, win more, own more, and have more. Misery is misery because it does not know the meaning of enough. Those who lack gratitude's vision do not possess things; things possess them. And that is misery."[8]

We need to learn to live in the here and now, as the Jews had to learn to live day-by-day in the wilderness depending upon God's provision of daily bread (manna). Think about it: how we live today becomes the past that will affect our future. As mentioned earlier, Jesus emphasized the importance of living in the present; he offered this advice to his disciples, "Do not worry about tomorrow . . . Each day has enough trouble of its own."[9] Worrying about what may or may not happen in the future robs us of the ability to enjoy and to fully experience the present.

Because of past disappointments and hurts, we attach ourselves to self-protective behaviors and inner attitudes that ultimately prevent us from fully experiencing the present. Part of being fully alive is to experience both joy and sorrow. But, because of incidences in the past that may have caused us pain, our joy is replaced with cynicism and our sorrow replaced with callousness.[10] Because we feel inadequate and are fearful of past failures repeating themselves in the future, we become anxious and attach ourselves to the habit of worry; or just as bad we attempt to hide from future responsibilities through means of escape. One Christian counselor writes, "Not admitting and understanding deeply held anxieties freezes the power of the crucifixion to take hold within the soul. Jesus Christ, and Him crucified, unleashes incredible healing energy as darkness within is faced and crucified. . The death process of crucifixion does not occur through denying negative emotions and interior states."[11]

When you find yourself in the middle of a stress-producing situation, your natural tendency may be to seek a means of escape. Reverting back to a familiar time-proven stress-relieving habit such as smoking will be very appealing to you at such a time as this. But religious wisdom from the East would suggest that when presented with stress "you can learn to hold your seat and move closer to that pain. Reverse the usual pattern, which is to split, to escape . . . If it's painful, you become willing not just to endure it, but also to let it awaken your heart and soften you . . ."[12] You may find the following story of life on the African plains both interesting and relevant: "The gazelles never learn. The lion's strategy always works. Downwind several lionesses hide. They send the mighty male lion upwind. He doesn't try to sneak up on the gazelles. He wants to be seen – and heard. When he gets close, he roars with all his might. The frightened gazelles charge off away from the roar – and right into the waiting jaws of the lionesses." In reference to this story, it has been written: "The devil sets traps for you all the time. Wise up; don't keep making it easy for him. Run toward the roar, and break the ambush trap."[13]

People who have been hurt deeply in the past may also have a tendency to try to prevent things from going awry in the future by means of 'control.' They become obsessive about control. They become attached to the illusion that they can protect themselves by ordering the routines, surroundings, and people in their lives. Smoking also offers the illusion of control, because the cigarette serves as a 'mood thermostat' – enabling the person to quickly regulate his/her moods and emotions. The person becomes addicted to instant gratification or the 'quick fix.' One author suggests that "superficiality is the curse of our age. The doctrine of instant satisfaction is a primarily spiritual problem."[14]

An aspect of the obsession to control is the tendency to plan every detail, so there are no surprises – so that nothing unforeseen happens. But, spiritual wisdom suggests a different way. In the words of Joseph Campbell, "We must be willing to get rid of the life we've planned, so as to have the life that is waiting for us." Plato suggested we have a choice whether to swim easily in the river of life as it returns to its source, or swim against it.[15] Excessive planning, while providing a sense of control, is nevertheless exhausting. Life is not meant to be that way, and regardless of what has happened in the past, one needs to learn to trust that the benevolent, guiding hand of the Divine Shepherd can get you through anything you might have to face in the future. [16] [17]

The person who is attempting to control everything down to the last detail will likely come across as a bit self-centered. He or she appears to be addicted to his or her own agendas. One writer suggests that "personal growth and transformation occur when egocentricity and life's 'shoulds' are abandoned."[18]

Another inner attachment that must be dealt with is the tendency towards perfectionism. One needs to detach from expecting perfection from oneself or from other people. Now that is not to say that we should cease striving to be responsible or to do our best in situations; nor are we wrong to expect that others do the same. But, we need to humbly acknowledge that for a variety of reasons humans are incapable of being perfect on a consistent basis. With respect to others, perfectionism leads to an intolerant, judgmental spirit; sometimes to prejudice. With respect to ourselves it prevents us from loving and accepting who we are. Francis T. Vincent, Jr., former Commissioner of Major League Baseball once said, "We learn at a very young age that failure is the norm in baseball and, precisely because we have failed, we hold in high regard those who fail less often – those who hit safely in one out of three chances and become star players."[19] Alcoholics Anonymous co-founder, Bill Wilson warned those trying to quit drinking, 'Our problem is that we try, even demand, to be 'all-or-nothing.'"[20] In other words, they see themselves as abject failures unless they achieve total abstinence, with absolutely no slip-ups. Another author perceptively notes: "If I have reduced holiness to a single behavior, then I am standing on one leg. One slip and I am nothing again, absolutely useless."[21]

What is important in our journey toward freedom is that we persevere. At one point in his classic allegory *Pilgrim's Progress,* 17th-century author John Bunyan describes two characters, 'Pliable' and 'Christian,' on a journey from the City of Destruction to the Celestial City. The journey is an allegory of life. "They had not gone far before they stumbled and fell into the Slough of Despond. They were up to their necks in sludge. Pliable managed to get out first because he climbed out the way that he already knew; which was on the side nearest the City of Destruction. He yielded to the temptation to shrink back. Christian, on the other hand, stayed in the mess until he could find the way out nearest the Celestial City. He moved by faith in the direction he had not yet gone but in which he had chosen to go."[22] One fell backwards and one fell forwards!

In faith, we must patiently allow the Spirit-guided purgation process to proceed! It is the earnestness of our efforts, evidenced by our willingness to get back up after each failure that is pleasing to God. I remember reading a story of a father traveling with his young son. They stopped at a service station, and while the Dad filled up the car with gas, the little tyke crawled out and attempted to wash the windshield. Unfortunately all he accomplished was to smear the dead bugs all over the window. But because he was beaming with pride, and he did it to please his Dad, the father drove home with the windshield just the way it was.[23] I have to believe that God is just as delighted with our feeble efforts to show him how much we love him, by our attempting to break free from our attachments and to forsake our idols.

Unfortunately, sometimes successfully overcoming a habit can lead to pride rather than grateful humility. I've heard it suggested that "God wants us to walk in obedience, not in victory." When asked if her ministry to the dying untouchables in the slums of Calcutta was effective, Mother Teresa said "God calls us to fidelity and not success."[24]

A final example of an inner attachment that needs to be dealt with is the tendency to attach to too many things at once. Sometimes we stay busy as a means of escaping or avoiding some deeper needs that are not being addressed. But, even if this is not the case, we live in an age when our hearts and minds are overloaded with distractions and choices; we learn to 'multi-task.' If we are not careful we can become addicted to busyness. Brian McLaren writes candidly, "In my busyness, in my many roles, in the context of many demands and projects and goals, it is easy to lose touch with myself. And when I am out of touch with myself, it's hard – perhaps impossible – to get in touch with God. Why? Because there is no solid 'me' to bring into contact with God. I am a composite of ghost images . . . an out of-focus TV."[25] It has been suggested that "when the heart is divided, progress is slow and painful; life is purgatorial."[26] One author asserts "We must start without delay on the painful, steep, humiliating path of undoing our busy, deliberately deluded selves. So only will the Kingdom come."[27] The Buddhists have a term for the state of being addicted to busyness: 'monkey mind.' The image is of the monkeys constantly jumping from limb to limb, never content, never at rest.[28]

We must learn to refrain from getting on the trains of thought that take us away from our Divine center. As the Apostle Paul wrote, we are to "take captive every thought to make it obedient to Christ."[29] It is only then that we can rest content and be at peace, and discern the next step in our Spirit-led journey to freedom! As we gain control of our thoughts, our emotions will follow.

Chapter 36

Aspects of Purgation: The In-Between Time

Embracing the Spaciousness of the In-Between Time

This brings us to the in-between time between purgation and the next phase of spiritual transformation: illumination. You have for some time now been relinquishing your hold of objects, behaviors, and ways of thinking and feeling as the Spirit and your conscience have guided you. Oh, you may have had some slip-ups, but for the most part you have made a lot of progress. But, time is dragging on and like the caterpillar in the chrysalis it seems that all that is happening is that 'you' are dissolving. But remember the words of Jesus: "If any man would come after me, let him deny himself and take up his cross and follow me."[1] He also told his would-be followers that "He who finds his life will lose it, and he who loses his life for my sake will find it."[2] But, in our culture we are much more attracted to words like self-actualization and self-fulfillment than we are to self-denial. However, one contemporary mystic suggests that the way to find our true identity is through self-denial. He writes "Jesus calls us to self-denial without self-hatred. . . Self-denial declares that we are of infinite worth and shows us how to realize it."[3]

This in-between time may be frightening in the sense that you feel like the trapeze artist who has released hold of one bar, but has not yet grabbed hold of the next bar; you are suspended in air, in anticipation. Perhaps you identify with the Jews in the wilderness: You are grateful for the exodus (being delivered from the bondage of nicotine addiction), but you are growing weary in the wilderness. You don't seem to be getting any closer to the Promised Land of freedom, and you find yourself missing being attached to things – things familiar and visible. But, I encourage you to keep on walking. Don't depend upon feelings; they will catch up with your actions. Like the person who has forsaken dependence upon the cistern, you are thirsty. But keep digging and removing the rubble that has stopped up the well. The underground spring is there. You may be closer than you think. Resist the temptation to turn back to Egypt or to return to the cistern.

Temptation has been referred to as the crucible of character formation; and honey is said to be what bees make in the 'in-between time!' Don't abandon the project! I remember reading that when a person engages in an extended fast, hunger pains usually subside within the first four days. Between twenty-one to forty days of the fast, intense hunger pains return signaling "that the body has used up its reserves and is beginning to draw on the living tissue."[4] In other words, this is the body's last cry for survival. Towards the end of the purgative stage – during this in-between time – is when the last strongholds of attachment are vanquished, if you just persevere.

One author suggests that "God is at work in the areas of our deadness to transform them." He goes on to write: "God's work is unique in each person, because none of us has exactly the same configuration of the 'dead body,' that complex structure of harmful habits, deeply ingrained attitudes, troubling perspectives, destructive ways of relating to others, unhealthy modes of reacting and responding to the world, is very individual."[5] In the words of the Apostle Paul, "If by the Spirit, you put to death the deeds of the body, you will live."[6] In describing the darkness of purgation, modern-day Catholic mystic Benedict Groeschel writes, "In a very real way one dies. Many important things are laid aside as trivia. One becomes detached, objective, 'disinterested,' to use Loyola's word. There is a dead person lying on the stage of life; he or she looks familiar; 'Oh, yes it's me.'" He goes on to encourage the reader and sojourner, "For most, this darkness ends rather abruptly. In an hour, or a day, or a week, a new world dawns – sharp, clear, free. The basic anxiety of life has been silenced because all is lost. All is quiet because the individual is resting at the bottom of the sea. A strange light breaks; strange because it has always been there, but it has been hidden behind the hill. It is as if great doors open in the eastern sky. In the silence music is heard; it is familiar, yet it was never heard before because there was so much scatter sound, so many distractions. There is a presence at once familiar and oddly new; soft, gentle, but commanding."[7]

While purgation may consist of "increasing levels of renunciation guided by the Holy Spirit," it may also be described as "a consistent posture of actively turning our whole being to God so that His presence, purpose, and power can be released through our lives into all situations." It has been suggested that what is needed is an "inner reorientation of life."[8] But this process takes time. Conversion, which represented the beginning of your journey, can be seen as the initial earthquake, whereas purgation represents the aftershocks. One author writes, "So remember, the issue is: are you willing to be born again and again? . . . This is not about God punishing you, instead it is about God giving you the opportunity to change through your efforts and labor pains and give birth to yourself."[9]

Just as a person whose leukemia is in remission must still weather a second-round of 'consolidation' chemotherapy to eradicate all traces of the blood cancer that may be lurking under the surface, the person on the road to freedom from addiction must also endure a consolidation phase. Purgation provides just such a follow-up to the initial quitting process in overcoming an addiction. Although there may be an initial conversion experience, salvation is an ongoing process. John Newton, the sea captain who wrote *Amazing Grace*, "was inspired by a transformational experience that happened while he was transporting a shipload of slaves. Yet he continued to make several more slaving voyages before finally redirecting his life."[10] Newton went on to become an Anglican priest and abolitionist in Britain.

A wise counselor and former smoker, Gerald May warned of the danger of rushing through this in-between time – i.e., attempting to take the short cut of reforming behavior rather than patiently allowing God to transform behavior. He has written of reformation: "[It] usually involves substituting one addiction for another, adapting to a new, possibly less destructive normality. . . In addition to minimizing withdrawal symptoms, the substitution of one normality for another allows us to avoid the open empty feeling that comes when an addictive behavior is curtailed. Although this emptiness is really freedom, it is so unconditioned that it feels strange, sometimes even horrible. If we are willing for a deeper transformation of desire, we would have to try to make friends with the spaciousness; we would need to appreciate it as openness to God."[11] He went on to write, "Because openness to God is threatening, and because our desire is more to overcome an addiction than to claim our deepest desire for God, we fill the space with something else. In so doing, we assent to continued slavery under a new master who, we hope, will be kinder. Two risks accompany our choice. First, if the new normality is indeed kinder, it will almost surely seem insufficient. Something in us will continue to remember the old addiction and the greater satisfaction it gave. . . Second, there is no guarantee that our new master will be kinder than the old. It might turn out to be worse. . . . When reformation 'works,' it is well worth it. It may even be life saving. But because it applies only to behavior and does not address the underlying processes of attachment, old addictive behavior will tend to resurface at a later date."[12] If Jesus is indeed the Son of God, as most Christians believe, I am sure he was tempted to come down off the cross. It certainly would have been within his supernatural abilities to do so! But his allegiance to his father's will kept him there; and the crucifixion became the doorway to the resurrection – for both himself and those who would follow him.

Remembering that God is at Work in Your Life

So, as you endure the mysterious dark night of purgation, hanging there as if in mid-air, remind yourself that God has called you there. Your feelings will catch up with your actions, when the Divine work is accomplished. Find encouragement in the words of the Hebrew prophet Isaiah: "Those who hope in the Lord will renew their strength. They will soar on wings like eagles; they will run and not grow weary, they will walk and not be faint."[13]

Allow the Apostle Paul, who was beaten and imprisoned for his faith on numerous occasions, to remind you that "God who began the good work within you will keep right on helping you to grow in his grace until his task within you is finally finished . . ."[14] Hear the words of the Apostle Peter: "Therefore, since Christ suffered in his body, arm yourselves also with the same attitude, because he who has suffered in his body is done with sin. As a result, he does not live the rest of his earthly life for evil human desires, but rather for the will of God. . . . And the God of all grace, who called you to his eternal glory in Christ, after you have suffered a little while, will himself restore you and make you strong, firm and steadfast."[15] Remember, Peter is the one who thought himself strong but proved himself to be weak in the face of stress; he was the confident, assertive right-hand man, who denied knowing Jesus three times after his master had been arrested. But in time, after his humiliation, he grew strong in his faith and was strengthened by the Holy Spirit. Peter became the leader of the fledgling band of believers referred to as the early Church. According to legend Peter went on to minister in Rome during the later years of his life, where eventually he is thought to have been martyred. The early Church Father Origen wrote that when Peter was crucified he requested to be done so with his head facing downward – a symbol of his humility. He did not consider himself worthy to be crucified in the same manner as his master, Jesus had been.

Purgation is the process of cleansing and preparing the vessel of the soul. It has been said that full surrender is the prelude to service. The detachment process only has meaning if it is followed by an attachment process; the emptying only makes sense if there is a subsequent filling; and that is where we are headed in the next section on illumination. But I will leave you with a final metaphor to meditate upon: Perhaps we come into this world a little like a simple laptop – essentially innocent but with the potential to be corrupted. As we begin to interact with the outside world through the internet we become corrupted by viruses and overloaded with spam. What we need is to return to innocence, but a laptop is incapable of doing that itself; someone else has to install new software (e.g. virus protection, spam-blocker, spyware), delete the trash, and empty the recycle bin. Likewise, we need the Holy Spirit to cleanse and sanctify us. If purgation represents the cleansing process; then illumination represents the sanctifying, reprogramming process. Let us continue onward and upward!

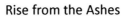

Section VI:

Maintenance & Illumination (Staying Quit – Part 2)

Rise from the Ashes

Rise from the Ashes

The caterpillar continues to be enveloped by its chrysalis. Outwardly things may seem dormant but inwardly much change is occurring. Subsequent to and perhaps simultaneously with the dissolving of the caterpillar into a soup of nutrients, 'imaginal cells' arise which contain the blueprint for what will become the butterfly. As memories of the former existence begin to fade, a new vision begins to formulate. Slowly, behind the scenes, the new creation begins to take shape.

This brings us to the next step in the journey to freedom: what the Christian mystics refer to as 'illumination.' Subsequent to or simultaneous with detaching from our idols, we must attach to the living God. The reason to leave the far country is to return home. The purpose in letting go of the 'old' is to embrace the 'new.' For every negative there is a positive. If purgation represents 'defense' then in a sense illumination corresponds with 'offense.' In our biblical discussion of purgation we have already unavoidably alluded to 'illumination.' For example, everything negative that the Jews were expected to let go of was replaced by something positive of which to grab hold. It was not good enough for the Jews to shed the skin of a slave mentality unless they clothed themselves with the mentality of beloved children of God; it wasn't good enough to forsake cisterns if a well was not dug and the spring of water not tapped; it wasn't good enough to secure the city wall or the house, if things were not prepared for the new king or inhabitant.

In the journey of Jesus, illumination corresponds to his ascension - when he rose to heaven to spend quality time with his Father after his earthly sojourn. If it is true that in conversion we have received a new heart or new nature, then through illumination we are making use of it; we are testing its limits. Persons who have received a lung and/or heart transplant go through an interesting process that is relevant to someone emerging from a longstanding habit such as smoking. Initially they have to learn to accept the fact that their new lungs and/or heart are capable of so much more than their old ones. Psychologically they need to stop seeing themselves as being limited in the old way. They need to let go, or be purged of this. But, indeed they are still limited in what they can do, not so much because of their lungs or heart, but because of the de-conditioning process that took place prior to the transplant. They must begin the slow process of rebuilding their muscular strength and stamina. Through this positive exercise and rehabilitation they will hopefully get to the point where they can live a full and healthy life; that is the goal.

This is analogous to the journey of recovery from an addiction. You terminate the offending habit, you change your lifestyle by eliminating other sources of addiction and by resisting temptation (i.e. purgation), and then you begin to adopt and embrace a new healthier lifestyle, which begins the process of 'illumination.

Chapter 38

Components of Illumination: Healthy Lifestyle - Part 1

As a new non-smoker it would behoove you to begin pursuing a healthier lifestyle. The more you do so, the more you will be unwilling to go backwards to habits that are both self-centered and self-destructive. Being more conscious of the types and amount of food you eat, beverages you drink, and things you read and view are all part of living healthier. The Buddhists have a word for this: 'mindful consuming.'[1] But, without exception all the major world religious traditions advocate living in such a way. Some traditions are more specific about the things we should or should not partake of, but in essence the rule is to avoid things that are harmful and/or addictive and to practice moderation in other things.[2] [3] [4] [5] From a Christian perspective, we are called to be good, responsible stewards of the bodies, minds, and spirits given to us by our Creator.

If you are not already active, it would be good to incorporate regular exercise into your lifestyle.[6] Of course it is important to tailor exercise to your age and overall health; if you have concerns, consult your physician first. In addition to improving your health, exercise enhances a sense of well-being through the release of substances like endorphins in the brain, and giving one feelings of self-mastery and -control. But, what we're primarily after in the illumination stage is the pursuit of 'spiritual health.' This is not to say that physical and psychological health do not impact spiritual health. But, think about it - even if you were unable to move or to eat, your spirit would need nourishment. And, unfortunately the spirit is usually the one aspect of our humanity that we neglect. The Apostle Paul wrote to his young apprentice in the faith, Timothy: "Train yourself to be godly. For physical training is of some value, but godliness has value for all things, holding promise for both the present life and the life to come."[7] Don't forget, whereas your body and your mind may be temporal, your spirit is eternal – at least this seems to be the consensus of the world's religious traditions. Perhaps while contemplating the severity and brevity of earthly life, the Apostle Paul wrote: "Therefore we do not lose heart. Though outwardly we are wasting away, yet inwardly we are being renewed day by day. For our light and momentary troubles are achieving for us an eternal glory that far outweighs them all. So we fix our eyes not on what is seen, but on what is unseen. For what is seen is temporary, but what is unseen is eternal."[8]

Whether you are young, middle-aged, or elderly the cultivation of your spirit is important. Without a healthy spiritual life, you are not truly alive. Joseph Campbell observed, "People say that what we're seeking is a meaning for life. I don't think that's what we're really seeking. I think that what we're seeking is an experience of being alive, so that we actually feel the rapture of being alive." Abraham Lincoln is quoted as having said "In the end it's not the years in your life that count; it's the life in your years." Jesus recognized that there is a malevolent, spiritual being or force that seeks to rob us of life, by tempting us with the enchanting things of this world. Once under the spell, we watch the years slip by while we're chained to habits and imprisoned by desire. But Jesus told his disciples whereas, "the thief comes only to steal and kill and destroy; I have come that they may have life, and to the full."[9] (In some translations of Scripture this is referred to as 'abundant' life.) He was comparing us to sheep and himself to a good shepherd. The illuminative way is following the Shepherd back to the fold, and beyond - to greener pastures.

During the purgative process of detaching and relinquishing, you have turned away from the cisterns of habit and are working to unstop the well, or you have attended to the breaks in the city wall, and are clearing away the rubble; but now you must strengthen the lining of the well and prime the pump, or you must get about the business of rebuilding the palace and the temple.[10] The illuminative process consists of implementing spiritual disciplines to facilitate this process – to prepare your heart and life for the indwelling presence of the Holy One. The Apostle Paul portrayed the goal of illumination when he wrote: "I pray that out of His glorious riches He [God] may strengthen you with power through His Spirit in your inner being, so that Christ may dwell in your hearts through faith. . ."[11] The Christian tradition is not alone in speaking of the need to have our inner beings strengthened for holy purposes.[12] [13] In the words of Carl Jung, "the inner self is a vessel filled with grace."[14]

One author recounts the story of a submarine known as *Thresher* that exceeded its maximum depth: "When the pressure became too great, the seawater crushed the sub's heavy steel bulkheads as if it were a plastic model." If one wants to descend deeper into the sea, one would have to be lowered by cable in a single-passenger steel ball with very thick glass windows. And yet, fish exist even at the depth of the ocean floor; and these fish are not heavily armored, but have normal skin. He poses the rhetorical question: "How can they survive under such pressure? They have a secret: equal and opposite pressure inside themselves." This same author goes on to draw the analogy that in real life, people "deal with pressure by putting on inches of steel plate. They shield themselves from the outside world and strap themselves into a narrow space, peering out into the darkness. They are safe inside. But God's kind of freedom is more like the fish's. We keep our shape not through steel plate, but by God's Spirit, who gives us inside strength to deal with each pressure point in our lives." [15] Referring to religion, it has been suggested that "the aim is not external conformity, whether to doctrine or deed, but the re-formation of the inner self – of the spiritual core, the place of thought and feeling, of will and character."[16]

Jesus invited the spiritually road-weary of his day to take his yoke upon them. He assured them they would find rest for their souls. When training oxen, the young ox learns the ropes by being yoked to a seasoned ox. In the ancient world, teachers would invite would-be disciples to join in step alongside of them, to be yoked to them to learn their wisdom and ways.[17] Jesus proclaimed that he was the way, the truth, and the life; he even said that knowing him was the key to knowing the Father.[18] Now, I realize there are several ways of interpreting this passage, which I have paraphrased. But, if nothing else, I think Jesus was inviting people to become acquainted with his ways, and to follow in his footsteps – to live in the manner that he lived his life. In the book of Hebrews, he is referred to as both high priest and 'apostle.'[19] We also learn from this epistle that "although he was a son, he learned obedience from what he suffered and once made perfect, he became the source of eternal salvation for all who obey him . . ."[20] He modeled certain disciplines: solitude; prayer; meditation; worship; human engagement; and service. The Illuminative way is to take on the yoke of religious wisdom, to begin practicing the classical spiritual disciplines.

Chapter 39

Components of Illumination: Healthy Lifestyle - Part 2

As I mentioned earlier, while the Jews were being led by their Divine bridegroom from the bondage of Egypt to the freedom of Canaan, they were engaged in both purgation and illumination. One author has written: "Let us never forget that deserts are gardens of courtship as well as fields of battle. Struggle with attachment can be seen as warfare with an insidious enemy, or it can be seen as a romance in which the soul seeks the beloved one for whom it thirsts."[1] If purgation represents letting go of the old abusive lovers in your life, then illumination is attaching to the Divine lover of your soul; the disciplines are the means by which you will be able to do this.

Cultivating a relationship with God, while we are in a fallen state, is a bit like trying to grow roses in the dead of winter in Ohio. It can only occur under the right conditions - in the temperature controlled climate of a greenhouse. Likewise, practicing the classical disciplines creates the right environment for spiritual growth. Those traveling on the spiritual path have compared the disciplines to training wheels, guard rails, and scaffolding. Richard Foster, who reintroduced his generation to the classical disciplines of the Christian faith through his 1978 book, *Celebration of Discipline*, writes: "The path of Spiritual disciplines places us or keeps us where inner spiritual change and transformation can occur."[2] There indeed is joy in the journey as the Divine presence invites us, through the disciplines, to greater freedom. Rather than being a "death march to holiness," author Nate Larkin describes this process as being like "a dance – a beautiful and intoxicating dance that God leads." He goes on to say, "For people who are accustomed to marching, the rhythm of the dance feels very awkward at first." He admits that "most of us trip and fall a lot in the beginning, but eventually we catch on."[3] I am reminded how during the T.V. show *Dancing with the Stars* the judges frequently remind the novices to stand up straight, keep their shoulders and head up, and to maintain the proper frame.

Martin Luther once said, "Sinfulness is the curvature of the self in upon the self." C.S. Lewis referred to fallen man as being "bent." Building upon these images, contemporary Christian counselor Leanne Payne writes: "The unfallen position was, as it were, a vertical one, one of standing erect, face turned upward to God in a listening-speaking relationship. It was a position of receiving continually one's true identity from God. But fallen man is bent toward the creature and trapped in the continual attempt to find his identity in the created rather than in the Uncreated."[4] She goes on to state that the cure is to "renounce our idols – those persons or things in which we attempt to find ourselves – and we straighten up into the vertical, listening relationship to God."[5] [6]

One of the most difficult addictions to overcome is crack cocaine. After interviewing a number of recovering crack-cocaine addicts, physician Dale Matthews made the observation that "these men were living, not one day at a time, as recovering alcoholics do, but one minute at a time." He goes on to say that these men indicated that "it was not the experience of conversion per se that helped them overcome addiction. They did not depend on the emotional 'high' of a 'zap' conversion in their daily struggle against crack. Rather, it was the structured, disciplined aspects of their spirituality – daily Bible study, prayer, and fellowship – that gave them the strength they needed."[7] Matthews also cites a 1991 study of alcoholics: "Researchers found that alcoholics who had achieved long-term sobriety (four to sixteen years) had developed spiritual practices in conjunction with their Alcoholics Anonymous participation; 100% said they meditated or had 'quiet time' daily, 100% prayed regularly, and 97% read a meditation book daily."[8] I have heard it said that "horses have bridles; dogs have leashes; we have discipline."[9]

The spiritual disciplines, like braces on the teeth, will help in the straightening process. But make no mistake it will still involve a certain amount of pain. One author refers to spiritual disciplines as "the act of releasing ourselves in a consistent manner to God . . ."[10] But he goes on to stress that "without God's transforming grace, our disciplines are empty, hollow motions, the form of godliness without the power."[11] It has been suggested that "trying to follow Jesus without the Spirit's indwelling empowerment is like trying to cross the ocean in a sailboat by blowing on the sails."[12] But, God is calling you on this journey and will certainly be with you in Spirit as you implement the disciplines, so take heart!

177

Before we continue, let me just bring to your attention that you have already begun practicing some of the disciplines. Of the classical disciplines presented by Foster, you have already essentially engaged in six. *Simplicity* and *fasting* are two disciplines that are purgative: letting go of things to which we have become attached, reducing the clutter. Some refer to these practices as 'blessed subtraction.' *Study* is essentially what you have been doing while reading this book: familiarizing yourself more and more with the literature of the spirit. *Confession* and *Submission* to God were disciplines you engaged in during the conversion process. And, *guidance* is what you are seeking of the Divine spirit as you continue your journey. We will now examine six additional disciplines: solitude; meditation; prayer; worship; service; and human interaction and connectedness.

Chapter 40

Components of Illumination: Solitude

We must be careful not to follow in the footsteps of the Jews who returned from Babylonian/Persian exile. They started working on repairing the Jerusalem wall, but before completing the project and before rebuilding the Temple they got side-tracked with building their own elaborately paneled houses. They got caught up in the pursuit of happiness and self-indulgence. Now that you have detached from habits and addictions, which had been limiting your ability to enjoy other things in life, it is understandable that you discover new healthier pursuits and objects of desire. But don't lose sight of your overall purpose; don't simply replace one form of addiction with another, even if it is a less destructive one. What you long for is freedom from addiction; you long to drink from that underground spring, to worship the living God in the temple of your heart.

One author noted, "There is a strange sadness in this growing freedom. Our souls may have been scarred by the chains with which our addictions have bound us, but at least they were familiar chains. We were used to them. And as they loosen, we are likely to feel a vague sense of loss. The things to which we were addicted may still be with us but we no longer give them the ultimate importance we once did. We are like caged animals beginning to experience freedom, and there is something we miss about the cage."[1] But the spirit of freedom beckons us, and now is our time. As Saint Augustine has suggested, God has always desired to give us good things, but our hands have been too full to receive them.[2] But now that we have let go of our attachments, and have reached this point of emptiness we need to embrace the spaciousness and mystery with joyful anticipation.

The discipline of 'solitude' forces us to sit still. It is likely a difficult thing for you to do, especially in this world of cell phones, iPods, computer screens and TVs. Our lives may be like a pond whose water is being constantly agitated. But, as one author says, "Clarity can come to the inner eye . . . only insofar as life attains a quiet that equals that of a deep and silent pool."[3] As we practice solitude, the silt settles to the bottom of the pond and the water becomes calm and clear. We are then able to see clear to the floor of the pond, and we also begin to see a true reflection of ourselves as well as the sky. The discipline of solitude is simple and yet profound; it enables us to see more clearly how things really are. We are better able to understand ourselves, the deeper needs that lie below the surface, and the outward masks we are wearing, and we can better see God in our midst. It has been suggested that "we're conditioned to act on problems rather than wait for answers to present themselves."[4] By scheduling breaks from all the surface noise and busyness of our lives, we can begin to hear the whisper of the Divine Spirit, and discern what things we need to attend to in order to continue on the journey of spiritual formation. The illuminative way, which follows purgation, has been described as "a spring morning after a bad storm. Even though everything is washed clean and the sky is filled with clouds and sunlight, there are many fallen trees and an occasional live wire blocking the road."[5]

Jesus modeled the practice of solitude when he slipped away from his followers and the crowds early in the morning to find a quiet garden or hillside. Prior to embarking on his three-year ministry the Spirit led him into the wilderness for forty days of solitude; before he chose his twelve apostles he spent the night alone in the hills; after getting the news of his predecessor John the Baptist's death he withdrew on a boat to a lonely place; and prior to his crucifixion he sought the quiet solace of the Garden of Gethsemane under the cover of night. But, Jesus also displayed an inner solitude, which may have been directly related to his practice of outward solitude. Possessing an inner contentment with life and with who he was, he did not feel compelled to adjust his image to please people. He was not interested in the latest gossip and was secure enough in himself that he felt no need to judge others or draw attention to their faults; and yet at the same time he was able to stand strong and true in the face of opposition, and to hold the mirror up to expose others' hypocrisy. He exhibited a sense of spiritual presence wherever he went. He knew when to speak and when to hold his tongue; even before his accusers, and those who had the power to sentence him to death, he was calm and controlled.

In teaching others to 'turn the other cheek' Jesus was encouraging assertiveness. In his day, if a Roman soldier was to hit a Jew, he would likely do so with the back of his hand – it was a gesture of condescension and derision. Jesus, was in effect telling people to stand up to this, especially if they were in the right. By turning the other cheek the person would be forcing the offender to hit them again, but with the front of the hand as if fighting an equal. In other words he was encouraging his followers to have the inner calm to take an assertive stand – not to run away in a passive manner nor fight back in an aggressive manner. He didn't feel the need to defend himself. He was able to forgive his enemies. This is inner solitude.

One author writes: "Solitude is more a state of mind and heart than it is a place. There is solitude of the heart that can be maintained at all times. Crowds, or the lack of them, have little to do with this inward attentiveness." He goes on to say that "our fear of being alone drives us to noise and crowds," but he insists that "loneliness or clatter are not our only alternatives. We can cultivate an inner solitude and silence that sets us free from loneliness and fear. Loneliness is inner emptiness. Solitude is inner fulfillment."[6] The discipline of solitude is an opportunity to allow the Divine Spirit to tame our restless, self-willed spirits.

Although we can practice the discipline of solitude in the quiet of our room, behind closed doors, we can also practice solitude sitting on a bench anonymously in the middle of a busy shopping mall. To some extent it is a matter of getting lost in the eternity of the moment. It can happen anywhere and anytime. You've already experienced it to some extent when you have gotten absorbed in something and lost track of time. The difference with solitude is you're not doing anything other than being present. It is in fact all about 'being' versus 'doing.' With that being said, often people find it easier to enter into solitude when they separate themselves from man-made activity and noise. Naturalist John Muir offered this advice: "Climb the mountains and get their good tidings. Nature's peace will flow into you as sunshine flows into trees. The winds will blow their own freshness into you . . . while cares will drop off like autumn leaves."[7] Now, we don't have to live near the mountains to benefit from the tonic of nature. Stepping outside for what would have been a smoking break and feeling the sunshine and the breeze, hearing the birds, smelling the trees and flowers, or taking a stroll will do. We need to discover the moments of solitude that fill the day and enter into them, in addition to setting aside regular retreats into the quiet.

One author compares fishing to the practice of solitude: "The charm of fishing is that it is the pursuit of what is elusive but attainable – a perpetual series of occasions for hope." He goes on to write: "And I suppose that is how it is with solitude and the other means of experiencing God . . . One can put oneself in the right place in the right frame of mind, and then one must wait, but not passively – rather actively, as a fisherman waits with his line in the water, or as a farmer waits after he has planted his crops –

leaving the outcome to God. That's where faith comes in . . . believing that there will be a tug on the line or that the fields will come to life and in time bear a harvest."[8] [9]

Charles Spurgeon once said "the sheep are never so safe from the wolf as when they are near the shepherd."[10] As you consistently practice solitude, you will discover that you are in the presence of God.[11] You will sense a fullness rather than lonely emptiness. You will understand what the Apostle Paul meant when he addressed the philosophers and the intellectual elite of Athens: "For in him [God] we live and move and have our being."[12] You will find that contentment will replace the restlessness of your soul. I am reminded of what Dorothy said after returning to Kansas from Oz, "If I ever go looking for my heart's desire again, I won't look any further than my own backyard . . . because if it isn't there, I never really lost it to begin with."[13]

One author writes, "I wonder about all this business of 'detachment' as taught in some spirituality courses. If we just practice 'attachment' to God, the detachment from all that is amiss in our lives will take care of itself. In fact, I am more and more impressed with the danger of 'emptying out' without 'filling up.' "[14] In solitude we may discover that the process of attaching to God is easier than we thought; it is an inside job. It has been observed that a common perception of being filled with the Holy Spirit is that it is "a work the Lord brings to people from above, as if they were an empty pitcher and He pours the Holy Spirit into them, much as one would pour water into a pitcher." A different image has been suggested: "The Holy Spirit is present deep within the inner places of the [person's] soul, much as an artesian well flows deep within the earth. He is there in all His power and truth. Being filled with the Spirit means surrendering to the full flow of His presence already within the [person's] life."[15]

Silence has also been referred to as "the discipline by which the inner fire of God is tended and kept alive."[16] This is an allusion to the passage from the Second Epistle to the Corinthians, where Paul stated that "we are the temple of the living God."[17] It is interesting to note the significance of the term 'naos' which Paul used for temple. "One of the uses for this word is of the little cell, the niche in the Greek temples where the image of the god was placed. The believer, then, is the very niche especially designed for God's residence."[18] This leads us to the next three disciplines, which are certainly fitting for a temple: meditation, prayer, and worship.

Chapter 41

Components of Illumination: Meditation

For many people, when they hear the word meditation they may think of the Eastern forms of meditation – e.g. 'transcendental.' One might picture a yogi in the lotus position going 'ohm' or softly repeating a mantra. In my limited western understanding, it is my impression that this approach seeks to empty or calm the mind, so that the person can for the moment sense oneness with the energy of the cosmos; as a dewdrop slipping into the stream. In a sense this type of meditation is a means to an end – a pathway into solitude; a means of reducing the scatter noise and clutter of this material life so that spiritual reality can be perceived more clearly and the unity of all life grasped more fully.[1]

Dr. Herbert Benson has coined the term *relaxation response*, which he says "can be evoked by any of a large number of techniques, including meditation, certain types of prayer, autogenic training, progressive muscular relaxation, jogging, swimming, Lamaze breathing exercises, yoga, tai chi chuan, chi gong, and even knitting and crocheting." He goes on to state that "only two basic steps need to be followed. You need to repeat a word, sound, prayer, phrase, or muscular activity. And when common, everyday thoughts intrude on your focus, passively disregard them and return to your repetition."[2]

Benson and his colleagues have found that "after exposure to the relaxation response the body requires more of the hormone nor-adrenaline to increase heart rate and blood pressure . . . so that the body does not react as radically to mildly stressful events but retains the ability to respond immediately to major threats."[3] They have also observed a drop in metabolism associated with the relaxation response.[4] [5]

Lest you think that meditation is only an eastern religious practice, let me assure you meditation is also a part of Judeo-Christian spirituality. The goal of western meditation is to establish communion with God: "to move beyond the superficialities of our culture . . . to go down into the recreating silences, into the inner world of contemplation."[6] We desire to hear God's voice and to be changed as a result. We seek to still our creaturely activities long enough to become aware of the Divine activity that is going on all around us. We want to be able to get in step with the Spirit. We seek to penetrate the mystery of God, ourselves, and the world around us. As has been suggested by one Christian mystic, our goal in meditation is to "create the emotional and spiritual space which allows Christ to construct an inner sanctuary in the heart."[7]

One author points out that "the Bible uses two different Hebrew words . . . to convey meditation, and together they are used fifty-eight times."[8] Way back in Genesis, the first book of the Hebrew Pentateuch, we read that Abraham's son, Isaac – who was the father of Israel – would go out into the fields to meditate under the starry sky.[9] [10] King David spoke frequently of meditating upon God's laws and promises – they were his inspiration during many a difficult time. In one of his psalms he sings, "I think of thee upon my bed, and meditate on thee in the watches of the night."[11] As I mentioned earlier it was the custom of Jesus to break away from the madding crowds on occasion to seek islands of solitude; and I'm sure he engaged in meditation. It is very evident in the Gospel accounts that Jesus had spent a lot of time meditating upon Scripture, because he would often quote it and would apply it to life situations. Since quitting smoking, you have been developing the practice of meditation upon Scripture yourself.

During meditation we turn our gaze God-ward and listen for the whisper of the Spirit. We can begin doing this by simply contemplating the natural world around us, as perhaps Isaac did in the fields at night so long ago.[12] We can also meditate upon the discoveries of science and marvel in wonder at the handiwork of the Creator. I majored in Biology as an undergraduate in college, and for me much of my study ended up in worship as I marveled at all of the beauty, order, complexity, and creativity in the natural world! Even if we cannot physically retreat to a place like 'Walden's Pond' to commune with nature and to meditate in the virgin woods, as did Henry David Thoreau, we can still do so in our imagination. I live in the city, and during inclement weather I walk on a treadmill for exercise. When I do so, I will often slowly leaf through a large book containing beautiful photos of nature. Using my imagination I enter into these scenes as if I were really there, and it is amazing how calming and invigorating it is.

Tapping the imagination is certainly an important aspect of meditation. We need to allow the Holy Spirit to penetrate the mind's faculties of abstraction and analysis and awaken the child-like capacity for imagination. As we gaze deeply into the face of God, we may gain a glimpse of our true selves – of who we are meant to be. Like the caterpillar in the chrysalis, we may sense 'imaginal' cells arising in our consciousness of what we should pursue and of who we are to become. Through the use of imagination we can also use the techniques of visualization and guided imagery to prepare for the challenges we know we are about to face. If you watch Olympic downhill skiers you will see them before their event, perched at the top of the run, going through the course in their minds – imagining every twist and turn they will encounter. To some extent, we can do this also in our daily lives – although we cannot anticipate everything that the future will bring.

Through imagery we can counteract daily stress by taking little breaks, perhaps in place of smoking breaks.[13] We can simply close our eyes and picture in our mind's eye being somewhere we have encountered peace in the past – perhaps by the ocean, or strolling in the woods. We can engage our senses by remembering the sounds of the seagulls and the waves, or the babbling brook; by recalling the smell of the salt air or the scent of pine.

The legendary basketball coach Phil Jackson has utilized a unique approach with his players: "During the fifteen or thirty seconds they have to grab a drink and towel off, I encourage them to picture themselves someplace where they feel secure. It's a way for them to take a short mental vacation before addressing the problem at hand. Simple as it may seem, the exercise helps players reduce their anxiety and focus their attention on what they need to do when they return to the court."[14] As I mentioned earlier it is important to look for the moments of potential solitude throughout your busy day. As a music lover once said "The pauses between the notes – ah, that is where the art resides!"[15] So, too in our lives.

Meditation can also have a lingering effect upon our lives. The Catholic Bishop of Geneva, Francis De Sales, who lived during the sixteenth and seventeenth centuries, spoke of the spiritual nosegay. "A nosegay was a bunch of sweet-smelling flowers that ladies and gentlemen of the period carried with them when they went outdoors so they would not be overcome by the stench of open sewers. This was De Sale's image of the aftereffect of meditation, a sweet aroma that freshens the day."[16]

Chapter 42

Components of Illumination: Prayer

This brings us to the discipline of prayer, which is the ultimate goal and privilege of sinking down into the inner sanctuary of the heart via means of solitude and meditation. It is to be in the presence of God where one can listen to and speak with the Divine. In the Beatitudes, Jesus emphasized the importance of 'purity of heart.' In fact he said: "Blessed are the pure in heart, for they will see God."[1] The practices of solitude and meditation are practiced largely to achieve this purity of heart.[2]

The Apostle Peter wrote, ". . . Be clear-minded and self-controlled so that you can pray."[3] A contemporary author suggests that "prayer involves a focused state of mind usually characterized by feelings of internal quiet, serenity, and stillness." He goes on to state that the great 16th-Century Spanish mystic Saint Teresa of Avila "compared the attempt to achieve this mental condition to trying to ride a bucking horse."[4]

The Apostle Paul encouraged people to pray without ceasing – on all occasions.[5] Thomas Merton once said "I pray by breathing."[6] This connotes a state of being – a posture of prayerfulness.[7] Although there is an active side to prayer, there is also an all-pervasive restfulness to it. According to one expert: "Being anxious carries with it several bodily responses. One of these, a shortening of breath, is embedded in the roots of the word itself: the Latin word is *angere*, meaning 'to choke in distress;' in Greek one word for anxiety is *stenochoreo*, meaning to 'to shorten the breath.'"[8] One of the natural and beneficial things that a smoker does is to periodically take time to breathe slowly and deeply. Believe it or not this sends a signal to the rest of the body to slow down and relax. Think about it, when one smokes a cigarette one doesn't inhale fast and furiously, but rather slowly - savoring the moment. One takes a slow deep drag and holds the breath momentarily, while perhaps looking off wistfully in the distance. As one exhales it's as if one is expelling worries and cares that have been bottled up inside.

Let me emphasize here that prayer is the real thing that can and should incorporate all of this. The difference is with prayer you can envision yourself breathing in the very Spirit or breath of God, rather than expensive, harmful smoke. *Pneuma* is an ancient Greek word for "breath," and in a religious context it denotes "spirit." In the Genesis account of creation, we are told that "the Lord God formed the [first] man from the dust of the ground and breathed into his nostrils the breath of life, and the man became a living being."[9] As you inhale, imagine God breathing new life into you – giving you a new start, making you a new creation. Runners often describe a 'second wind' that kicks in during the final leg of a race – just when they feel like collapsing. This second wind enables them to finish strong. As you are re-inventing yourself as a non-smoker, envision the Divine Spirit giving you a second wind! This type of 'breath' prayer can be done anywhere, anytime! It can even become gloriously addictive in itself. As Calvin Miller has written: "Heady inebriation this Spirit intoxication. . . If we but take one sip, we *pneumaholics* must have more of the Pneuma!'"[10]

When you breathe in you can imagine yourself fanning the flame of faith in the sanctuary of your heart. Throughout the Bible, from the Old Testament descriptions of the Jewish Temple to the apocalyptic vision of John in Revelation, the continual burning of incense represents the prayers of the people going up to God; it is said to be a pleasing aroma to God. Just as the purpose of breathing is twofold, so is prayer. During respiration we breathe in to get fresh oxygen into our bodies to support our metabolism, to keep us alive. We breathe out to expel carbon-dioxide, which is the natural by-product of metabolism. Both phases of respiration are critical for life. Prayer involves listening to God, so that we can be inspired by the Holy Spirit; it also involves casting down our cares and confessing our sins to God, so that we can be unburdened and cleansed.

Jesus invited all the weary and burdened to come to him so that he could give them rest.[11] After a lifetime of personal trials and tribulation, the Apostle Paul wrote to the believers in Philippi, "The Lord is near. Do not be anxious about anything, but in everything, by prayer and petition, with thanksgiving, present your requests to God." But, listen to this! This is the good part: If you cultivate the discipline of doing this rather than resorting to familiar dysfunctional means of relieving stress, such as smoking, "the peace of God, which transcends all understanding, will guard your hearts and your minds . . ."[12] This is a wonderful promise which I have benefited from.

Prayer involves bringing our own needs before God - like uncovering our wounds in the healing sunlight of His love; but it also involves bringing the needs of others before Him. The privilege of praying on the behalf of others follows in the footsteps of countless individuals described in the Gospels, who approached Jesus asking for the healing of loved ones. God delights in this. A real prayer life gets us in tune with a compassionate God; it does not demand immediate answers from God but rather patiently rests and waits for God's timing, and then motivates us to act appropriately in season and out of season.[13]

I've heard it said that we are never more than co-authors with God, when it comes to our lives. But that in itself is remarkable. God is still creating and we are invited to join in the process. He beckons us in the here and now. With each new dawn, as God provided daily manna for the Jews in the wilderness, he presents us with new solutions to our problems, new goals to pursue, and new inspiration if we are but expectant and receptive. If all this talk of prayer is still a bit new and uncomfortable to you, don't fret. You will get the hang of it – as we have been emphasizing, it is as natural as breathing! In fact I dare say the ongoing monologue that has been going on between your ears since the day you were born, is essentially ceaseless prayer. The difference now is that you are acknowledging the Divine presence who is listening and who is inviting you to dialogue. I've also heard it said that prayer evolves from dialogue to duet.

The Apostle Paul provided insight into prayer when he wrote, "The Spirit helps us in our weakness. We do not know what we ought to pray, but the Spirit himself intercedes for us with groans that words cannot express . . . in accordance with God's will."[14] As we attempt to pray as best we can, we may eventually sense the Divine presence, much like the little child in the following story experienced the thrill of accompaniment from the master pianist: "Ignace Paderwski was Poland's prime minister and most famous pianist. He set up a tour of rural Poland in hopes of cultivating an appreciation for the arts. At one village the concert was about to begin. Imagine the gasp of the audience when the stage lights came on. There was Paderewski's grand piano, all right. But crawling up onto the bench was a little boy. Oblivious to the crowd he began to pick out with two fingers 'Twinkle, Twinkle, Little Star.' The audience groaned, the child's mother nearly passed out, and the stagehands surged forward. But Paderewski appeared and waved them away. The world's premier pianist stepped up behind the boy and whispered, 'Don't quit.

Keep playing.' Leaning over, Paderewski put his left hand around the boy and began to fill in some bass notes. Then his right arm reached around the other side of the boy and began to add a running obbligato. The crowd was mesmerized."[15] The feeblest attempt at prayer is like the 'faith' which Jesus compared to the smallest of all seeds – the mustard seed – which grows to become the largest of all garden plants.[16]

Phyllis Tickle has written about the Catholic tradition of keeping the Divine Hours: appointed times of prayer and reflection throughout the day. When asked why she observes this practice or discipline, she responded: "[That] is like asking me why I go to Church. One, granted is a place of bricks and mortar, but the other is a chapel of the heart, as powerful a place, albeit one of the spirit. The offices open me four times a day and call me to remember who owns time and why it is, as a part of creation. All that means really is that four times a day the watchmaker and I have conversation about the clock and my place as a nano-second in it."[17]

Prayer does not need to be confined to sitting or kneeling, or any position or activity for that matter. However, people often find it helpful when desiring to devote time to prayer, to withdraw to a quiet, uninterrupted private place. But some people enjoy taking 'prayer walks', and others enjoy writing out their dialogue with God in a 'prayer journal.' Both of these techniques can be helpful when attempting to break a habit such as smoking, because they are activities that can be implemented in place of smoking breaks, and they utilize a combination of mind, hands, and feet. The Labyrinth is an ancient type of maze designed for participants to meditatively and prayerfully walk. One begins walking in toward the center of the labyrinth and then back out again slowly. It has been suggested that "the walk inward becomes a journey of purification, meditation in the center is compared to illumination, and the journey outward becomes union, a return to service in the world for the walking meditator who is refreshed and healed."[18]

Chapter 43

Components of Illumination: Worship

Worship is prayer taken to the streets; a prayerful attitude infused into our daily lives. It has been suggested "The spiritual life is not something we add onto an already busy life . . . [It] is to impregnate and infiltrate and control what we already do with an attitude of service to God."[1] The Apostle Paul urged fellow First-Century believers to offer their "bodies as living sacrifices", and he referred to this as a "spiritual act of worship."[2] I think what he was getting at is that everything we do can be viewed as spiritual worship: as our senses perceive things we can engage in worship: as we go about doing our work or activities of daily living we can do them in an attitude of worship; and as we interact with other people we can turn it into worship.

There was a lay monk, named Brother Lawrence, who worked in the kitchen of a Carmelite monastery in Paris in the Seventeenth century. A little book of his correspondence, *The Practice of the Presence of God* has become a classic of devotional literature. In his writings he reveals how even washing pots and pans was a worshipful experience for him, simply because of his intimate friendship with God. French philosopher and Jesuit Priest, Pierre Tielhard De Chardin once wrote "Do not forget that the value and interest of life is not so much to do conspicuous things . . . as to do ordinary things with the perception of their enormous value."[3] Concurring with this line of reasoning, a modern-day devotional writer notes "In the realm of the spirit we soon discover that the real issues are found in the tiny, insignificant corners of life." Elaborating further he writes, "The great virtues are a rare occurrence; the ministry of small things is a daily service. Large tasks require great sacrifice for a moment; small things require constant sacrifice."[4] [5]

In a way, this type of worship involves bringing new meaning to the ordinary and extraordinary events of life; reframing how we view things based upon our faith and life of prayer. It is a new way of feeling, almost like learning a new language of the heart consisting of words like: faith, hope, joy, love, gratitude, forgiveness, respect, and compassion. While these qualities are the fruit of a Spirit-filled life, they also become the spiritual weapons we use in the trenches of everyday life. The painter Marc Chagal suggests that qualities such as "faith and hope are our primal instincts, a kind of light to which we are naturally drawn."[6] Author Emily Dickinson once wrote, "Hope is the thing with feathers, that perches in the soul, and sings the tune without the words, and never stops at all."[7] Instead of seeing the proverbial glass of life half empty, we practice and learn through the eyes of faith to see it half-full! One medical expert states: "Endless studies show that optimists have better health and longer lives than pessimists, even if they are less accurate about the reality of life . . ."[8] We exhibit what researchers refer to as 'hardiness,' which may be defined as "the ability to view challenges as opportunities to grow."[9] I've heard that Gandhi used to say "Be the change you wish to see!"[10]

Throughout the Old and New Testaments we are encouraged to offer thanks and gratitude to our Creator.[11] The Jews were to regularly celebrate God's deliverance and provision, remembering yearly the Exodus, and seasonally the planting and harvesting of crops. The Apostle Paul told believers in Christ to keep the Spirit's fire burning bright by finding reasons for joy and thankfulness in all circumstances.[12] The Pilgrims who landed on Plymouth Rock understood the importance of offering thanks to God and celebrating His providence. That first Thanksgiving Day, which included feasting and friendly competitive games, was a grand celebration which the Pilgrims shared with the Native Americans; in fact it was so grand that it was extended for three days![13]

Abraham Maslow, founder of humanistic psychology and creator of Maslow's hierarchy of needs, recommended that people "appreciate again and again, freshly and naively, the basic goods of life with awe, pleasure, wonder, and even ecstasy."[14] I love the saying from the Muslim tradition which suggests that "every time a bird drinks a drop of water it lifts its eyes in gratitude toward heaven."[15] Medical missionary Albert Schweitzer, who received the 1952 Nobel Peace Prize for his philosophy of 'Reverence for Life', said "there is within each of us . . . an inner exaltation, which lifts us above dependence upon the gifts of events for our joy."[16]

But, did you know that the practice of this discipline benefits us physiologically? Researchers have observed that "cultivating appreciation and gratitude for life lowers stress hormones like cortisol."[17] Just a short fifteen-minute focusing on appreciation has been shown to increase levels of an immune antibody called secretory IgA.[18] The practice of appreciation has also been "correlated with a physiological state known as resonance (or parasympathetic dominance) – where heart, breathing, blood pressure, as well as brain rhythm and even the electrical potential of the skin are synchronized."[19] New brain research suggests that "consciously focusing on gratitude may help us subvert our own insatiability [i.e. craving for new pleasure]."[20]

Another heart attitude associated with worship is forgiveness. Jesus emphasized the importance of having a clear conscience when we approach God in worship.[21] Before we will be free to fully worship we must forgive and be forgiven; at least we must take the initiative. Jesus also taught that we should forgive others because we ourselves have been forgiven by the Father; and he indicated that in the future we will be forgiven as we have forgiven others. Researchers have found that "people who score high on forgiveness as a personality trait are less likely to be depressed, anxious, hostile, narcissistic, or exploitative and are also less likely to become dependent on drugs or nicotine."[22]

Joyfulness is like an inner spring that bubbles forth with good humor and laughter. It is evidence of being in sync with the Holy Spirit - a type of worship in its own right. Joseph Campbell is someone who understood the importance of joy and 'bliss.' He told people that if they find joy, it will burn out the pain; and if they follow their bliss, walls will become doors. It has been suggested that "humor releases us from time, and a moment of laughter is a hint of eternity.[23] Referring to Jesus, one author noted: "He never jests as Socrates does, but He often lets the ripple of a happy breeze play over the surface of His mighty deep."[24] We should find the humor in life. It is healthy to laugh when appropriate.

Experts suggest that "one hundred laughs is the aerobic equivalent of ten minutes spent rowing." Laughter has been observed to elevate the secretion of our natural mood-enhancing catecholamines and endorphins and decreases levels of the stress hormone cortisol. According to research, "one reason laughter is exhilarating may be that it releases the feel-good chemical, dopamine." If this isn't enough, "humor –used in a benign, uplifting way – is linked to . . . heart health, higher self-esteem, and psychological well-being."[25] One physician even asserts that "cancer patients who laugh live longer."[26]

Another aspect of day-to-day worship is to respect other people around us as beloved of God - whether we think they are deserving of our

192

respect or not.[27] In an attempt to convey God's perspective, the Fourteenth-Century Catholic Saint Catherine of Sienna once wrote: "I [i.e. God] require that you should love Me with the same love with which I love you. This, indeed, you cannot do because I love you without being loved. All the love which you have from Me you owe to Me, so that it is not of grace that you love Me, but because you ought to do so, while I love you out of grace and not because I owe you My love. Therefore, to me, in person, you cannot repay the love which I require of you, and I have placed you in the midst of your fellows, that you may do to them that which you cannot do to Me, that is to say, that you may love your neighbor of free grace, without expecting any return from him, and what you do to him I count as done to Me. . ."[28]

In their excellent book *Why Good Things Happen to Good People*, bio-ethicist Stephen Post and Jill Neimark write: "Respect is love's careful guardian. Its essence is acceptance – to hold another as 'irreducibly valuable,'" a term which they attribute to Christian philosopher Gene Outka. They go on to state: "The Latin root of 'respect' – *respectare* – means 'to look again.'"[29] The implication is that out of respect, we will look past first impressions, prejudices, and even glaring faults to see the person whom God has created in His image – one worthy of love.

Respect naturally leads to the final aspect of worship which I am going to mention: compassion. The Hebrew book of Lamentations was written as if for a national funeral, portraying the capture and destruction of Jerusalem. But, buried in this book is a jewel of a passage revealing God's longsuffering heart: "Because of the Lord's great love we are not consumed, for his compassions never fail. They are new every morning; great is your faithfulness."[30] In the New Testament, the Apostle Paul wrote "The Father of compassion . . . comforts us in all our troubles, so that we can comfort those in any trouble with the comfort we have received from God."[31]

Researchers suggest that compassion is tied to the release of the hormone oxytocin, which causes 'calm and connection' – "the exact opposite of the well-known fight-or-flight hormones."[32] Another expert notes that studies indicate compassion results in an increase in the antibody salivary IgA, which "provides major protection against cold an upper respiratory infection." He goes on to state "The ability to love and care about others also seems to precipitate lower levels of the stress hormone, nor-epinephrine, and a higher ration of suppressor T-cells that produce an important balance in a healthy immune system."[33] This leads us to the next of the disciplines: Service.

Chapter 44

Components of Illumination: Service

It has been suggested that "true ecstasy comes when we transcend self-interest and serve others, particularly those in need."[1] [2] [3] One physician writes, "People who volunteer also have better health, especially when they have a disease and are helping others with the same affliction."[4] The Apostle Paul encouraged people to "serve one another in love."[5] But, really he was just following the lead of his Master, Jesus who set the example by stooping to wash his disciples feet and who gave the following instructions to them: "Whoever wants to become great among you must be your servant, and whoever wants to be first must be your slave – just as the Son of Man [Jesus] did not come to be served, but to serve, and to give his life as a ransom for many."[6]

One wise, contemporary author draws a distinction between being a servant and merely rendering service: "When we choose to serve we are still in charge. We decide whom we will serve and when we will serve. And if we are in charge we will worry a great deal about anyone stepping on us, i.e. taking charge over us. But when we choose to be a servant we give up the right to be in charge. There is a great freedom in this. If we voluntarily choose to be a servant we surrender the right to decide who and when we will serve. We become available and vulnerable."[7] The ability to serve altruistically does not necessarily come easily or naturally. But, as has been suggested: "The Spirit's infilling not only refreshes our desire to serve but also purifies our motives to serve."[8] The Apostle Paul offers good advice for one who would become a true servant: "Whatever you do, work at it with all your heart, as working for the Lord, not for men . . ."[9] The more single-minded is our devotion to God in the little and big things that we set our hand to do, the more pure will be the service rendered. In the words of Oswald Chambers, "If the mainspring of your service is love for Jesus, you can serve men although they treat you as a door-mat."[10]

In the sport of road cycling, a unique member of the team, referred to as a 'domestique,' provides a perfect example of what being a servant is all about. Domestiques are cyclists who work solely for the benefit of their teammates and leader. They are like the unsung heroes in the race; their goal is simply to help the leader achieve a better position in the race. They don't share in the limelight. An author familiar with sport of competitive cycling writes: "Some important tasks carried out by the domestiques include retrieving water and nutrition from team cars and bringing it back up to the rest of the team and shielding teammates from aggressive opponents. They are also vital in helping teammates cope with mechanical disasters – should the leader get a flat tire, the domestique will shield them as they pull over, wait with them until they have replaced the wheel, then cycle in front of them to create an aerodynamic advantage allowing them to quickly reclaim their position. A domestique may also be called upon to sacrifice his or her bicycle if the leader crashes."[11] Domestique is a French word for servant.

Intercessory prayer (i.e. lifting other's needs before God in prayer) is another way that we can serve people. This is a form of worship too. There is growing scientific evidence of the efficacy of this type of prayer. A study published by Randolph Byrd, M.D. in 1988 was conducted in the coronary-care unit of San Francisco General Hospital: "393 patients were randomly assigned to two groups. One group of 192 patients was prayed for by outside intercessors ("born again" Christians from around the country), who were committed to pray regularly for each patient until the patient's discharge. The second group of 201 patients, the control group, did not receive this experimental prayer, in order to provide a basis for comparison for the prayed-for group."[12] "The findings were statistically significant: Patients in the control group were nearly twice as likely to suffer complications than were patients in the prayer group (27 percent as opposed to 15 percent)."[13] Another prayer study of special interest to smokers was published in 1987: "In this study, conducted by Drs. M. Gmur and A. Tschopp in Switzerland, a faith-healing practitioner laid his hands on the heads of 532 smokers. This was the only treatment the smokers received, yet 40% of them abstained from smoking for at least four months after the laying on of hands – a remarkable miracle. . . . After one year, 33% of patients in the Swiss study had stayed smoke-free; after five years, 20%. When participants were interviewed twelve years after the initial treatment, 16% were continuing to abstain from smoking."[14]

Larry Dossey, M.D. has studied extensively the scientific evidence of the healing properties of prayer. He suggests that what appears to be paramount is that the intercessory prayer is genuine, and sincere, and that it comes from the heart. Whether the person praying is a novice or a veteran is not so much the issue. Whereas God certainly hears the prayers of everyone, the Apostle James suggests that the personal integrity of the person offering the prayer may be a factor. In James own words, "The prayer of a righteous man is powerful and effective."[15] But, what Dossey suggests is most important is love. He writes, "If I were sick I would enlist the prayers of people I love and who love me. I would want compassionate, empathetic individuals on my side."[16]

In reflecting upon the difficulty of serving others through intercessory prayer, Henri Nouwen wrote in his journal: "Today I imagined my inner self as a place crowded with pins and needles. How could I receive anyone in my prayer when there is no real place for them to be free and relaxed when I am still so full of preoccupations, jealousies, angry feelings, anyone who enters will get hurt. I had a very vivid realization that I must create some free space in my innermost self so that I may indeed invite others to enter and be healed. To pray for others means to offer others a hospitable place where I can really listen to their needs and pains. Compassion, therefore, calls for a self-scrutiny that can lead to inner gentleness."[17] I seem to remember Henri Nouwen also saying something to the effect that the primary reason we don't engage in intercessory prayer as much as we should, is not so much because we lack faith but rather that we lack compassion!

One author warns, "We can all recognize the tendency for spiritual practice, including prayer, to spiral into inactivity."[18] As good and important as prayer is, there comes a time when action is needed to truly love and serve others. C.S. Lewis once said, "I am often praying for others when I should be doing things for them. It's so much easier to pray for a bore than to go and see him."[19] In addition to stepping out of the private prayer closet to physically help meet people's needs, we also may need to join together with others to pray in concert for specific needs. In reference to this type of concerted prayer, British theologian and physicist John Polkinhorne invokes the metaphor of the laser. According to one expert, "laser light is unusually powerful because it is 'coherent'; that is, all the crests and troughs of the waves making up the light are in step."[20] Polkinhorne believes that "divine and human coherence in prayer . . . can make things possible which would not be so if we and God were at cross-purposes." He goes on to suggest "It is appropriate to encourage many people to pray for the same thing. That is not because there are more fists beating on the heavenly doors, but because there are more wills to be aligned with the divine will."[21] There would therefore be "more coherence, more order, more power, like the light of the laser."[22]

This leads us to a final type of discipline of the illuminative way: human interaction and connectedness.

Chapter 45

Components of Illumination: Human Connection

Although Jesus sought out times of solitude for the purposes of prayer and meditation, he was a social person – one connected with people. He was never too busy or preoccupied to entertain people who sought him out; even when he was dead tired or in the middle of something, he would stop and compassionately heal or teach as the needs presented themselves. He exhibited solidarity with common people; he identified with humanity. He had a close band of twelve disciples who became his entourage. As he approached his final days, he shared with them his premonitions of what lay ahead. Certainly it was to prepare them for what was coming, but it also seemed that he was seeking support from them. The night he was betrayed, he asked his three closest friends to join him in prayer as he sought to discern his Father's will. Although they fell asleep during his night of anguished prayer, he nevertheless sought to draw strength from their fellowship and support.

You and I also need to interact with and be connected to other people. This final aspect of illumination involves attaching ourselves not only to God, but to those created in God's image. Oftentimes habits thrive in secrecy, loneliness, and boredom. We are not meant to go through life in solitaire; to bleed and hurt alone. Even in the Garden of Eden, God recognized that Adam needed a flesh and blood companion to share earthly existence; the Divine-human relationship was not sufficient to dispel loneliness. We too, even the most spiritual, need to see and embrace the image of God in people; we also need to be embraced and to be seen by real-live, flesh-and-blood people. By this, I do not mean to suggest that everyone needs to be married or be in a romantic relationship to find fulfillment; but I do believe that one needs to have a friend or to be a part of a community of people to fully experience what it means to be human.

In a song from the 1960's, entitled *I am a Rock*, Simon & Garfunkel described the sentiment of a person disconnected from the rest of humanity: ". . . I've built my walls - a fortress deep and mighty, that none may penetrate. I have no need of friendship; friendship causes pain - its laughter and its loving I disdain. . . Don't talk of love, I've heard the words before; it's sleeping in my memory. I won't disturb the slumber of feelings that have died. If I never loved I never would have cried. . . I have my books and my poetry to protect me; I am shielded in my armor, hiding in my room, safe within my womb. I touch no one and no one touches me. I am a rock, I am an island. And a rock feels no pain; and an island never cries." In contrast, the 17th-Century English poet John Donne revealed his sense of connection with humanity: "No man is an island, entire of itself . . . any man's death diminishes me, because I am involved in mankind."

One author presents a rather eloquent case that love is a universal human need: "My friends, now desperately do we need to be loved and to love. . . Love is something you and I must have. We must have it because our spirit feeds upon it. We must have it because without it we become weak and faint. Without love our self-esteem weakens. Without it our courage fails. Without love we can no longer look out confidently at the world. We turn inward and begin to feed upon our own personalities, and little by little we destroy ourselves. With it we are creative. With it we march tirelessly. With it and with it alone, we are able to sacrifice for others."[1]

Experts in the treatment of alcoholism, Ernest Kurtz & Katherine Ketchem write: "Modern humankind feels homeless in the deepest meaning of the word: not in the transient sense of having no place to sleep for the night, not even in the wider sense of poverty's homelessness, but in a monstrous, universal sense of having no place wherein we fit. . . Those broken within, also cut off from what is without, find themselves fundamentally estranged – not at home with self, not at home with family, not at home with the world. This is a terrible feeling, a terrible be-ing – this . . . sense of a bone ripped out of its socket. The experience is of lost souls circling endlessly, seeking the place where they 'fit.' For, only in finding that 'fit' is the bone re-healed into its socket, and only thus does one find a place to rest, a place to hide, a place to be one's self. . . a home."[2] [3]

Christian psychologist, Larry Crabb defines 'disconnection' as "a condition of existence where the deepest part of who we are is vibrantly attached to no one, where we are profoundly unknown and therefore experience neither the thrill of being believed in nor the joy of loving or being loved."[4] Citing a recent study, one physician writes ". . . Loneliness affects the genes that regulate immune function and makes . . . [people] . . . vulnerable to cancer and to auto-immune and viral diseases."[5] Another physician states "We do not know how having many and frequent social contacts might boost the immune system, but . . . studies offer the possibility that social support is one of the main building blocks of health."[6] He goes on to suggest that we were built to interact with one another; that human interaction and connectedness are vital.

It has been suggested that because we are "born lonely we try hard to fit in to be the kind of person that will cause others to like us."[7] But we have a hard time letting down our guard to reveal our true selves for fear of not being accepted or worse yet of being rejected. One writer reveals an appreciation of the need to move beyond this surface type of human relationship to true friendship: "Oh, the comfort, the inexpressible comfort of feeling safe with a person, having neither to weigh thought nor measure words, but pouring them all right out, just as they are, chaff and grain together, certain that a faithful hand will take and sift them, keep what is worth keeping, and with a breath of kindness, blow the rest away."[8]

Catholic priest, Adrian Van Kaam wrote "When the dark recesses of our spirit become manifest, we especially need at least a friend to share our fears, and assure us that ours is not an uncommon experience."[9] It is common for people attempting to break free from a habit, to feel alone and somehow unique in their struggle. But as the Apostle Paul pointed out "No temptation has seized you except what is common to man."[10] For this reason we need to find someone to confide in – to be real with; someone who can identify with what we are going through. In fact, the Apostle James wrote "Confess your sins to each other and pray for each other so that you may be healed."[11] One author has suggested that in order to make our own wounds a source of healing, we need to see our own pain and suffering as "rising form the depth of human condition which all men share."[12] Not only do others' need our prayers, compassion, and forgiveness but we also need to receive these things ourselves. Human interaction and connectedness facilitate this process.

As a new nonsmoker and someone on a new spiritual journey, it is advisable to find others who can encourage you on toward freedom and spiritual maturity. The concept of a traveling companion or a 'soul friend' to accompany you on your journey and to provide a listening supportive ear is one that has a rich history in spirituality.[13] [14] [15] One author suggests: "We are, each of us, angels with only one wing, and we can only fly embracing each other."[16]

In addition to finding a good confidant, if you don't already have one, it would be beneficial to attach yourself to a group or community of people who share your passion for both freedom from smoking and for spiritual growth. Some remarkable trees provide an excellent example of the strength associated with being part of a community: "The giant redwoods of California have stood tall against the howling storms for centuries now. You would think that with such an endurance record they would have deep roots that burrow deep into the mountainside and wrap themselves around huge boulders. You could think that – but you would be wrong. Actually, they have shallow roots. How can they survive so long? They grow in groves, and the roots of many trees entwine. Thus they stand together against the storms as if to announce to the north wind, 'We stand together. If you are going to take one of us out, you will have to take us all.' Sometimes a redwood does fall, almost always one that sprouted up some distance from the others. Its roots could not reach those of the other trees. Even a giant redwood cannot stand when it has to stand alone."[17]

One of the reasons Alcoholics Anonymous has been so successful is the group support it provides its participants. But long before AA, the value of group support was recognized by religious communities throughout history and throughout the world. There are many benefits of being connected with a group of people - providing that the group is healthy, and is not of the toxic variety: exclusive, intolerant, controlling, and/or cult-like. If you are not connected with a good group or community, then I would suggest that you prayerfully seek out one, and trust that God will guide you to where you belong – but don't exhaust yourself looking for the perfect group. You won't find it. As someone has said, we are all works in progress. Look rather for a place to serve others and you will find reciprocation.

Consider the following quote from a Trappist monk: "A monk is simply a sinner who joins a community of sinners who are confident in God's mercy and who strive to recognize their weaknesses in the presence of their brothers."[18] To stay on track with your smoke-free lifestyle, you may want to visit a local 'Nicotine Anonymous' group. But even more important, for spiritual nourishment and encouragement, you will want to find a church, fellowship, or other religious group to become a part of. If you don't know where to begin looking, ask around. You may also benefit from doing an internet search and pulling up websites of groups in your area; then narrow down your search and take your time visiting them.

One of the benefits of being part of a group of like-minded, spiritually-motivated individuals is that you will harness the power of accountability. If there is an openness and vulnerability present, then others can call your bluff when you are being less than honest about yourself and your behavior, and when perhaps you are tempted to return to your former dysfunctional ways of living. The writer of the New Testament book of Hebrews recognized the importance of accountability in community, as evidenced by the following admonition: "See to it, brothers, that none of you has a sinful, unbelieving heart that turns away from the living God. But encourage one another daily, as long as it is called today, so that none of you may be hardened by sin's deceitfulness. We have come to share in Christ if we hold firmly till the end the confidence we had at the first."[19] Involving others in your life destroys the inner secrecy where compulsions tend to thrive. I have heard it said that in telling others the truth about ourselves, we discover the truth! I've also heard it said that the strength of good spiritual communion is in the sharing of weaknesses; that is when we grow strong. We need each other to "grow strong in the broken places."[20]

Another benefit of being a part of a loving spiritual community is the prayer support one receives. During my wife's recent illness we have been sustained on the wings of others' prayers, especially from different church congregations we have been a part of. Likewise, for a person struggling to break free of a habit such as smoking, intercessory prayer can make a real difference. Another advantage of community is the love and acceptance one receives. Experts would agree that wounded people heal best and live best (i.e. survive and thrive) in a supportive community.

A wonderful example from nature of the benefits of community can be observed in geese. This mobile tight-knit community displays teamwork. You have probably seen them migrating, and what you will notice is that they fly in 'V' formation. They fly in this manner to extend their flying range by as much as 71%; as each goose flaps its wing it creates an uplift for the geese that follow. If a goose falls out of formation it quickly senses an increase in drag and resistance, which compels it to get back in formation with the flock. The sound of honking that you hear as geese are flying overhead is their way of cheering on and encouraging the geese up front to maintain their speed. As the lead goose tires out it simply falls back in formation and another willing goose moves to the front of the flock to lead. If a goose should become ill or wounded and fall out of formation, two other geese will follow it to the ground where they will offer help and protection.

Being a part of community also opens up greater opportunities for service, which is healthy. As Catholic priest, Benedict Groeschel points out: "Unless they have the opportunity to share in a service-oriented volunteer activity with uplifting ideals, many people sink into a life of enclosed self-seeking. We have all seen couples who, often in isolation, become totally preoccupied with a house, which then becomes both castle and prison." He goes on to suggest "Doing good works and sharing the lot of the unfortunate, involvement with people of totally different values (or none at all) are all antidotes to false intimacy and emotionalism which can impede spiritual growth."[21] The author of the New Testament book of Hebrews wrote to the early Christian community ". . . Let us consider how we may spur one another on toward love and good deeds. Let us not give up meeting together, as some are in the habit of doing, but let us encourage one another . . . ."[22] Working together with others creates a bond much like the bond forged between soldiers fighting side-by-side in battle. Often times while serving together, even though the needs might be both grave and great, great love and joy bursts forth.[23] Accompanying the joy of comradery is often good natured humor and laughter, and some have suggested that the power in humor and laughter is of a spiritual nature.[24]

This leads to a final benefit of being in community: a deepening experience of worship. The beloved Psalms of the Hebrew Scriptures were thought to have been corporate songs of worship. In a letter to the Christian community of believers in Colassae, the Apostle Paul wrote "Let the peace of Christ rule in your hearts, since as members of one body you were called to peace. And be thankful. Let the word of Christ dwell in you richly as you teach and admonish one another with all wisdom, and as you sing psalms, hymns and spiritual songs with gratitude in your hearts to God."[25]

This brings us to the close of our discussion of illumination, or the process of Divine attachment. We will now proceed to the final stage in the spiritual journey, what the Christian mystics refer to as 'Union.' This final stage is the place of 'freedom.'[26]

Section VII:

Termination & Union (Living Smoke-Free)

Rise from the Ashes

After surrendering its former identity, and patiently enduring the long process of death and rebirth, the earthbound caterpillar has been transformed into a creature of free-flight. What first appeared to be a tomb has become a womb – the caterpillar has broken on through to the other side and has emerged from the chrysalis a butterfly! Like the mythical phoenix, it has risen from the ashes of its former self.

You have finally reached a point of stability in your journey. Your new healthier lifestyle has essentially replaced your old smoking lifestyle. You are feeling comfortable with the new you! Sure, every now and then you may have an urge to smoke, but it is manageable; you just let the urge subside and move on. By now you have established a nonsmoking history: you've weathered the seasons, stood the test of time, and created new smoke-free memories. But more important, through the processes of conversion, purgation, and illumination you are experiencing an oneness with God as never before; you may have reached what the Christian mystics refer to as the state of "Union." Of course you must realize that everyone is on a unique timetable when it comes to their spiritual development. Some reach this state of union sooner than others. But, ultimately as one author notes ". . . the awareness of God's presence grows because of a simple desire to accept the divine will and live according to it."[1]

The metaphor of sheep is a common one used throughout the Judeo-Christian Scriptures. The Apostle Peter compares us to sheep that were going astray but now have returned to the Shepherd and Overseer of our souls.[2] The beloved 23rd Psalm provides a wonderful description of the state of a contented sheep in the fold of a good shepherd. This is really a portrayal of a person who is in a state of union with his/her maker – it is a picture of health, satisfaction, safety and rest. This psalm was written by David, who knew firsthand what it was like to care for sheep - remember, he was a shepherd boy before he became a giant-slayer and king. Listen to a modern paraphrase of David's prayer of thankfulness to God: "God, my shepherd! I don't need a thing. You have bedded me down in lush

207

meadows, you find me quiet pools to drink from. True to your word, you let me catch my breath and send me in the right direction. Even when the way goes through Death Valley, I'm not afraid when you walk at my side. Your trusty shepherd's crook makes me feel secure. You serve me a six-course dinner right in front of my enemies. You revive my drooping head; my cup brims with blessing. Your beauty and love chase me every day of my life. I'm back home in the house of God for the rest of my life."[3]

Another common type of metaphor used throughout the Scriptures is that of seeds, plants, and trees.[4] [5] Two examples stand out: one from the Old and one from the New Testament. The 1st Psalm describes a person who is in a state of union with God: "Blessed is the man who does not walk in the counsel of the wicked or stand in the way of sinners or sit in the seat of mockers. But his delight is in the law of the Lord, and on his law he meditates day and night. He is like a tree planted by streams of water which yields its fruit in season and whose leaf does not wither. Whatever he does prospers. . . ."[6] The Apostle Paul compares the person who is in a state of union with God to a seed that has grown to maturity, as evidenced by its fruitfulness: ". . . The fruit of the Spirit is love, joy, peace, patience, kindness, goodness, faithfulness, gentleness and self-control."[7] This goal of reaching a state of spiritual maturity and fruitfulness is seen in every tradition.

Other Biblical themes that we have discussed, which illustrate this spiritual state of union, include: the Jews safe and secure in the Promised Land of Canaan – where the crops are plentiful and lush enough for the bees to make honey and for the lambs to be content enough to produce milk; the well that has been dug and/or unstopped so that a dependable source of fresh water from the underground spring is now readily available as opposed to dependence upon rainfall to fill cisterns; the Temple which has been rebuilt in the secured city and the palace that has been renovated for the new King; and the new master who has established residence in the house.

As we discussed earlier, it has been suggested that there are only four places to be in the cycle of life and faith: endings, in-between times, new beginnings, and settled places."[8] Conversion in the broadest sense of the word is the process of moving from a settled place of brokenness and alienation to a settled place of wholeness and union with God. If you think about it, this describes the journey you have been on. You started out broken and addicted to nicotine - on a plateau in your spiritual life.

Through the act of repentance you made an about-face and followed God's lead by leaving the settled place of addiction. From there you descended from the static plateau of your dysfunctional existence into the valley of the shadow of death. The more you let go of the things you were attached to the deeper the purgative path took you until you felt almost buried in the deep dark canyon. This was certainly an in-between time, where you found yourself longing for the familiarity of the plateau. But, then you began to ascend on the illuminative path – a new beginning. You continued to attach yourself to your guides, the disciplines of the Spirit, and now you have reached the summit with its grand vistas. This mountain peak represents the settled place of Divine union. After your long hard journey, you have reached a place of rest, where you sense more than ever the Divine presence in your life.

As a result of consecrating, or surrendering fully one's life to God – which purgation and illumination represent – one reaches a point of sanctification. Union and sanctification are Christian terms that essentially refer to the same condition. Oswald Chambers suggested "Sanctification is not something Jesus Christ puts into me: it is Himself in me."[9] Remember we had said previously that the purpose of illumination was to strengthen the inner core of a person – making it inhabitable for the Divine Spirit. Once this happens, the inner spring of living water bursts forth and the Spirit of God fills the temple of the human heart. In Chambers words "The last aching abyss of the human heart is filled to overflowing with the love of God."[10] In the journey of Jesus, this represents Pentecost. Remember, we had said that the death and resurrection of Jesus is analogous to conversion; the time he spent in his resurrected body saying goodbye to his disciples represents purgation; and his ascension to the Heavenly Father corresponds to illumination. Pentecost was when the Holy Spirit of Jesus returned to earth to be united with his followers, while the person of Jesus remained in God the Father's presence in heaven. The Church, as a collective people, has been referred to in the New Testament as the Bride of Christ. For our purposes as individuals, this union represents the consummation of our commitment or covenant with the Divine lover of our souls.

This state of being, referred to as union or the 'unitive' way, has been described as "a posture of yieldedness to God's presence and purpose, . . . [with] a purity of intention. . ."[11] Gregory of Nyssa, a Bishop from the fourth century A.D., wrote "The effect of prayer is union with God, and if someone is with God, he is separated from the enemy."[12] As a result the person is free to be the person he or she was meant to be. One author has observed: "Watching a person in the unitive way is like watching a great musician playing an instrument over which he or she has complete mastery and control."[13] But, as you most likely already know firsthand, the process of reaching union is not easy. In the words of St. John of the Cross: "The soul is purged and prepared for union with the divine light just as the wood is prepared for transformation into the fire. Fire, when applied to wood, first dehumidifies it, dispelling all moisture and making it give off any water it contains. Then it gradually turns the wood black, makes it dark and ugly, and even causes it to emit a bad odor. By drying out the wood, the fire brings to light and expels all those ugly and dark accidents which are contrary to fire. Finally, by heating and enkindling it from without, the fire transforms the wood into itself and makes it as beautiful as itself."[14] [15]

Union can be described as a state of 'simplicity.' One author writes "Simplicity brings joy and balance. Duplicity brings anxiety and fear."[16] He goes on to state that "simplicity begins in inward focus and unity."[17] [18] Soren Kierkegaard suggested that purity of heart consists of willing one thing. An old Shaker hymn describes simplicity: "Tis the gift to be simple, 'Tis the gift to be free, 'Tis the gift to come down where you ought to be. And when we find ourselves in the place just right, 'Twil be in the valley of love and delight."[19]

Chapter 47

Characteristics of Union: Altruism & Compassion

While it is wonderful to linger in the settled place of Divine union, at some point one must move on. Spiritual health is not static, but rather dynamic. The basic insight of developmental psychology is that "human beings are in a constant process of becoming."[1] As Yuichiro Miura, the author of *The Man Who Skied down Everest*, wrote "The end of one thing is the beginning of another. I am a pilgrim again."[2] Religious traditions across the board encourage adherents to become altruistic. Within each tradition one can find inspiring examples of revered individuals who have overcome the lure of settling into a self-preoccupied spiritual lifestyle.[3] [4] [5] [6]

According to the Christian Scriptures, Jesus Christ, the Son of God, left his throne in Heaven to become incarnate – one of us humans – in order to bring us salvation; and after his resurrection and ascension to Heaven, he returned again to earth in Spirit to encourage his followers on in their journey. He provided an example for others to follow - that of a 'suffering servant.' Part of the purpose for which God rescued you, is likely for you to help others move along in their spiritual journeys from bondage to freedom. Holocaust survivor and psychiatrist, Viktor Frankl, once remarked that what made his life meaningful was "helping others to find their meaning."[7] Being a former smoker, you may be able to encourage and help others who are attempting to break free from nicotine addiction. This may truly be a way for you to give back.

It has been suggested that "if indeed we are in intimate union with God in the center, then the soul's desire is God's desire."[8] Because God's desire is to show compassion, we will desire this as well. One author contends this type of compassion "is not knowing *about* the suffering and pain of others. It is, in some way, *knowing* that pain, entering into it, sharing it and tasting it in so far as possible."[9] [10] [11] By following the purgative and illuminative paths you have reached the summit of Divine union, and although the views are grand, you must descend back into the valley to fulfill your God-given destiny. As the founders of Alcoholics Anonymous were known to say, the spiritual approach is as useless as others if you soak it up like a sponge and keep it to yourself.[12] You must continue on the

Spirit-led journey to reach places "where your deep gladness and the world's deep hunger meet."[13]

It has been suggested that what sustains all novices is that "they know there is a sense of pleasure, enjoyment, and joy in mastery."[14] So by all means celebrate your freedom and recovery from addiction; throw your hats up in the air because of the newfound intimacy you have with God. And if you are so compelled by the Spirit, follow the joyous lead of the 16th-Century Saint, Francis Xavier who exclaimed "the world is full of closed doors and I have to open as many . . . as I can to let the sunshine in."[15] God can use this compelling and contagious type of joy to inspire and benefit others.

But let me issue a gentle warning. While you are sharing your joy and helping others to quit smoking and/or to grow spiritually, stay humble and centered upon God and don't neglect your own self-care. Don't think that you have fully arrived, or that you are immune to falling back. One sage spiritual counselor and psychiatrist has written: "Sadly, the brain never completely forgets what it has learned. Because of the deep and pervasive physical power of strong attachments, their potential exists forever in us, even after we have effectively broken the habit of acting upon them. We may joke about never forgetting how to ride a bicycle, saying, 'Don't worry; it will come back to you.' But the permanence of addiction memory is not funny. It stands ready to come back to us with only the slightest encouragement. The brain learns how to 'do' its attachments far better than it learns to ride a bicycle or drive a car, and it remembers them more powerfully. Years after a major addiction has been conquered, the smallest association, the tiniest taste, can fire up old cellular patterns once again."[16] As it has been said of sanctification, while sin may no longer 'reign' the potential for sin still does 'remain' in the person.

When you think you are invincible or home-free, beware. As the wise King Solomon wrote, "Pride goes before destruction, a haughty spirit before a fall."[17] The Apostle Paul, who was a mentor and pastor to countless of first-century Christians, offered some wise and practical words of counsel: "Brothers, if someone is caught in a sin, you who are spiritual should restore him gently. But watch yourself, or you also may be tempted."[18] He also warned "if you think you are standing firm, be careful that you don't fall."[19] After encouraging his readers to rigorously pursue the spiritual life as if they were Olympic athletes in training, he then turned the spotlight on himself: "I do not run like a man running aimlessly; I do not fight like a man beating the air. No, I beat my body and make it my slave so that after I have preached to others, I myself will not be disqualified for the prize."[20]

Chapter 48

Characteristics of Union: Joy, Celebration & Peace

Divine union also results in joy. It has been suggested that "God's normal means of bringing His joy is by redeeming and sanctifying the ordinary junctures of human life. . . Joy is the end-result of the Spiritual Disciplines' functioning in our lives."[1] One well-known devotional writer points out "when faithfully pursued, the . . . disciplines bring us deliverance from those things that have made our lives miserable for years, which, in turn, evokes increased celebration, thus, an unbroken circle of life and power is formed."[2] He goes on to state he is inclined to think that "joy is the motor, the thing that keeps everything else going. Without joyous celebration to infuse the other Disciplines, we will sooner or later abandon them. Joy produces energy. Joy makes us strong."[3]

Richard Foster has written: "Celebration is at the heart of the way of Christ. He entered the world on a high note of jubilation: 'I bring you good news of great joy,' cried the angel, 'which shall come to all the people' (Luke 2:10). He left the world bequeathing his joy to the disciples . . ."[4] In chapters 14-17 of the Gospel of John, we get a glimpse of what Jesus had to say to his closest disciples just prior to his arrest and crucifixion. He was comforting his little flock, preparing them for the events that were soon to transpire. He assured them that after he was gone, he would send the Holy Spirit who would comfort and guide to them. Then he spoke to them about maturing in their faith and bearing fruit, as branches abiding in the vine. But, listen to what he said next: "If you obey my commands, you will remain in my love, just as I have obeyed my Father's commands and remain in his love. I have told you this so that my joy may be in you and that your joy may be complete. My command is this: Love each other as I have loved you. Greater love has no one than this, that one lay down his life for his friends. You are my friends if you do what I command you. . . You did not choose me, but I chose you to go and bear fruit – fruit that will last."[5] This describes what we have been talking about. The disciplines are means by which we can attach ourselves to God like branches to the vine. As the life-giving Spirit flows freely through our lives, the spiritual fruit or qualities we long for will be produced – joy being one, and love being the greatest of all.

By gaining self-control, which is another fruit of the spirit, we actually begin to treat ourselves with the love and respect befitting persons created in the image of God. In addition to loving ourselves in a healthy manner, our love for God grows because of the deliverance we have experienced. But at some point we begin to love God not only for what he has accomplished in our lives, but for who he is. John Wesley, the Father of Methodism described this process as being 'perfected in love.' In his own words it consists of "love excluding sin, love filling the heart, taking up the whole capacity of the soul."[6]

15th-Century Saint, Catherine of Genoa pointed out it is only natural that when we are "confused and virtually desperate, we turn to Him [God] . . . because of the use we can make of Him rather than out of pure charity as He would rather have us do."[7] Recovery from an addiction can become an idol; and God can become the means for us to worship that idol.[8] Eventually however, we see God as not just a deliverer but a lover. We become more enamored with the giver of good gifts than with the gifts themselves.[9] We become what one author refers to as "presence-oriented" rather than gift-oriented or even fruit-oriented.[10]

There is yet another aspect of love that flowers during this unitive stage – our love for other people. As one author puts it, to fully love God, we "must escape from the prison of . . . self-love and love those who are loved by [God]."[11] The 'Golden Rule' has been described as the birthright of humans created in the Divine image: to love God, ourselves, and others. The 19th-Century Carmelite nun, Saint Therese of Lisieux, said what matters most in life is "not great deeds but great love."[12] Therese was known as the 'little flower' because of her loving attention to the little, unseen details and chores of life. In the early centuries of Christendom, some individuals desiring a deeper spirituality retreated from the busy, noisy cities to the solitude of the desert. It has been noted that these monks, the Desert Fathers and Mothers as they are now referred, "confronted their own weakness and developed a deep sense of their own sinfulness. But their spirituality did not stop there – it only began there. For out of that awareness of their own weakness, they developed a compassion for the weaknesses of others, the outstanding virtue that all of their sayings highlight."[13]

All of the world's enduring religious traditions teach, in their own unique ways, that reaching a 'unitive' stage of spirituality produces an enduring sense of calm, peace, harmony, and well-being.[14] [15] [16] [17] [18] It is what the Hebrew Scriptures refer to as 'shalom.' It is to recognize that "as a sponge is in the ocean and the ocean is in a sponge, so we are in God and He in us."[19] One author writes: "Struggling against the requirements of the present moment creates unnecessary frustration and interior distress. God provides the necessary grace each moment to fulfill the task at hand. Putting off life's demands wastes the grace of the present moment. Wasted grace propagates psychological malaise. . . Resting contentedly in God alone summarizes the purity of the Christian way."[20] The ability to rest in the moment, trusting in God, is a hallmark of Divine union.

Chapter 49

Characteristics of Union: Growth

Although we have been emphasizing the process of moving from spiritual brokenness to spiritual wholeness, it would be incorrect to assume that the spiritual saga is over once we reach a state of maturity and fruitfulness. We may be out of the woods and back on the path, but the journey must continue. As one author writes, "We must strive to take the next good step, rather than striving for a static reality of perfection to be arrived at."[1] In the words of the Apostle Paul, we must "keep in step with the Spirit."[2] We have been rescued for a purpose – to enjoy the good things of this earth in a way intended by the Creator, and to use our unique gifts and abilities in a responsible humble manner that honors God, respects ourselves, and benefits others. Spread your wings and fly. Embrace your newfound freedom, but always remain tethered to the spiritual way of life by means of the disciplines, "like a jazz musician who knows the score so well he can freely improvise but without the foolishness of those naïve, would-be musicians who think they can soar in ecstasy without knowing their chords or being tutored by the tradition itself."[3]

In conclusion, let me just say that as long as you are alive, there is opportunity for continued spiritual transformation. It has been suggested that "spirituality is one of those realities that you have only so long as you seek it; as soon as you think you have it, you've lost it . . . Spirituality is boundless, unable to be fenced in: We do not capture it; it captures us."[4] One expert points out, "As we have observed in any developmental sequence, we are in some way at all stages of the journey at any particular time."[5] It is the opinion of Asbury Seminary professor, M. Robert Mulholland that the classical pilgrimage toward wholeness, characterized by the stages of awakening, conversion, purgation, illumination, and union "can be thought of either as the overall path of . . . spirituality through life or as the path toward wholeness in any given area of our lives." He goes on to suggest "This means that we can be at different stages in various areas. In one area we may be well along the path to wholeness, while in another area God is just beginning to awaken us to another part of our life that needs transformation."[6]

217

With respect to the spiritual journey, it has been suggested: "Life is not a matter of reaching a stagnant end point, but is rather an ongoing process in which one, hopefully and with grace, grows ever more deeply in love."[7] Also speaking about life's journey, another author has written: "Our destination is never a place, but rather a new way of looking at things."[8] [9] To be in a right relationship with our Creator is in a sense to return to the Garden of Eden.[10] Only, this time you bring with you the wisdom and humility of age.

Developmental psychologist, Erik Erikson suggested that a major achievement of the last adult stage of life is "personal integrity." This is when a person is able to look back upon their life and find congruence between their values and actions.[11] I would suggest that the goal of spiritual transformation should be to reach that point, before the end of life, where one finds congruence between one's 'ideal' self and 'real' self – to live in such a way, day-to-day, that is both true to oneself, to one's fellow humanity, and to one's God. It is the Judaic concept of an actualized and/or righteous person, who "accepts responsibility of choice in his or her life regardless of circumstances" and demonstrates "courage for making choices that are in concert with their values."[12] This is the unitive way! This is real freedom!

One psychiatrist has observed: "No step forward is maintained unless it is followed by further steps. He who does not go forward, goes back. Physical, psychical, and spiritual health is not a haven in which we can take refuge in a sort of final security, but a daily battle in which our destiny is constantly at stake."[13] Another wise psychiatrist and spiritual counselor has written: "Authentic spiritual wholeness, by its very nature, is open-ended. It is always in the process of becoming, always incomplete. Thus we ourselves must also be always incomplete. If it were otherwise, we could never exercise our God-given right to participate in ongoing creation."[14] It has been suggested that 'gradual sanctification' is an aspect of the spiritual journey that continues beyond the point of reaching Divine union. The Twelfth-Century Christian mystic and Saint, Hildegarde of Bingen used the term *viriditas* or 'greening power' to signify spiritual fertility and growth.[15] It is an ongoing process where "submerged longings to be free from every stain of sin burst forth like tulips on an inordinately warm spring day. As the sunflower follows the sun, you are drawn to the transforming Light."[16] In the final chapter of the final book of the Old Testament, the Hebrew prophet Malachi recorded God's words to Israel: "But for you who revere my name, the sun of righteousness will rise with healing in its wings. And you will go out and leap like calves released from the stall. Then you will trample down the wicked; they will be ashes under the soles of your feet . . ."[17] By making a habit of looking and responding to God, in all things, you will not only rise from the ashes of your smoking habit, but you will continue to rise from the limitations of the past into newness of life – you will keep on becoming.

Postscript

Two years have passed since I sat down to begin writing this book. It is now January, 2013 and publication is imminent. We have just celebrated the two-year anniversary of my wife Linda's bone-marrow transplant. She is doing well. There is no sign of leukemia and it appears from her most recent blood-work that the donor's immune system is fully engrafted and working fine. She has just been cleared by her doctor's to return to work, which she has done this month. She is once again working in the area of smoking intervention.

For those of you who are on the journey of rising from the ashes, I pray that two years from now your new spiritual immune system will be fully engrafted and you will be able to celebrate the two-year anniversary of being smoke-free.

Endnotes

Chapter 1
[1] Alan Blum (editor), *The Cigarette Underworld: A Front-line Report on the War Against Your Lungs* (Secaucus NJ:Lyle Stuart Inc., Medical Society of New York, 1985), 7.
[2] Judith Mackay and Michael Eriksen, *The Tobacco Atlas* (Geneva: World Health Organization, 2002), 36.
[3] Centers for Disease Control and Prevention. Annual Smoking-Attributable Mortality, Years of Potential Life Lost, and Productivity Losses – United States, 1997-2001. Morbidity and Mortality Weekly Report (serial online). 2005:54 [cited 2006 Sep 23]. Available from: http://www.cdc.gov/mmwrhtml/mm5425al.htm.
[4] Alan Blum (ed.), *The Cigarette Underworld: A Front-line Report on the War Against Your Lungs,* 59.
[5] American Lung Association, *Smoking Fact Sheet,* (accessed from www.lungusa.org 1/19/2010.)
[6] U.S. Department of Health and Human Services. *The Health Consequences of Smoking: A Report of the Surgeon General.* Atlanta: U.S. Department of Health and Human Services, Centers for Disease Control and Prevention, National center for Chronic Disease Prevention and Health Promotion, Office on Smoking and Health, 2004. (accessed on 1/19/2010 from www.cdc.gov, *Health Effects of Cigarette Smoking* fact sheet.)
[7] American Cancer Society, *Prevention and Early Detection: Guide to Quitting Smoking.* (accessed from www.cancer.org, on 1/19/2010.
[8] Samuel Zelman, "Correlation of Smoking History with Hearing Loss," JAMA 1973; 223:920.
[9] JA Nisker and MA Maruncic, "Cigarette Smoking and Bone Loss During Hormone Replacement After Menopause," N Engl J Med 1986; 314:854.
[10] J Jensen, C Christiansen, P Rodbro, "Cigarette Smoking, Serum Estrogen, and Bone Loss During Hormone-Replacement Therapy Early After Menopause," N Engl J Med 1985; 313:973-5.
[11] If you have heart disease you need to visualize just how nicotine and carbon monoxide forces your heart to work overtime (increased heart rate) under the worst possible conditions (constricted blood vessels and reduced oxygen-carrying capacity of the blood). Quitting smoking is probably the most significant thing you can do to prevent the worsening of your condition. E Ackley and S Valentine,

"Smoking Cessation by Patients with Coronary Artery Disease," Focus on Critical Care, April 12, 1985; (2):50-56.
[12] Within 20 minutes of quitting smoking, your heart rate and blood pressure will drop. A Mahmud and J Feely, "Effect of Smoking on Arterial Stiffness and Pulse Pressure Amplification," Hypertension. 2003; 41:183 (cited in American Cancer Society, *Prevention and Early Detection: Guide to Quitting Smoking* (accessed from www.cancer.org on 1/19/2010).
[13] If you have been diagnosed with COPD, you need to realize how cigarette smoke can cause further deterioration of alveolar (air-sac) tissue and hasten the progression of emphysema. You should also be aware of how cigarette smoke tends to paralyze and destroy cilia (the tiny hair-like structures that line the airways and move mucus up and out of the lungs), cause airway-wall inflammation, and increase mucus production – further aggravating asthmatic and chronic bronchitis symptoms. If you have hypoxemia (low blood oxygen), you should be aware that carbon monoxide from cigarette smoke binds tightly to the hemoglobin of red blood cells and ties up space that would normally be transporting oxygen throughout your body. Smoking cessation will enable the blood to carry more oxygen and should translate to an increased exercise/activity tolerance, with less shortness of breath.
[14] AG Lipman, "How Smoking Interferes with Drug Therapy," Modern Medicine, Aug 1985; 141-142 (cited in *Clinical Opportunities for Smoking Intervention*, U.S. Dept. of Health and Human Services, Aug 1986).

[15] I am reminded of an unrelated and yet strangely relevant tragic story that took place in Brazil. Two unemployed men found some metal parts in a partially demolished cancer radiation clinic. They in turn sold a stainless steel cylinder from the clinic to a junk dealer, who ended up taking it home. The cylinder contained what appeared to be a magical glowing blue powder, which the man's six-year old niece proceeded to spread over her body and then danced around for everyone's entertainment. The tragedy is that the blue powder was cesium 137, a substance used to kill cancer cells. The little girl died as did several others who were exposed; and more than 200 others got sick. (Wes Tracy, Gary Cockerill, Donald Demaray, Steve Harper, *Reflecting God* (Kansas City MS: Beacon Hill Press of Kansas City, 2000), 148.)

Chapter 2
[1] Freedom from Smoking Manual, American Lung Association.
[2] Tom Ferguson, *The Smoker's Book of Health* (New York: G.P. Putnam's Sons, 1987), 26-32.
[3] Ibid, 26-32.
[4] The Taoists' term *chi*, which refers to the life-force or vital energy that flows

through us, may be analogous to what we westerners refer to as spirit. They would suggest that not only are addictions an indication that this life force is not flowing as it should, but also that these very behaviors may indeed block the flow of the spirit.

Chapter 3
[1] Paul Tournier, *The Healing of Persons* (New York: Harper & Row Publishers, 1965), 4-5.
[2] Philip Yancey, *What Good is God? In Search of a Faith that Matters* (New York: FaithWords – Hachette Book Group, 2010), 234.
[3] Jerome Dollard as quoted by Ernest Kurtz and Katherine Ketcham, *The Spirituality of Imperfection: Storytelling and the Search for Meaning* (New York: Bantam Books, 1992), 17.
[4] Pierre Teilhard de Chardin, quoted by Joey Green in *The Zen of Oz: Ten Spiritual Lessons from Over the Rainbow* (Los Angeles: Renaissance Books, 1998), 132.
[5] Dale A. Matthews, *The Faith Factor: Proof of the Healing Power of* Prayer (New York: Viking Penguin, Penguin Putnam, 1998), 279.
[6] Sigmund Freud, *New Introductory Lectures on Psychoanalysis*, 1933; and *The Future of Illusion*, 1927.
[7] Elaine E. Hartsman, "Jewish Anthropology: The Stuff Between," in *Religious Theories of Personality and Psychotherapy*, ed., R. Paul Olson, 236.
[8] Ibid, 236-237.
[9] WL Adeyamo, "Sigmund Freud: smoking habit, oral cancer and euthanasia," Niger J Med 2004 Apr-Jun; 13(2):189-195.
[10] Ernest Jones, *The Life and Work of Sigmund Freud* (New York: Basic Books, 1953), vol.1:309 -311 and vol. 3:238., quoted by Edward M Brecher and the Editors of Consumer Reports Magazine, 1972, *The Consumers Union Report on Licit and Illicit Drugs, Chapter 24. The case of Dr. Sigmund Freud* (accessed from www.druglibrary.org)
[11] Carl Gustav Jung as quoted in David G. Benner, *Psychotherapy and the Spiritual Quest* (Grand Rapids: Baker Book House Company, 1988), 112.
[12] Sigmund Freud as quoted in Kurtz & Ketchem, *The Spirituality of* Imperfection, 128.
[13] Philip Yancey, *Reaching for the Invisible God: What Can We Expect to Find?* (Grand Rapids: Zondervan Publishing House, 2000), 197.
[14] R. Paul Olson, *Religious Theories of Personality and Psychotherapy: East Meets West*, ed., R. Paul Olson (New York: Hayworth Press, 2002), 288.

Chapter 4
[1] William James quoted by Philip Yancey in *Rumors of Another World: What on Earth are We Missing?* (Grand Rapids: Zondervan Publishing House, 2003), 163.

[2] William R. Miller and Janet C' de Baca, *Quantum Change: When Epiphanies and Sudden Insights Transform Ordinary Lives* (New York: The Guilford Press, 2001.)

[3] Dale A. Matthews, *The Faith Factor: Proof of the Healing Power of* Prayer (New York: Viking Penguin, Penguin Putnam, 1998), 108.

[4] Ibid, 107.

Chapter 5

[1] Proverbs 19:2 (NIV)

[2] Anodea Judith, *Waking the Global Heart: Humanity's Rite of Passage* (Santa Rosa, CA: Elite Books, 2006), 35-36.

[3] Huston Smith, *Why Religion Matters: The Fate of the Human Spirit in an Age of Disbelief* (San Francisco: Harper Collins Publisher, 2001), 1.

[4] Huston Smith, *The World's Religions: Our Great Wisdom Traditions* (San Francisco: HarperCollins, 1991), 4-5.

[5] Ernest Kurtz and Katherine Ketcham, *The Spirituality of Imperfection: Storytelling and the Search for Meaning* (New York: Bantam Books, 1992), 8.

[6] Tony Jones, *The Sacred Way: Spiritual Practices for Everyday* Life (Grand Rapids: Zondervan Publishing House, 2005), 242.

[7] Joseph Campbell, quoted by P. Scott Richards in Foreword of *Religious Theories of Personality and Psychotherapy,* ed. R. Paul Olson (New York: Hayworth Press, 2002), xvi.

[8] Fyodor Dostoeyevsky quoted in Philip Yancey in *Rumors of Another World: What on Earth are We Missing?* (Grand Rapids: Zondervan Publishing House, 2003), 11.

[9] Hugh Derr quoted by Ernest Kurtz and Katherine Ketcham, *The Spirituality of Imperfection: Storytelling and the Search for Meaning* (New York: Bantam Books, 1992), 245.

[10] Job 12:13.

Chapter 6

[1] Apollonius of Tyana quoted in Larry Dossey, *Healing Words: The Power of Prayer and the Practice of Medicine* (New York, HarperCollins Publishers, 1993), 197.

[2] Paul Tournier, *The Healing of Persons* (New York: Harper & Row Publishers, 1965), 34, 55.

[3] Brian Mockenhaupt,"The Tunnel" (Esquire: August 2008, vol. 150, no.2), 89.

[4] The First Noble Truth of Buddhism suggests that the common symptom of the human condition is "dukkha," or suffering. It is the kind of suffering that is experienced when a bone is dislocated – slipped out of its socket; or when the axle of a wheel is off center. It has been suggested that living in this world sometimes takes on the frustration of pushing a shopping cart from the wrong end. Huston Smith, *The World's Religions: Our Great Wisdom Traditions* (San Francisco: HarperCollins, 1991), 99, 101.

---

5 Taoism, like Buddhism, "affirms as a fundamental principle that suffering is a natural part of life." Lynne Hagen, "Taoism and Psychology" in *Religious Theories of Personality and Psychotherapy: East Meets West,* ed., R. Paul Olson (New York: Hayworth Press, 2002), 167.

6 The Sand People of the Kalahari suggest that the common human symptom is the "big hunger' that lies deeper in the stomach than the 'little hunger." Huston Smith, *The Soul of Christianity: Restoring the Great Tradition* (San Francisco: Harper San Francisco, 2005), xii.

7 Frederick Buechner, *Wishful Thinking: A Theological ABC* (San Francisco: Harper & Row Publishers, 1973), 54.

8 Romans 7:15-17 (NLT)

9 Huston Smith, *The Soul of Christianity: Restoring the Great Tradition*, xii-xiii.

10 The Second Noble Truth of Buddhism diagnoses the problem as "tanha," or desire; but it is a specific kind of desire – the desire for private fulfillment. "When we are selfless we are free, but that is precisely the difficulty – to maintain that state. Tanha is the force that ruptures it, pulling us back from the freedom of the all to seek fulfillment in our egos, which ooze like secret sores."[10] Tanha has been described as "those inclinations which tend to continue or increase separateness, the separate existence of the subject of desire; in fact, all forms of selfishness, the essence of which is desire for self at the expense, if necessary, of all other forms of life." Christmas Humphreys, quoted in Huston Smith, *The World's Religions*, 102-103.

11 The Taoist tradition suggests that "from birth, humans encounter experiences that teach separateness and narcissism," and "distress results when humans are disconnected from themselves, other human beings, nature, and the universe that supports them." Psychologist Lynne Hagen writes "The Tao is 'The Way' to dynamic peace. It is eternal and the source of creation and fulfillment." She goes on to say that "if we lose 'The Way,' we become alienated from others and nature, and many difficulties ensue." Lynne Hagen, in *Religious Theories of Personality and Psychotherapy, ed., R. Paul* Olson, 166-167, 172.

12 Sikhism, a religious movement born around 1500 A.D. in a Hindu culture under Muslim domination, believes that "apart from God life has no meaning; it is separation from God that causes human suffering." Huston Smith, *The World's Religions*, 77.

13 The Sufis, the love-intoxicated mystics of Islam, propose that the spiritual hunger so prevalent "is a living, radiant fire put by God into the hearts of His servants so that their ego can be burned. . ." Abu Said Ibn Abi Khayr, quoted by Andrew Harvey and Eryk Hanut, *Perfume of the Desert: Inspiration from Sufi Wisdom* (Wheaton IL: Quest Books Theosophical Publishing House, 1999), 48.

14 Huston Smith, *The Soul of Christianity*, xii-xiii.

[15] Ibid, *xi-xii.*

[16] Karen Armstrong, *The Great Transformation: the Beginning of Our Religious Traditions* (New York: Alfred A. Knopf, 2006), *319-320.*

[17] Philip Yancey in *Rumors of Another World: What on Earth are We Missing?* (Grand Rapids: Zondervan Publishing House, 2003), 35-36.

[18] David G. Benner, *Psychotherapy and the Spiritual* Quest (Grand Rapids: Baker Book House Company, 1988), 146.

[19] R. Paul Olson, *"Christian Humanism"* in *Religious Theories of Personality and Psychotherapy: East Meets West*, ed., R. Paul Olson, 248.

Chapter 7

[1] "The Hindu and Christian God stands in relation to the world as an artist to one's handiwork." R. Paul Olson (editor), *Religious Theories of Personality and Psychotherapy: East Meets West* (New York: Hayworth Press, 2002), 286.

[2] According to Hindu tradition, "Humans first came into being on earth at a time of truth and goodness. Conflict, tensions, and behavioral deviations from values were minimal. The individual and society were in a congenial balance; with needs of the majority being met, everyone was happy. The population was small and resources were abundant. It was an idyllic time suggested by the myth of paradise. Brahmins [holy persons] were the leaders of society during this era. . . Brahmin leadership was relinquished to Kshatriya leadership due to lack of physical and financial power among the Brahmins. Although they could preach great ideals and set examples with their own conduct, the vegetarian Brahmins lacked the physical capacity to enforce appropriate consequences for the inappropriate conduct of the deviant. The Kshatriyas were a muscular, hunting, and meat-eating group, with physical and financial powers. Conquering other territories through battles to increase their own prosperity was the norm for the kings." Asha Mukherjee, "Hindu Psychology and the *Bhagavad Gita*" in *Religious Theories of Personality and Psychotherapy: East Meets West*, ed., R. Paul Olson (New York: Hayworth Press, 2002), 25-26.

[3] Chinese philosopher Mo Tzu, founder of Mohism and rival of Confucius in the sixth century B.C., attributed his love-based philosophy to 'Shang Ti', the Sovereign on High, a personal god who "loves people dearly; ordered the sun, the moon, and the stars; sent down snow, frost, rain, and dew; established the hills and rivers, ravines and valleys; appointed dukes and lords to reward the virtuous and punish the wicked. Heaven loves the whole world universally. Everything is prepared for the good of human beings." Yi-pao Mei quoted by Huston Smith, *The World's Religions: Our Great Wisdom Traditions* (San Francisco: HarperCollins, 1991), 166-167.

[4] Taoist philosopher, Chuang Tzu, who lived in China during the fourth-century

B.C. referred to a by-gone era when humanity was in its infancy – a 'Golden Age of Perfect Virtue.' In describing this golden age, Lynne Hagen writes: "During the Age of Perfect Virtue, all of nature lived together in egalitarian harmony where none were separated or classified as better than or less than the other. All remained genuine to their true selves and lived simply and purely. All were accepting of one another despite their intellectual ability, achievement, or level of wisdom. During this age, all creatures loved, respected, and supported each other without laws and regulation. . . . As time went by, however, humans grew to believe that they were more important than other forms of life and began to act in ways that upset the cooperative harmony among life. The Great Separation occurred when humans separated themselves and placed themselves above nature. In an effort to help the humans realize the importance of cooperation, equality, and interdependence, nature exiled the humans from their paradise where they were cut off from food, social support, and peace. As in consequence of being cast out and alienated from nature, humans began experiencing isolation and loneliness. Thus began the frenetic quest to recover the happiness they had known. They tried to regain their lost happiness though the collection of things, but found it only brought them short-term contentment. In fact, this process brought even more distress into their lives because they needed to continually search for more and more things to sustain peace and happiness. Eventually, humans learned that 'things' were only a substitute for the belongingness, contentment, peace, and joy they had known before the Great Separation. . . Ever since the Great Separation, the goal of Taoists has been to attain the state of Perfect Virtue by abandoning all that thwarts harmony in the universe." Lynne Hagen, "Taoism and Psychology" in *Religious Theories of Personality and Psychotherapy: East Meets West*, ed., R. Paul Olson (New York: Hayworth Press, 2002), 148-149.

[5] Lao Tzu, Tao Te Ching, 53; quoted in Joseph A Loya, Wan-Li Ho, and Chang-Shin Jih, *The Tao of Jesus: An Experiment in Inter-Traditional Understanding* (New York/Mahwah NJ: Paulist Press, 1998), 44.

[6] Romans 1:18-28 (NIV)

[7] Philip Yancey, *What Good is God? In Search of a Faith that Matters* (New York: FaithWords –Hachette Book Group, 2010), 109.

[8] Richard Foster, *Life with God: Reading the Bible for Spiritual Transformation* (New York: Harper One, 2008), viii.

[9] Frederick Buechner quoted by Bob Benson Sr. and Michael W Benson in *Disciplines for the Inner Life* (Nashville TN: Generoux Nelson, 1989), 124-125.

[10] Rob Bell, *Velvet Elvis: Repainting the Christian Faith* (Grand Rapids MI: Zondervan, 2005), 58-59.

[11] Karl Menninger, *Whatever Became of Sin?* (New York: Hawthorn Books, 1973),

20-21.

[12] Paul Tournier, *Guilt and Grace* (New York: Harper & Row Publishers,1983), p 13.

[13] Philip Yancey in *Rumors of Another World: What on Earth are We Missing?* (Grand Rapids: Zondervan Publishing House, 2003), 146.

Chapter 8

[1] It is interesting to note that in Islam, human nature is viewed as being dialectical. "The body with its biological instincts and needs is one pole, and the spirit with its abstract and subliminal (spiritual) goals is the other. The psychological component of human personality, referred interchangeably in Islamic philosophy as soul, self (nafs), overlaps the body and spirit, and acts as a mediator between the two." Zehra Ansari, "Islamic Psychology" in *Religious Theories of Personality and Psychotherapy: East Meets West,* ed., R. Paul Olson (New York: Hayworth Press, 2002), 332.

[2] Brian D. McLaren, *A Search for What Makes Sense: Finding Faith* (Grand Rapids, MI: Zondervan, 1999), 138-139.

[3] Leanne Payne, *The Healing Presence* (Westchester, IL: Crossway Books, 1989), 52.

[4] Tony Jones, *The Sacred Way: Spiritual Practices for Everyday* Life (Grand Rapids: Zondervan, 2005), 127.

[5] Richard J. Foster, *Celebration of Discipline: The Path to Spiritual Growth,* Revised Edition (San Francisco: Harper & Row, 1988), p 80.

[6] Wayne E. Oates, *Temptation: A Biblical and Psychological Approach* (Louisville KY: Westminster/John Knox Press, 1991), p 54.

[7] Ibid, 54.

[8] Scott Kamilar, "A Buddhist Psychology" in *Religious Theories of Personality and Psychotherapy*, ed., R. Paul Olson (New York: Hayworth Press, 2002), 90-91.

[9] Paul Tournier, *The Healing of Persons* (New York: Harper & Row Publishers, 1965), 5.

[10] In Islamic literature there is a term for a soul addicted to passion – it is nafs Ammarah. It is descriptive of the soul that has been pulled away from the spirit by the body and attached to this world. Zehra Ansari, "Islamic Psychology" in *Religious Theories of Personality and Psychotherapy: East Meets West,* ed., R. Paul Olson , 333.

[11] Gerald G. May, *Addiction & Grace: Love and Spirituality in the Healing of Addictions* (New York: Harper Collins Publishers, 1988), p 3.

[12] John Shelby Spong, *This Hebrew Lord: A Bishop's Search for the Authentic Jesus* (New York: Harper Collins Publishers, 1993), 156.

[13]Philip Yancey, *Rumors of Another World: What on Earth are We Missing?* (Grand Rapids: Zondervan Publishing House, 2003), 31.

[14] Ibid, 32.

[15] Wayne E. Oates, *Temptation: A Biblical and Psychological Approach* (Louisville KY: Westminster/John Knox Press, 1991), 47-48.

[16] Ibid, 49.

[17] Gerald G. May, *Addiction & Grace: Love and Spirituality in the Healing of Addictions* (New York: Harper Collins Publishers, 1988), 23.

[18] Ibid, 73.

[19] Richard J. Foster, *Celebration of Discipline: The Path to Spiritual Growth,* Revised Edition (San Francisco: Harper & Row, 1988), 88.

[20] Philip Yancey, *What Good is God? In Search of a Faith that Matters* (New York: FaithWords –Hachette Book Group, 2010), 241-242.

[21] Quote from "Campaign for Tobacco Free Kids" in Judith Mackay and Michael Eriksen, *The Tobacco Atlas* (Geneva: World Health Organization, 2002) , 57.

Chapter 9

[1] Psalm 8:3-6.

[2] Genesis 1:26-31.

[3] Leanne Payne, *The Healing Presence* (Westchester, IL: Crossway Books, 1989), 52.

[4] Wes D Tracy, E Dee Freeborn, Janine Tartaglia, Morris A Weigelt, *The Upward Call: Spiritual Formation and the Holy Life* (Kansas City MS: Beacon Hill Press of Kansas City, 1994), 27.

[5] Nobel Laureate author and Holocaust survivor, Elie Wiesel retells an old Hasidic legend: "In a distant land, a prince lost his mind and imagined himself a rooster. He sought refuge under the table and lived there, naked, refusing to partake of the royal delicacies served in golden dishes – all he wanted and accepted was the grain reserved for the roosters." Elie Wiesel, *Souls on Fire: Portraits and Legends of Hasidic Masters* (New York: Random House, 1972), 170-171.

[6] Dale A. Matthews, *The Faith Factor: Proof of the Healing Power of* Prayer (New York: Viking Penguin, Penguin Putnam, 1998), 104.

[7] Philip Yancey, *What Good is God? In Search of a Faith that Matters* (New York: FaithWords –Hachette Book Group, 2010), 109.

[8] Richard J. Foster, *Celebration of Discipline: The Path to Spiritual Growth,* Revised Edition (San Francisco: Harper & Row, 1988), 56.

[9] Aristotle, quoted in Gerald G. May, *Addiction & Grace: Love and Spirituality in the Healing of Addictions* (New York: Harper Collins Publishers, 1988), 21.

[10] Gerald May, quoted in Wayne E. Oates, *Temptation: A Biblical and Psychological Approach* (Louisville KY: Westminster/John Knox Press, 1991), 70.

[11] Philip Yancey, *Rumors of Another World: What on Earth are We Missing?* (Grand Rapids: Zondervan Publishing House, 2003), 244.

[12] Wes Tracy, Gary Cockerill, Donald Demaray, Steve Harper, *Reflecting God*

(Kansas City MS: Beacon Hill Press of Kansas City, 2000), 35.

[13] Ibid, 25.

[14] Deuteronomy 28:65.

[15] Wes D Tracy, E Dee Freeborn, Janine Tartaglia, Morris A Weigelt, *The Upward Call: Spiritual Formation and the Holy Life* (Kansas City MS: Beacon Hill Press of Kansas City, 1994) , 88.

[16] Dietrich Bonhoeffer, quoted in Wayne E. Oates, *Temptation: A Biblical and Psychological Approach* (Louisville KY: Westminster/John Knox Press, 1991), 85-86.

[17] Paul DeBlassie III, *Deep Prayer: Healing for the Hurting* Soul (New York: The Crossroad Publishing House, 1990), 11.

Chapter 10

[1] Scott Kamilar, "A Buddhist Psychology" in *Religious Theories of Personality and Psychotherapy*, ed., R. Paul Olson (New York: Hayworth Press, 2002), 104-105.

[2] Paul Tournier, *The Whole Person in a Broken World* (San Francisco: Harper & Row Publishers, 1964), 148.

[3] Brian D. McLaren, *A Search for What Makes Sense: Finding Faith* (Grand Rapids, MI: Zondervan, 1999), 138-139.

[4] According to Huston Smith, "The Third Noble Truth [of Buddhism] follows logically from the Second. If the cause of life's dislocation is selfish craving, its cure lies in the overcoming of such craving. If we could be released from the narrow limits of self-interest into the vast expanse of universal life, we would be relieved of our torment." The Fourth Noble Truth suggests that this can be achieved through adherence to a prescribed, disciplined way of life known as the Eight-fold Path. Huston Smith, *The World's Religions: Our Great Wisdom Traditions* (San Francisco: HarperCollins, 1991), 103-112.

[5] The Hindu concept of "karma denotes the principle that each soul reaps what it has sown in its past through many different lifetimes or rebirths." Asha Mukherjee, "Hindu Psychology and the *Bhagavad Gita*" in *Religious Theories of Personality and Psychotherapy: East Meets West*, ed., R. Paul Olson (New York: Hayworth Press, 2002), 20.

[6] Hindu mysticism encourages people to seek God now so that they can find liberation and cut the 'noose of karma' while living. The four types of yoga (i.e. knowledge, love, work, and exercise) are paths or methods of training "designed to unite the human spirit with the God who lies concealed in its deepest recesses." Huston Smith, *The World's Religions: Our Great Wisdom Traditions* (San Francisco: HarperCollins, 1991), 27.

[7] Hindu mystic, Kabir writes, "Only spiritual practice will get you across; be addicted to this practice." Andrew Harvey and Eryk Hanut, *Perfume of the Desert: Inspiration from Sufi Wisdom* (Wheaton IL: Quest Books Theosophical Publishing

House, 1999), 82-83.

[8] A special term, 'Jeevan-mukta' is used to refer to someone who has achieved liberation during this life. Asha Mukherjee, "Hindu Psychology and the *Bhagavad Gita*" in *Religious Theories of Personality and Psychotherapy: East Meets West*, ed., R. Paul Olson (New York: Hayworth Press, 2002), 20.

[9] The Bhagavad Gita speaks of the Causal layer of the self and the area of action. These are similar to what psychologist Carl Rogers has referred to as the 'ideal' self and the 'real' self. In her discussion of Hindu psychology, Asha Mukherjee writes, "The greater the congruence between the two, the higher the mental health and personal adjustment level of the individual. In other words, in our civilization a person feels comfortable as their actions and behavior become similar to values." Ibid, 68.

[10] Taoism's prescription for the human condition center's on the concept of "ch'i" which literally means breath, but actually means vital energy. According to Huston Smith, "The Taoists used it to refer to the power of the Tao that they experienced coursing through them – or not coursing because it was blocked – and their main object was to further its flow." Such harmful addictions as smoking certainly block the flow of ch'i. To maximize ch'i, Taoists focus on such things as nutrition, calisthenics, dance, yoga, and meditation. Huston Smith, *The World's Religions: Our Great Wisdom Traditions* (San Francisco: HarperCollins, 1991), 200.

[11] Richard J. Foster, *Celebration of Discipline: The Path to Spiritual Growth*, Revised Edition (San Francisco: Harper & Row, 1988), p 4-5.

[12] Gerald G. May, *Addiction & Grace: Love and Spirituality in the Healing of Addictions* (New York: Harper Collins Publishers, 1988), p 4.

[13] John Baker, *Life's Healing Choices: Freedom from Your Hurts, Hang-Ups, and Habits* (New York: Howard Books, 2007), 17.

[14] Wes Tracy, Gary Cockerill, Donald Demaray, Steve Harper, *Reflecting God* (Kansas City MS: Beacon Hill Press of Kansas City, 2000), 39-40.

[15] John Baker, *Life's Healing Choices: Freedom from Your Hurts, Hang-Ups, and Habits* (New York: Howard Books, 2007), 129-130.

[16] Wes D Tracy, E Dee Freeborn, Janine Tartaglia, Morris A Weigelt, *The Upward Call: Spiritual Formation and the Holy Life* (Kansas City MS: Beacon Hill Press of Kansas City, 1994), 13.

[17] Gerald G. May, *Addiction & Grace: Love and Spirituality in the Healing of Addictions* (New York: Harper Collins Publishers, 1988), 123.

[18] Mark 2:17

[19] Frederick Buechner quoted in Bob Benson Sr. and Michael W Benson in *Disciplines for the Inner Life* (Nashville TN: Generoux Nelson, 1989), 128.

[20] Richard J. Foster, *Celebration of Discipline: The Path to Spiritual Growth*, Revised Edition (San Francisco: Harper & Row, 1988), 4.

---

[21] Ralph Waldo Emerson once wrote, "There is a crack in everything God has made!" Ernest Kurtz and Katherine Ketcham, *The Spirituality of Imperfection: Storytelling and the Search for Meaning* (New York: Bantam Books, 1992), 42.
[22] Ibid, 29.
[23] Ibid, 29.

[24] William R. Miller and Janet C' de Baca, *Quantum Change: When Epiphanies and Sudden Insights Transform Ordinary Lives* (New York: The Guilford Press, 2001), 32.
[25] J. Keith Miller, *A Hunger for Healing: The Twelve Steps as a Classic Model for Christian Spiritual Growth* (San Francisco: Harper Collins Publishers, 1991), 32.
[26] Romans 7:21-24
[27] Matthew 5:3 (New Living Translation)
[28] Mark 10:27
[29] Huston Smith, *The World's Religions: Our Great Wisdom Traditions* (San Francisco: HarperCollins, 1991), 265.
[30] William R. Miller and Janet C' de Baca, *Quantum Change: When Epiphanies and Sudden Insights Transform Ordinary Lives* (New York: The Guilford Press, 2001), 71.

Chapter 11
[1] William R. Miller and Janet C' de Baca, *Quantum Change: When Epiphanies and Sudden Insights Transform Ordinary Lives* (New York: The Guilford Press, 2001), 11.
[2] Rob Bell and Don Golden, *Jesus Wants to Save Christians: A Manifesto for the Church in Exile* (Grand Rapids, MI: Zondervan, 2008), 017.
[3] 2 Corinthians 5:2-3.
[4] Brian Mockenhaupt, "The Tunnel" (Esquire: August 2008, vol. 150, no.2), 89.

[5] Perhaps this Garden of Shalom is analogous to the state of innocence, purity and simplicity described by Taoists as the "un-carved block."
[6] Isaiah 53:6.
[7] Romans 3:23.
[8] Gerald G. May, *Addiction & Grace: Love and Spirituality in the Healing of Addictions* (New York: Harper Collins Publishers, 1988), 3.
[9] Ibid, 146-147.
[10] Simon Tugwell quoted in Ernest Kurtz and Katherine Ketcham, *The Spirituality of Imperfection: Storytelling and the Search for Meaning* (New York: Bantam Books, 1992), 21.
[11] John 16:8.

[12] Psalm 32:4-5 (The Living Bible).
[13] Psalm 139:23.

Chapter 12

[1] Larry Dossey, *Healing Words: The Power of Prayer and the Practice of Medicine* (New York, HarperCollins Publishers, 1993), 154.

[2] Ibid, 154.

[3] Walter Brueggemann, quoted in Wes D Tracy, E Dee Freeborn, Janine Tartaglia, Morris A Weigelt, *The Upward Call: Spiritual Formation and the Holy Life* (Kansas City MS: Beacon Hill Press of Kansas City, 1994), 27.

[4] Proverbs 28:13 (The English Version)

[5] Jay E. Adams, *Competent to Counsel* (Grand Rapids, MI: Baker Book House, 1970), 14.

[6] Karl Menninger, *Whatever Became of Sin?* (New York: Hawthorn Books, 1973), 20-21.

[7] As the Taoists counsel, what is important is to get into the flow of the Eternal – to return to the right path.

[8] Terry Wardle, *Healing Care Healing Prayer: Helping the Broken Find Wholeness in Christ* (Abilene TX: Leafwood Publishers, 2001), 150.

[9] Gerald G. May, *Addiction & Grace: Love and Spirituality in the Healing of Addictions* (New York: Harper Collins Publishers, 1988), 12.

[10] Elaine E. Hartsman, "Jewish Anthropology: The Stuff Between," in *Religious Theories of Personality and Psychotherapy*, ed., R. Paul Olson (New York: Hayworth Press, 2002), 221.

[11] Becca Cowan Johnson, *Good Guilt, Bad Guilt: And What to Do with Each* (Downer's Grove IL: InterVarsity Press, 1996), 62-64.

[12] 2 Samuel 12:13.

[13] Luke 15:18.

[14] Chuck Colson, "The Everyday Business of Holiness" in *Victory over Temptation*, ed., Bruce H. Wilkinson (Eugene Oregon: Harvest House Publishers, 1998), 50.

[15] C.S. Lewis, *Mere Christianity* (New York: Macmillan Publishing Company, 1960), 35.

Chapter 13

[1] It has been suggested that peace comes to us "when crucifixion-like events are transformed through Jesus Christ into resurrection-like fulfillments." Paul S. Minear, quoted by Joseph A Loya, Wan-Li Ho, and Chang-Shin Jih, *The Tao of Jesus: An Experiment in Inter-Traditional Understanding* (New York/Mahwah NJ: Paulist Press, 1998), 103.

[2] As Soren Kierkegaard once said "In order to move from the spot, a person must move at the spot."

[3] L.B. Cowman, *Streams in the Desert*, ed., James Reimann (Grand Rapids, MI: Zondervan, 1997), 141-142.

[4] 2 Samuel 14:14.

[5] Richard J. Foster, *Celebration of Discipline: The Path to Spiritual Growth,* Revised Edition (San Francisco: Harper & Row, 1988), 11.

[6] John Baker, *Life's Healing Choices: Freedom from Your Hurts, Hang-Ups, and Habits* (New York: Howard Books, 2007), 1.

[7] David G. Benner, *Psychotherapy and the Spiritual* Quest (Grand Rapids: Baker Book House Company, 1988), 68.

[8] Dale A. Matthews, *The Faith Factor: Proof of the Healing Power of* Prayer (New York: Viking Penguin, Penguin Putnam, 1998), 92.

[9] William R. Miller and Janet C' de Baca, *Quantum Change: When Epiphanies and Sudden Insights Transform Ordinary Lives* (New York: The Guilford Press, 2001), 184.

[10] Ibid, 11.

[11] Ibid, 127.

[12] Perhaps this 'grace' is analogous to what Taoists refer to as the 'power of the Tao.'

[13] Brian D. McLaren, *A Search for What is Real: Finding Faith* (Grand Rapids: Zondervan, 1999), 54.

Chapter 14

[1] Paul Valery, quoted in Phil Jackson, *Sacred Hoops: Spiritual Lessons of a Hardwood Warrior* (New York: Hyperion, 1995), 9.

[2] American Cancer Society, *Prevention and Early Detection: Guide to Quitting Smoking*, quoting Mark Twain (accessed from www.cancer,org, on 1/19/2010).

[3] Arden G Christen and Kenneth H Cooper, "Strategic Withdrawal from Cigarette Smoking," CA:A Cancer Journal for Clinicians, Vol. 29, No. 2, March/April 1979, 96-107 quoted in Tom Ferguson, *The Smoker's Book of Health* (New York: G.P. Putnam's Sons, 1987), 96.

[4] MAH Russell, "Cigarette Dependence: II-Doctor's Role in Management," Br Med J 1971;2:393-395, quoted in JA Peters and VJ Lim, "Smoking Cessation Techniques," in JE Hodgkin, EG Zorn, GL Connors (editors) *Pulmonary Rehabilitation: Guidelines to Success*, (Stoneham, MA: Butterworth Publishers, 1984), 95.

[5] JA Peters and VJ Lim, "Smoking Cessation Techniques," in JE Hodgkin, EG Zorn, GL Connors (editors) *Pulmonary Rehabilitation: Guidelines to Success*, (Stoneham, MA: Butterworth Publishers, 1984), 95.

[6] Philippians 2:12-13.

[7] Quoted in *Pathways to Freedom: Winning the Fight Against Tobacco.* Department of Health and Human Services, CDC.

[8] American Lung Association, *A Lifetime of Freedom From Smoking* Maintenance Manual, 1986, 14.

[9] Tom Ferguson, *The Smoker's Book of Health* (New York: G.P. Putnam's Sons, 1987), 60.

[10] Lesley Sussman and Sally Bordwell, *An Ex-Smoker's Survival Guide: Positive Steps to a Slim, Tranquil, Smoker-Free Life* (New York: McGraw-Hill Book Company, 1986), 110-111.

[11] John Jerome, "The Conditioning Effect: Getting it All Back," American Health, March/April 1982.

[12] AG Christen and KH Cooper, "Strategic Withdrawal from Cigarette Smoking," CA-A Cancer Journal for Clinicians, March/April 1979, 104 quoted in Tom Ferguson, *The Smoker's Book of Health* (New York: G.P. Putnam's Sons, 1987).

[13] Tom Ferguson, *The Smoker's Book of Health* (New York: G.P. Putnam's Sons, 1987), 161-163.

[14] American Cancer Society, *Prevention and Early Detection: Guide to Quitting Smoking* (accessed from www.cancer.org on 1/19/2010).

[15] Lesley Sussman and Sally Bordwell, *An Ex-Smoker's Survival Guide: Positive Steps to a Slim, Tranquil, Smoker-Free Life* (New York: McGraw-Hill Book Company, 1986), Ch. 4.

[16] Ibid, 136-140.

[17] American Cancer Society, *Prevention and Early Detection: Guide to Quitting Smoking,* (accessed from www.cancer.org, on 1/19/2010).

[18] Ibid.

[19] R Kanigel and T Yulsman, "By Smoke Possessed," American Health, June 1986, 37-43.

[20] KH Cooper, *Running Without Fear: How to Reduce the Risk of Heart Attack and Sudden Death During Aerobic Exercise,* (New York: M. Evans, 1985), 185 quoted in Tom Ferguson, *The Smoker's Book of Health* (New York: G.P. Putnam's Sons, 1987), 62.

[21] American Cancer Society, *Great American Smokeout* materials, 1987.

Chapter 15

[1] JA Peters and VJ Lim, "Smoking Cessation Techniques," in JE Hodgkin, EG Zorn, GL Connors (editors) *Pulmonary Rehabilitation: Guidelines to Success*, (Stoneham, MA: Butterworth Publishers, 1984), 96.

[2] Tom Ferguson, *The Smoker's Book of Health* (New York: G.P. Putnam's Sons, 1987), Ch. 6.

[3] JA Peters and VJ Lim, "Smoking Cessation Techniques," in JE Hodgkin, EG Zorn, GL Connors (editors) *Pulmonary Rehabilitation: Guidelines to Success*, (Stoneham, MA: Butterworth Publishers, 1984), 100.

[4] MC Fiore, CR Jaen, TB Baker, et al, *Treating Tobacco Use and Dependence: 2008 Update. Clinical Practice Guidelines*. Rockville, MD: U.S. Department of Health and Human Services. Public Health Service. May 2008. (Cited in American Lung

Association: Smoking Fact Sheet, accessed from www.lungusa.org on 1/19/2010.
[5] American Cancer Society, *Prevention and Early Detection: Guide to Quitting Smoking* (accessed from www.cancer.org, on 1/19/2010.
[6] Ibid.
[7] Ibid.
[8] Centers for Disease Control and Prevention. National Center for Health Statistics. National Health Interview Survey Raw Data, 2008. Analysis by the American Lung Association, Research and Program Services Division using SPSS software.
[9] American Cancer Society, *Prevention and Early Detection: Guide to Quitting Smoking* (accessed from www.cancer.org, on 1/19/2010.

Chapter 16
[1] Sun Tzu, *The Art of War: A Treatise on Chinese Military Science*, quoted in Judith Mackay and Michael Eriksen, *The Tobacco Atlas* (Geneva: World Health Organization, 2002).
[2] John 10:10.
[3] John 8:44.
[4] Judith Mackay and Michael Eriksen, *The Tobacco Atlas* (Geneva: World Health Organization, 2002), 58.
[5] American Lung Association, Research and Program Services Epidemiology and Statistics Unit, July 2008.
[6] Judith Mackay and Michael Eriksen, *The Tobacco Atlas* (Geneva: World Health Organization, 2002), 24-26.
[7] Centers for Disease Control and Prevention. National Center for Health Statistics. National Health Interview Survey Raw Data, 2008. Analysis by the American Lung Association, Research and Program Services Division using SPSS software.
[8] Judith Mackay and Michael Eriksen, *The Tobacco Atlas* (Geneva: World Health Organization, 2002), 30.
[9] Consumer Reports, "Ban Cigarette Advertising?" Sept 1987, 565.
[10] The majority of smokers begin at an early age (during adolescent years). The cigarette industry, although claiming not to directly target teenagers with their marketing, certainly reaches this population in a variety of ways. Youthful-looking adults are portrayed in smoking ads. Teenagers are often in a hurry to grow up, so they respond to this type of advertising.
[11] Back in the 1940's well-known athletes (from speed swimmers to rodeo stars and everyone in between) were featured in cigarette ads. Famous movie stars and other celebrities were often shown smoking their favorite brands. Right up to present times there are still ads depicting healthy individuals, who smoke, pursuing rugged outdoor activities. One brand of cigarettes was promoted as

being "Alive with Pleasure!" Back in the 1930's, at a time when female smoking was frowned upon, socialite women were featured in cigarette ads. Success and professionalism have always been emphasized. Certain brands have been highly promoted among minority groups. An example might be "Kools" or "Black & Milds" promoted among the African-American population. Cigarette advertising has also tried to make smoking seem as natural and commonly accepted as drinking milk or eating apple pie. Back in the earlier days of advertising, Santa Clause was a favorite subject of the ads, as was Uncle Sam. The subliminal message was: If everyone's doing it and if it feels good, how bad can smoking really be? This line was bought early on by the smoking public, and still to this day it has the effect of *luring* people into 'Marlboro Country.' The propaganda of cigarette advertising also has the effect of *keeping* people among the ranks of smokers. The advertising continues to perpetuate the myth that if all the beautiful, successful, happy people in the ads are smoking, then it can't be as bad for you as the little warning labels on the packs claim.

[12] Years ago through advertizing, medical studies were commonly cited which claimed that certain cigarettes were proven to be mild on the throat because of a new added ingredient, the removal of an ingredient, or a new process of preparing tobacco (e.g. 'toasting"). In the ads, official-looking doctors in white lab coats were portrayed giving their support of specific brands. Well-known show-biz personalities, who depended on their voices for a living, endorsed certain brands as being mild on the throat. Menthol was added to cigarettes and "Dr. Kool' was depicted in ads advising health-conscious smokers to make the switch to the latest breakthrough. In more recent years the emphasis has been on the development of an array of filtered, low- tar brands.

Back in 1984, sixty-four percent of total advertising and promotional expenditures were for cigarettes yielding 15 mg or less of tar; tobacco industry executives appeared confident that this explosion of low-tar, low-nicotine brands had stopped health-conscious smokers from quitting. Business Week, "Cigarette Sales Keep Rising," Dec 15, 1980:52, 57 cited in Ronald Davis, "Current Trends in Cigarette Advertising and Marketing," New England Journal of Medicine, March 19, 1987, 727.

[13] What about the tobacco industry's attempts to come up with safer cigarettes for their loyal customers? The filter-tipped, 'low-yield,' 'light' cigarettes might be in themselves slightly less dangerous than conventional ones. But, unfortunately it is suspected that smokers attempt to compensate for the lower amount of nicotine in these smokes, by inhaling deeper, smoking more of each cigarette, and by smoking more cigarettes per day. NL Benowitz, et al, "Influence of smoking Fewer Cigarettes on Exposure to Tar, Nicotine, and Carbon Monoxide." NEngl J Med 1986; 315:1310-1313.

[14] There is no guarantee that switching to lower tar, lower nicotine brands will mean the smoker will be exposed to less of these substances. This is not to mention exposure to carbon monoxide and the countless other potentially hazardous chemicals in cigarette smoke that enter the smokers' lungs unchallenged! To make matters even worse, it is known that additional substances are added to some of the newer 'low-yield' cigarettes for flavor enhancement. These additives may present additional risks to smokers. Their identity, as of yet, has not been disclosed to the public. The only thing for sure is that the tobacco industry does stand to benefit monetarily if it is able to deter smokers from quitting and to introduce them to cigarettes which they will ultimately end up smoking in a larger quantity. RM Davis, "Current Trends in Cigarette Advertising and Marketing." N Engl J Med 1987; 316:727-8.

[15] To some extent these alternatives may be safer than cigarettes, but by no means are they safe! These alternatives might make the use of tobacco somewhat less offensive and less hazardous to people who are around the users (although the chewing and spitting of tobacco was condemned in the late 1800's by such eminent medical and scientific leaders as Pasteur, Koch, and Lister on the grounds that it contributed to the transmission of communicable disease). The use of snuff is associated with the development of cancers of the gums and buccal mucosa, and chewing tobacco is associated with cancers of the oral cavity and hypopharynx. Council on Scientific Affair, "Health Effects of Smokeless Tobacco." JAMA 1986; 255:1038-39.

[16] Smokeless tobacco products across the board (because they contain nicotine) are known to elevate blood pressure. GN Connelly, et al, "The Re-emergence of Smokeless Tobacco." N Engl J Med 1986; 314:1023.

[17] The effects of the newer 'smokeless' cigarettes on health have not been adequately tested to assure us that there is no danger.

[18] It was noted that between 1963 and 1987 in the U.S.A., while the cigarette marketing strategists targeted the female population, lung cancer overtook breast cancer as the leading cause of cancer deaths among women. American Cancer Society, *Great American Smokeout* materials, 1987.

[19] Judith Mackay and Michael Eriksen, *The Tobacco Atlas* (Geneva: World Health Organization, 2002), 32.

[20] Ibid, 36.

[21] Ibid, 21.

[22] The White House: Office of the Press Secretary, *Fact sheet: the Family Smoking and Prevention and Tobacco Control Act of 2009,* Immediate Release June 22, 2009 (accessed from www.whitehouse.gov on 1/19/2010).

[23] Wikipedia, *Family Smoking Prevention and Tobacco Control Act* (accessed from www.wikipedia.org on 1/19/2010).

[24] Judith Mackay and Michael Eriksen, *The Tobacco Atlas* (Geneva: World Health

Organization, 2002), 66.

[25] Terry Martin, "Global Smoking Statistics, About.com Guide, Updated January 2, 2007.

[26] Judith Mackay and Michael Eriksen, *The Tobacco Atlas* (Geneva: World Health Organization, 2002), 66.

[27] Luke 23:34.

[28] Ephesians 6:12.

[29] Yancey, Philip, *The Jesus I Never Knew* (Grand Rapids MI: Zondervan Publishing House, 1995), 76-77.

[30] John 10:10.

Chapter 17

[1] Ernest Kurtz and Katherine Ketcham, *The Spirituality of Imperfection: Storytelling and the Search for Meaning* (New York: Bantam Books, 1992), 44.

[2] Luke 22:40, 46.

[3] Matthew 6:13.

[4] Philippians 2:12-13.

[5] Terry Wardle, *Healing Care Healing Prayer: Helping the Broken Find Wholeness in Christ* (Abilene TX: Leafwood Publishers, 2001), 225.

[6] Proverbs 26:11; 2 Peter 2:22.

[7] Isaiah 41:10; Exodus 14:13; Deuteronomy 1:23, 26, 29, 3:21, 31:7; Nehemiah 4:19.

[8] John 14:27, 16:33.

[9] Hebrews 4:3-10.

[10] James 4: 7-8.

[11] Hebrews 2:18, 4:14-16; Romans 8:34.

[12] 1 Corinthians 10:13.

Chapter 18

[1] Warren Wiersbe, "We Grow Through Exercise" in *Victory over Temptation*, ed., Bruce H. Wilkinson (Eugene Oregon: Harvest House Publishers, 1998), 76.

[2] Tim Stafford, "The Squeeze" in *Victory over Temptation*, ed., Bruce H. Wilkinson (Eugene Oregon: Harvest House Publishers, 1998), 107.

[3] Bernie Siegel and Jennifer Sander, *Faith, Hope & Healing: Inspiring Lessons Learned from People Living with Cancer* (Hoboken, NJ: John Wiley & Sons, Inc., 2009), 170.

[4] Ibid, 215.

[5] Rhonda Byrne, *The Secret* (New York: Aria Books, 2006), 141.

[6] Ibid, 142.

[7] Ibid, 143.

[8] Bernie Siegel and Jennifer Sander, *Faith, Hope & Healing: Inspiring Lessons*

Learned from People Living with Cancer (Hoboken, NJ: John Wiley & Sons, Inc., 2009), 11.

[9] Romans 12:21.

[10] It is also interesting to note that one of the most decisive victories for Muhammad and his loyal followers from Medina, over the rival Meccans, was achieved through non-violence. Religious historian, Karen Armstrong writes: "During the five-year war with Mecca, atrocities were committed on both sides, as was customary in the bloodbath of pre-Islamic Arabia. . . But as soon as the balance shifted in his favor, Muhammad cut the destructive cycle of strike and counterstrike, and pursued an astonishingly daring nonviolent policy." Armstrong goes on to describe a rather remarkable event that took place in 621 AD, when Muhammad announced that he wanted to make the hajj pilgrimage to Mecca, where the holy Kabah was located. "During the hajj, Arab pilgrims could not carry arms; all violence was forbidden in the Meccan sanctuary. It was even forbidden to speak a cross word or kill an insect. In going unarmed into Mecca, Muhammad was, therefore, walking into the lion's den. Nevertheless, a thousand Muslims chose to accompany him. The Meccans sent their cavalry to kill the pilgrims, but local Bedouins guided them into the sanctuary by another route. Once they had entered the sacred territory, Muhammad made the Muslims sit down in a peaceful demonstration, knowing that he was putting the Meccans in a difficult position. . . . During the homeward journey, Muhammad received a revelation from God, who called this apparent defeat a 'manifest victory.' While the Meccans, inspired by the violence of the old religion, had 'harboured a stubborn disdain in their heart,' God had sent down the 'gift of inner peace [sakinah]' upon the Muslims, so that they had been able to respond to their enemies with calm serenity." Armstrong points out that "two years later the Meccans voluntarily opened their gates to Muhammad, who took the city without bloodshed." Karen Armstrong, *The Great Transformation: the Beginning of Our Religious Traditions* (New York: Alfred A. Knopf, 2006), 389-390.

[11] The Taoist concept of 'wu wei' is a "way of being that comes from an internal sensitivity to the natural rhythms of the universe, similar to water flowing over or around rocks, logs, or islands in a stream." This way of thinking would accept temptation as a natural part of life, although certainly not something to be directly sought. Lynne Hagen, "Taoism and Psychology" in *Religious Theories of Personality and Psychotherapy: East Meets West,* ed., R. Paul Olson (New York: Hayworth Press, 2002), 152.

[12] Scott Kamilar, "A Buddhist Psychology" in *Religious Theories of Personality and Psychotherapy*, ed., R. Paul Olson (New York: Hayworth Press, 2002), 100.

[13] Lynne Hagen, "Taoism and Psychology" in *Religious Theories of Personality and Psychotherapy: East Meets West,* ed., R. Paul Olson (New York: Hayworth Press,

2002), 153.

14 Tim Stafford, "The Squeeze" in *Victory over Temptation*, ed., Bruce H. Wilkinson (Eugene Oregon: Harvest House Publishers, 1998), 108.

Chapter 19

1 Matthew 4:1-11; Luke 4:1-13.

2 Wes Tracy, Gary Cockerill, Donald Demaray, Steve Harper, *Reflecting God* (Kansas City MS: Beacon Hill Press of Kansas City, 2000), 104.

3 Wes D Tracy, E Dee Freeborn, Janine Tartaglia, Morris A Weigelt, *The Upward Call: Spiritual Formation and the Holy Life* (Kansas City MS: Beacon Hill Press of Kansas City, 1994), 214.

4 Marcus Borg, *The Heart of Christianity: Rediscovering a Life of Faith* (San Francisco: Harper San Francisco, 2003), 233.

5 Writing from a Zen perspective, one author encourages us to center our lives "on the source of correct morals, ethics, and principles." He goes on to suggest that this source is our intrinsic essence, our true self, the inner spark within us. While I am not in agreement that 'we' are the source; I do believe that as we center our lives through meditation upon God, who is the true Source, we will discover our true identity – a person created in the image of God. Joey Green, *The Zen of Oz: Ten Spiritual Lessons from Over the Rainbow* (Los Angeles: Renaissance Books, 1998), 131-132.

6 Philip Yancey, *What Good is God? In Search of a Faith that Matters* (New York: FaithWords –Hachette Book Group, 2010), 184-185.

7 Wes Tracy, Gary Cockerill, Donald Demaray, Steve Harper, *Reflecting God* (Kansas City MS: Beacon Hill Press of Kansas City, 2000), 104.

8 Ibid, 104

9 Psalm 119:11.

10 Herbert Benson, *Timeless Healing: the Power and Biology of* Belief (New York: Scribner, 1996), 90-91.

11 Ibid, 92-93

12 Abraham Lincoln, Letter to Isham Reavis, Nov.5, 1855.

13 Wes D Tracy, E Dee Freeborn, Janine Tartaglia, Morris A Weigelt, *The Upward Call: Spiritual Formation and the Holy Life* (Kansas City MS: Beacon Hill Press of Kansas City, 1994), 76.

14 Richard Foster, *Life with God: Reading the Bible for Spiritual Transformation* (New York: Harper One, 2008), 7.

15 Wes D Tracy, E Dee Freeborn, Janine Tartaglia, Morris A Weigelt, *The Upward Call: Spiritual Formation and the Holy Life* (Kansas City MS: Beacon Hill Press of Kansas City, 1994), 77.

16 Ibid, 69.

17 Proverbs 3:5-6.

[18] Looking outside of the Judeo-Christian tradition for a moment, I believe the words of Chang-tzu to be both relevant and profoundly simple: "Don't analyze Tao, live it!" Bryan Walker, *Hua Hu Ching: The Unkown Teachings off Lao-TzuJoseph* (Harper Collins Publishers, 1992), 41 cited in A Loya, Wan-Li Ho, and Chang-Shin Jih, *The Tao of Jesus: An Experiment in Inter-Traditional Understanding* (New York/Mahwah NJ: Paulist Press, 1998), 156.

[19] John Baker, *Life's Healing Choices: Freedom from Your Hurts, Hang-Ups, and Habits* (New York: Howard Books, 2007), 24.

[20] Psalm 32:8-9.

Chapter 20

Chapter 21

[1] John Baker, *Life's Healing Choices: Freedom from Your Hurts, Hang-Ups, and Habits* (New York: Howard Books, 2007), 133.

[2] M. Robert Mulholland, Jr., *Invitation to a Journey: A Road Map for Spiritual Formation* (Downer's Grove, IL: InterVarsity Press, 1993), 80-81.

[3] Lynne Hagen, "Taoism and Psychology" in *Religious Theories of Personality and Psychotherapy: East Meets West,* ed., R. Paul Olson (New York: Hayworth Press, 2002), 190.

[4] Romans 11:32 (J.B. Phillips Version)

[5] Romans 11:32 (The Message)

[6] Interestingly we find support for this line of reasoning in the Quran: "If God should touch thee with misfortune, there is none who could remove it but He" (Quran 6:17) Zehra Ansari, "Islamic Psychology" in *Religious Theories of Personality and Psychotherapy: East Meets West,* ed., R. Paul Olson (New York: Hayworth Press, 2002), 344.

[7] Psalm 25:15

[8] Exodus 8:1, 20; 9:1, 13; 10:3

[9] Philip Yancey, *Rumors of Another World: What on Earth are We Missing?* (Grand Rapids: Zondervan Publishing House, 2003), 151.

[10] Philip Yancey, *What Good is God? In Search of a Faith that Matters* (New York: FaithWords –Hachette Book Group, 2010), 233.

[11] Terry Wardle, *Healing Care Healing Prayer: Helping the Broken Find Wholeness in Christ* (Abilene TX: Leafwood Publishers, 2001), 151.

[12] Alphonsus Liguori, quoted in Richard J. Foster, *Celebration of Discipline: The Path to Spiritual Growth,* Revised Edition (San Francisco: Harper & Row, 1988), 151.

[13] Wes D Tracy, E Dee Freeborn, Janine Tartaglia, Morris A Weigelt, *The Upward Call: Spiritual Formation and the Holy Life* (Kansas City MS: Beacon Hill Press of Kansas City, 1994), 85.

[14] Wes Tracy, Gary Cockerill, Donald Demaray, Steve Harper, *Reflecting God* (Kansas City MS: Beacon Hill Press of Kansas City, 2000), 71.

[15] "Oswald Chambers called repentance the 'threshold' to the Kingdom. John Wesley called repentance the 'porch' that leads to a life of intimacy with God." Wes Tracy, Gary Cockerill, Donald Demaray, Steve Harper, *Reflecting God* (Kansas City MS: Beacon Hill Press of Kansas City, 2000), 71.

[16] Agnes Sanford, *The Healing Light* (New York: Ballantine Books, 1972), 123.

[17] Matthew 11:28.

[18] In Islam, there is a term for a repentant person: "Nafs Lawwamah – the reproaching soul (Quran 75:1; 9:102) . . . This soul is conscious of evil and resists it, and asks for God's grace and pardon . . ." Zehra Ansari, "Islamic Psychology" in *Religious Theories of Personality and Psychotherapy: East Meets West,* ed., R. Paul Olson (New York: Hayworth Press, 2002), 341.

[19] In the Quran, Allah is quoted ". . . Self-surrender unto Me shall be your religion."(Quran 5:3) Ibid, 325.

[20] Most Christians are familiar with the words of surrender that Jesus spoke, but, Lao Tzu, the author of the 'Tao Te Ching,' also spoke of laying down one's load. Joseph A Loya, Wan-Li Ho, and Chang-Shin Jih, *The Tao of Jesus: An Experiment in Inter-Traditional Understanding* (New York/Mahwah NJ: Paulist Press, 1998), 151.

[21] Dale A. Matthews, *The Faith Factor: Proof of the Healing Power of* Prayer (New York: Viking Penguin, Penguin Putnam, 1998), 227.

[22] Herbert Benson, *Timeless Healing: the Power and Biology of* Belief (New York: Scribner, 1996), 68.

[23] In addition to the Chinese belief in a spiritual energy (ch'i) that pulses through us and the natural world, It has been pointed out that "many other cultures have named and believed in a mysterious healing energy. The ancient Egyptians called it 'Ka,' the Hawaiians 'Mana,' and the Indians 'Prana.'" Ibid, 157.

[24] Ibid, 161.

[25] Leanne Payne, *The Healing Presence* (Westchester, IL: Crossway Books, 1989), xv.

[26] Richard J. Foster, *Celebration of Discipline: The Path to Spiritual Growth,* Revised Edition (San Francisco: Harper & Row, 1988), 159.

[27] Ibid, 143.

[28] Ibid, 153.

[29] Isaiah 4:22.

[30] A phrase from the opening surah of the Koran, which is repeated many times in the Muslim's five daily prayers acknowledges Allah as "The Merciful," "The Compassionate," and "The Creator of the Worlds!" Huston Smith, *The World's Religions: Our Great Wisdom Traditions* (San Francisco: HarperCollins, 1991), 242.

[31] In the Tao Te Ching, Lao Tzu wrote: "Tao is the source of the ten thousand things. It is the treasure of the good man, and the refuge of the bad . . . Why

does everyone like the Tao at first? Isn't it because you find what you seek and are forgiven when you sin? Therefore this is the greatest treasure of the universe." Lynne Hagen, "Taoism and Psychology" in *Religious Theories of Personality and Psychotherapy: East Meets West,* ed., R. Paul Olson (New York: Hayworth Press, 2002 , 141.

[32] William R. Miller and Janet C' de Baca, *Quantum Change: When Epiphanies and Sudden Insights Transform Ordinary Lives* (New York: The Guilford Press, 2001), 73.

[33] Ibid, 117.

[34] Richard J. Foster, *Celebration of Discipline: The Path to Spiritual Growth,* Revised Edition (San Francisco: Harper & Row, 1988), 153.

[35] Ernest Kurtz and Katherine Ketcham, *The Spirituality of Imperfection: Storytelling and the Search for Meaning* (New York: Bantam Books, 1992), 27.

[36] Isaiah 61:1-2; Luke 4:17-21; John 1:29.

[37] Leviticus Ch. 25.

[38] Terry Wardle, *Healing Care Healing Prayer: Helping the Broken Find Wholeness in Christ* (Abilene TX: Leafwood Publishers, 2001), 224, 226.

Chapter 22

[1] American Lung Association, *A Lifetime of Freedom From Smoking* Maintenance Manual, 1986, 14.

[2] American Lung Association, Freedom from Smoking Facilitator Manual, p. 69, 2007.

[3] Centers for Disease Control and Prevention. National Center for Health Statistics. National Health Interview Survey Raw Data, 2008. Analysis by the American Lung Association, Research and Program Services Division using SPSS software.

[4]Centers for Disease Control and Prevention. *Vital Signs: Current Cigarette Smoking Among Adults Aged ≥ 18 Years—United States, 2005–2010.* Morbidity and Mortality Weekly Report 2011;60(35):1207–12.

[5] Judith Mackay and Michael Eriksen, *The Tobacco Atlas* (Geneva: World Health Organization, 2002), 24-26, 36.

[6] American Cancer Society, *Prevention and Early Detection: Guide to Quitting Smoking,* citing U.S. Surgeon General's Reports 1988 and 1990 (accessed from www.cancer.org, on 1/19/2010).

[7] Paul Tournier, *The Healing of Persons* (New York: Harper & Row Publishers, 1965), 5.

[8] Dale A. Matthews, *The Faith Factor: Proof of the Healing Power of* Prayer (New York: Viking Penguin, Penguin Putnam, 1998), 104.

[9] Philip Yancey, *What Good is God? In Search of a Faith that Matters* (New York: FaithWords –Hachette Book Group, 2010), 109.

---

[10] Richard J. Foster, *Celebration of Discipline: The Path to Spiritual Growth,* Revised Edition (San Francisco: Harper & Row, 1988), 56.
[11] Aristotle, quoted in Gerald G. May, *Addiction & Grace: Love and Spirituality in the Healing of Addictions* (New York: Harper Collins Publishers, 1988), 21.

Chapter 23
[1] AG Christen and KH Cooper, "Strategic Withdrawal from Cigarette Smoking," CA-A Cancer Journal for Clinicians, March/April 1979, 104.
[2] American Cancer Society, *Prevention and Early Detection: Guide to Quitting Smoking*, citing U.S. Surgeon General's Reports 1988 and 1990 (accessed from www.cancer.org, on 1/19/2010).
[3] John Shelby Spong, *This Hebrew Lord: A Bishop's Search for the Authentic Jesus* (New York: Harper Collins Publishers, 1993), 156.
[4] Terry Wardle, *Healing Care Healing Prayer: Helping the Broken Find Wholeness in Christ* (Abilene TX: Leafwood Publishers, 2001), 150.
[5] Gerald G. May, *Addiction & Grace: Love and Spirituality in the Healing of Addictions* (New York: Harper Collins Publishers, 1988), 4.
[6] Stephen Post and Jill Neimark, *Why Good Things Happen to Good People* (New York: Broadway Books, 2007), 108.

Chapter 24
[1] Tom Ferguson, *The Smoker's Book of Health* (New York: G.P. Putnam's Sons, 1987), 51.
[2] American Cancer Society, *Prevention and Early Detection: Guide to Quitting Smoking*, citing U.S. Surgeon General's Reports 1988 and 1990 (accessed from www.cancer.org, on 1/19/2010).
[3] Frank Moore, *Breaking Free from Sin's Grip: Holiness Defined for a New Generation* (Kansas City: Beacon Hill Press, 2001), 66.
[4] Paul DeBlassie III, *Deep Prayer: Healing for the Hurting* Soul (New York: The Crossroad Publishing House, 1990), 9.

[5] Gerald G. May, *Addiction & Grace: Love and Spirituality in the Healing of Addictions* (New York: Harper Collins Publishers, 1988), 51.
[6] Abraham Lincoln, Letter to Isham Reavis, Nov.5, 1855

Chapter 25
[1] Lowell Ponte, "Radioactivity: The New-Found Danger in Cigarettes," Reader's Digest, March, 1986, 123-127.
[2] American Cancer Society, *Prevention and Early Detection: Guide to Quitting Smoking*, citing U.S. Surgeon General's Reports 1988 and 1990 (accessed from www.cancer.org, on 1/19/2010).

[3] Wayne E. Oates, *Temptation: A Biblical and Psychological Approach* (Louisville KY: Westminster/John Knox Press, 1991), 92.

[4] Thomas Merton, *New Seeds of Contemplation* (New York: New Directions Publishing, Inc., 1962), 86.

[5] Herbert Benson, *Timeless Healing: the Power and Biology of* Belief (New York: Scribner, 1996), 110.

[6] Paul DeBlassie III, *Deep Prayer: Healing for the Hurting* Soul (New York: The Crossroad Publishing House, 1990), 39.

[7] Ernest Kurtz and Katherine Ketcham, *The Spirituality of Imperfection: Storytelling and the Search for Meaning* (New York: Bantam Books, 1992), 91.

Chapter 26

[1] Sir Richard Doll, quoted in Judith Mackay and Michael Eriksen, *The Tobacco Atlas* (Geneva: World Health Organization, 2002), 34.

[2] American Cancer Society, *Prevention and Early Detection: Guide to Quitting Smoking*, citing U.S. Surgeon General's Reports 1988 and 1990 (accessed from www.cancer.org, on 1/19/2010).

[3] Tony Jones, *The Sacred Way: Spiritual Practices for Everyday* Life (Grand Rapids: Zondervan, 2005), 127.

[4] Larry Dossey, *Healing Words: The Power of Prayer and the Practice of Medicine* (New York, HarperCollins Publishers, 1993), 101.

[5] Richard J. Foster, *Celebration of Discipline: The Path to Spiritual Growth,* Revised Edition (San Francisco: Harper & Row, 1988), 113-115.

[6] Ibid, 90-91.

[7] Ernest Kurtz and Katherine Ketcham, *The Spirituality of Imperfection: Storytelling and the Search for Meaning* (New York: Bantam Books, 1992), 134.

Chapter 27

[1] Tom Ferguson, *The Smoker's Book of Health* (New York: G.P. Putnam's Sons, 1987), 31.

[2] American Cancer Society, *Prevention and Early Detection: Guide to Quitting Smoking*, citing U.S. Surgeon General's Reports 1988 and 1990 (accessed from www.cancer.org, on 1/19/2010).

[3] Gerald G. May, *Addiction & Grace: Love and Spirituality in the Healing of Addictions* (New York: Harper Collins Publishers, 1988), 136.

[4] Ibid, 105.

[5] Terry Wardle, *Healing Care Healing Prayer: Helping the Broken Find Wholeness in Christ* (Abilene TX: Leafwood Publishers, 2001), 102.

[6] Rhonda Byrne, *The Secret* (New York: Aria Books, 2006), 169.

Chapter 28
[1] Judith Mackay and Michael Eriksen, *The Tobacco Atlas* (Geneva: World Health Organization, 2002), 35.
[2] American Cancer Society, *Prevention and Early Detection: Guide to Quitting Smoking*, citing U.S. Surgeon General's Reports 1988 and 1990 (accessed from www.cancer.org, on 1/19/2010).
[3] American Lung Association, *Smoking Fact Sheet*, (accessed from www.lungusa.org 1/19/2010.)
[4] Paul Tournier, *The Healing of Persons* (New York: Harper & Row Publishers, 1965), xx.
[5] Quoted in *Pathways to Freedom: Winning the Fight Against Tobacco*. Department of Health and Human Services, CDC.
[6] Ibid.
[7] Ibid.
[8] Ibid.

Chapter 29
[1] Karl Menninger, *Whatever Became of Sin?* (New York: Hawthorn Books, 1973), 48.
[2] David G. Benner, *Psychotherapy and the Spiritual* Quest (Grand Rapids: Baker Book House Company, 1988), 30.
[3] Wes Tracy, Gary Cockerill, Donald Demaray, Steve Harper, *Reflecting God* (Kansas City MS: Beacon Hill Press of Kansas City, 2000), 79.
[4] Gerald G. May, *Addiction & Grace: Love and Spirituality in the Healing of Addictions* (New York: Harper Collins Publishers, 1988), 154.
[5] Joseph P. Weaver, *The Tao of Quitting Smoking*, (Oregon IL: Quality Books, Inc., 2004), 30.
[6] The Sufi, Sultan Valad has written "You must be born twice, once from your mother, and the second time from yourself." Andrew Harvey and Eryk Hanut, *Perfume of the Desert: Inspiration from Sufi Wisdom* (Wheaton IL: Quest Books Theosophical Publishing House, 1999), 37-38.
[7] Catholic priest and author, Henri Nouwen wrote "The closer we come to God the stronger will be His demand to let go of the many 'safe' structures we have built around ourselves . . . dying to all that we consider to be our own and of being born to a new existence which is not of this world." M. Robert Mulholland, Jr., *Invitation to a Journey: A Road Map for Spiritual Formation* (Downer's Grove, IL: InterVarsity Press, 1993), 106.
[8] Dale A. Matthews, *The Faith Factor: Proof of the Healing Power of* Prayer (New York: Viking Penguin, Penguin Putnam, 1998), 226-227.

Chapter 30

[1] Wes Tracy, Gary Cockerill, Donald Demaray, Steve Harper, *Reflecting God* (Kansas City MS: Beacon Hill Press of Kansas City, 2000), 32.

[2] I Corinthians 10:1-12 (The Message)

Chapter 31

[1] It is interesting to note that when we look to the Muslim tradition, we see that Mohammed drew a distinction between the 'lesser jihad' of physical warfare and the 'greater jihad' of spiritual warfare. Today when we hear the word 'jihad' we think of a 'holy war' being waged by wild-eyed extremists against their enemies, whom they consider infidels. But, it is interesting that "the prophet of Islam is quoted as having said after returning from a battle with unbelievers that he had returned from a lesser jihad to a greater jihad, referring to the inner struggle against temptation with which every individual personally experiences. Muslims believe that there is always a negative force, personified as Satan (Iblis), tempting humans away from the right path." Zehra Ansari, "Islamic Psychology" in *Religious Theories of Personality and Psychotherapy: East Meets West,* ed., R. Paul Olson (New York: Hayworth Press, 2002), 338.

[2] Romans 12:1-2.

[3] Proverbs 25:28.

[4] John Baker, *Life's Healing Choices: Freedom from Your Hurts, Hang-Ups, and Habits* (New York: Howard Books, 2007), 19.

[5] Jeremiah 2:13.

[6] John 4:1-26.

[7] I've heard that upon arriving in the New World, the conquistador Cortez instructed his men to burn their ships. He did this so that they would not be tempted to return home before they had accomplished their mission – as greedy and barbaric as it was. Your mission on the other hand is noble – holy in fact!

Chapter 32

[1] Luke 11:14-26.

[2] Bruce H.Wilkinson, "Turning to Holiness: The Defining Moment" in *Victory over Temptation*, ed., Bruce H. Wilkinson (Eugene Oregon: Harvest House Publishers, 1998), 15.

[3] Wes Tracy, Gary Cockerill, Donald Demaray, Steve Harper, *Reflecting God* (Kansas City MS: Beacon Hill Press of Kansas City, 2000), 86.

[4] Colossians 3:1-13.

[5] Romans 13: 11-14.

[6] Gerald G. May, *Addiction & Grace: Love and Spirituality in the Healing of Addictions* (New York: Harper Collins Publishers, 1988), 14.

Chapter 33
[1] In the *Taittiriya Upanishad* of Hinduism we are told to "master the passions," Andrew Harvey (editor), *Teachings of the Hindu Mystics* (Boston: Shambhala Publications, Inc., 2001), 34.
[2] The Hindu mystic Kabir has written, ". . . cut the noose of your karma while living . . ." Andrew Harvey (editor), *Teachings of the Hindu Mystics* (Boston: Shambhala Publications, Inc., 2001), 82.
[3] In Taoism we are told to remove anything that blocks the flow of vital energy (ch'i) in our lives. In the *Hua Hu Ching*, a collection of the purported oral teachings of Lao Tzu, we read "The cleansing of spiritual contamination is not the responsibility of the teacher, but of the student." Joseph A Loya, Wan-Li Ho, and Chang-Shin Jih, *The Tao of Jesus: An Experiment in Inter-Traditional Understanding* (New York/Mahwah NJ: Paulist Press, 1998), 118.
[4] In the Third Noble Truth of Buddhism we are told to turn from selfish desire and its pursuits. Islam prohibits substances of an addictive nature, and expects people to live in a self-controlled manner. Zehra Ansari, "Islamic Psychology" in *Religious Theories of Personality and Psychotherapy: East Meets West,* ed., R. Paul Olson (New York: Hayworth Press, 2002), 348.
[5] In the Quran 13:11, we are told that "God does not change men's condition unless they change their inner-selves" Ibid, 343.
[6] Genesis 4:7.
[7] Psalm 101:1-4.
[8] Wes D Tracy, E Dee Freeborn, Janine Tartaglia, Morris A Weigelt, *The Upward Call: Spiritual Formation and the Holy Life* (Kansas City MS: Beacon Hill Press of Kansas City, 1994), 40.
[9] J. Keith Miller, *A Hunger for Healing: The Twelve Steps as a Classic Model for Christian Spiritual Growth* (San Francisco: Harper Collins Publishers, 1991), 6.
[10] Gerald G. May, *Addiction & Grace: Love and Spirituality in the Healing of Addictions* (New York: Harper Collins Publishers, 1988), 85.
[11] Terry Wardle, *Healing Care Healing Prayer: Helping the Broken Find Wholeness in Christ* (Abilene TX: Leafwood Publishers, 2001), 164.
[12] Paul DeBlassie III, *Deep Prayer: Healing for the Hurting Soul* (New York: The Crossroad Publishing House, 1990), 135-138.
[13] Philip Yancey, *What Good is God? In Search of a Faith that Matters* (New York: FaithWords –Hachette Book Group, 2010), 247.
[14] In their book 'The Cultural Atlas of Islam,' authors Faruqi and Faruqi, state

"Man is the only creation in which the will of God is actualized not necessarily but with man's own personal consent." Faruqi and Faruqui quoted by Zehra Ansari, "Islamic Psychology" in *Religious Theories of Personality and Psychotherapy: East Meets West,* ed., R. Paul Olson (New York: Hayworth Press, 2002), 335.

[15] Paul DeBlassie III, *Deep Prayer: Healing for the Hurting* Soul (New York: The Crossroad Publishing House, 1990), 128.

[16] Philip Yancey, *What Good is God? In Search of a Faith that Matters* (New York: FaithWords –Hachette Book Group, 2010), 111.

[17] Benedict J. Groeschel, *Spiritual Passages: The Psychology of Spiritual Development* (New York: The Crossroad Publishing Company, 1983), 4.

[18] Ibid, 11.

[19] If we resist moving through the purgative phase, life can take on "the aspects of a lingering, terminal illness." Ibid, 82.

[20] Wayne E. Oates, *Temptation: A Biblical and Psychological Approach* (Louisville KY: Westminster/John Knox Press, 1991), 92.

[21] Arsenio Orteza, "The Nominees are . . ." WORLD, Feb 12, 2011, p 32.

[22] Benedict J. Groeschel, *Spiritual Passages: The Psychology of Spiritual Development* (New York: The Crossroad Publishing Company, 1983), 56.

[23] Ibid, 23.

[24] 2 Timothy 2:22.

[25] 1 Corinthians 13:11.

[26] Mark 12:28-31.

Chapter 34

[1] Gerald G. May, *Addiction & Grace: Love and Spirituality in the Healing of Addictions* (New York: Harper Collins Publishers, 1988), 58-62.

[2] Ibid, 82.

[3] Richard J. Foster, *Celebration of Discipline: The Path to Spiritual Growth,* Revised Edition (San Francisco: Harper & Row, 1988), 95.

[4] 1 Corinthians 6:12.

[5] 1 Corinthians 9:26-27.

[6] Hebrews 12:1.

[7] Philip Yancey, *What Good is God? In Search of a Faith that Matters* (New York: FaithWords –Hachette Book Group, 2010), 241.

[8] Frederick Brotherton Meyer and Charles Erlandson, *F.B. Meyer: The Best from All His Works (The Christian Classics Collection, Vol. 3* (Nashville: Thomas Nelson Inc., 1988), 14-15.

[9] Gerald G. May, *The Dark Night of the Soul: A Psychiatrist Explores the Connection Between Darkness and Spiritual Growth* (New York: Harper Collins Publishers, Inc., 2004), 55.

---

[10] Philip Yancey, *What Good is God? In Search of a Faith that Matters* (New York: FaithWords –Hachette Book Group, 2010), 109.

[11] Gerald G. May, *The Dark Night of the Soul: A Psychiatrist Explores the Connection Between Darkness and Spiritual Growth* (New York: Harper Collins Publishers, Inc., 2004), 58-62.

[12] Ibid, 65.

[13] Frank Moore, *Breaking Free from Sin's Grip: Holiness Defined for a New Generation* (Kansas City: Beacon Hill Press, 2001), 9-10.

[14] In a paraphrase of the *Tao Te Ching* we read of the danger of pinning our hopes of satisfaction on material things: "In attaching so much importance to gaining these things, you are really just expending energy and wearing yourself out, making your existence anxious and precarious by staking so much on what can easily be lost. You should learn to stop this flow of your energy outward, and to rest content in your own being. This is ultimate security." Joseph A Loya, Wan-Li Ho, and Chang-Shin Jih, *The Tao of Jesus: An Experiment in Inter-Traditional Understanding* (New York/Mahwah NJ: Paulist Press, 1998), 78.

[15] Offering a Hindu perspective, Asha Mukerjee suggests that while it may be natural for our desires to become attached to pleasurable experiences, "this attachment creates illusions (maya), which denotes ideas and experiences divorced from 'supreme reality.'" She goes on to state that "actions without a spiritual rationale/intent are self-defeating behaviors and cause distress." Asha Mukherjee, "Hindu Psychology and the *Bhagavad Gita*" in *Religious Theories of Personality and Psychotherapy: East Meets West*, ed., R. Paul Olson (New York: Hayworth Press, 2002), 39.

[16] Wes D Tracy, E Dee Freeborn, Janine Tartaglia, Morris A Weigelt, *The Upward Call: Spiritual Formation and the Holy Life* (Kansas City MS: Beacon Hill Press of Kansas City, 1994), 40.

[17] Offering a Zen/New Age spin on this advice, Joey Green writes: "Your heart's desire is your destiny. But to fulfill that destiny, you must first give up your attachment to the outcome. You don't give up your 'intention' to realize your desire. You simply detach yourself from the result. In other words, you surrender to the creative intelligence of the cosmic nexus and allow it to unfold before you." Joey Green, *The Zen of Oz: Ten Spiritual Lessons from Over the Rainbow* (Los Angeles: Renaissance Books, 1998), 89.

[18] Richard J. Foster, *Celebration of Discipline: The Path to Spiritual Growth*, Revised Edition (San Francisco: Harper & Row, 1988), 103.

[19] Paul DeBlassie III, *Deep Prayer: Healing for the Hurting Soul* (New York: The Crossroad Publishing House, 1990), 25.

Chapter 35

[1] Lynne Hagen, "Taoism and Psychology" in *Religious Theories of Personality and*

Psychotherapy: East Meets West, ed., R. Paul Olson (New York: Hayworth Press, 2002), 183.

[2] Doug Pagitt and Tony Jones (editors), *An Emergent Manifesto of Hope* (Grand Rapids, MI: Baker Books, 2007), 306.

[3] John Baker, *Life's Healing Choices: Freedom from Your Hurts, Hang-Ups, and Habits* (New York: Howard Books, 2007), 104.

[4] Wes Tracy, Gary Cockerill, Donald Demaray, Steve Harper, *Reflecting God* (Kansas City MS: Beacon Hill Press of Kansas City, 2000), 41.

[5] In Buddhism there is an emphasis on the here and now, so as to avoid "the trap of reinforcing the tendency to replay and become stuck in past experiences." Scott Kamilar, "A Buddhist Psychology" in *Religious Theories of Personality and Psychotherapy,* ed., R. Paul Olson (New York: Hayworth Press, 2002), 102.

[6] This was the attitude of Taoist philosopher Chang Tzu. Joseph A Loya, Wan-Li Ho, and Chang-Shin Jih, *The Tao of Jesus: An Experiment in Inter-Traditional Understanding* (New York/Mahwah NJ: Paulist Press, 1998), 78.

[7] Ernest Kurtz and Katherine Ketcham, *The Spirituality of Imperfection: Storytelling and the Search for Meaning* (New York: Bantam Books, 1992), 171.

[8] Ibid, 180.

[9] Matthew 6:34.

[10] Ernest Kurtz and Katherine Ketcham, *The Spirituality of Imperfection: Storytelling and the Search for Meaning* (New York: Bantam Books, 1992), 183.

[11] Paul DeBlassie III, *Deep Prayer: Healing for the Hurting Soul* (New York: The Crossroad Publishing House, 1990), 135-138.

[12] From the Lojong Teachings of Buddhism. Scott Kamilar, "A Buddhist Psychology" in *Religious Theories of Personality and Psychotherapy,* ed., R. Paul Olson (New York: Hayworth Press, 2002), 115.

[13] Wes Tracy, Gary Cockerill, Donald Demaray, Steve Harper, *Reflecting God* (Kansas City MS: Beacon Hill Press of Kansas City, 2000), 178.

[14] Richard J. Foster, *Celebration of Discipline: The Path to Spiritual Growth,* Revised Edition (San Francisco: Harper & Row, 1988), 1.

[15] Benedict J. Groeschel, *Spiritual Passages: The Psychology of Spiritual Development* (New York: The Crossroad Publishing Company, 1983), 15.

[16] A Taoist might suggest, one must learn "to work with the flow of life rather than against it and to act spontaneously." If we do, we will find that "actions and events harmonious with Tao are effortless . . . and inexhaustible." Lynne Hagen, "Taoism and Psychology" in *Religious Theories of Personality and Psychotherapy: East Meets West,* ed., R. Paul Olson (New York: Hayworth Press, 2002), 150-151.

[17] A goal of Taoist therapy is to help the client to become accustomed to ceaseless change. If this is accomplished, the client will be "free to be in a state of relaxed alertness, always open to new opportunities, and ready for growth and transformation." Ibid, 174.

[18] Ibid, 174.

[19] Ernest Kurtz and Katherine Ketcham, *The Spirituality of Imperfection: Storytelling and the Search for Meaning* (New York: Bantam Books, 1992), 1.
[20] Ibid, 188.
[21] Nate Larkin, *Samson and the Pirate Monks: Calling Men to Authentic Brotherhood* (Nashville: Thomas Nelson, Inc., 2006), 132.
[22] Wayne E. Oates, *Temptation: A Biblical and Psychological Approach* (Louisville KY: Westminster/John Knox Press, 1991), 23-24.
[23] Frank Moore, *Breaking Free from Sin's Grip: Holiness Defined for a New Generation* (Kansas City: Beacon Hill Press, 2001), 93-94.
[24] Benedict J. Groeschel, *Spiritual Passages: The Psychology of Spiritual Development* (New York: The Crossroad Publishing Company, 1983), 156.
[25] Brian D. McLaren, *A Search for What is Real: Finding Faith* (Grand Rapids: Zondervan, 1999), 59.
[26] Benedict J. Groeschel, *Spiritual Passages: The Psychology of Spiritual Development* (New York: The Crossroad Publishing Company, 1983), 11.
[27] Ibid, 133.
[28] The emphasis among Buddhists and Taoists is to tame and de-clutter the mind. According to Wu-Men "If your mind isn't clouded by unnecessary things, this is the best season of your life." Phil Jackson, *Sacred Hoops: Spiritual Lessons of a Hardwood Warrior* (New York: Hyperion, 1995), 113.
[29] 2 Corinthians 10:5.

Chapter 36
[1] Mark 8:34.
[2] Matthew 10:39.
[3] Richard J. Foster, *Celebration of Discipline: The Path to Spiritual Growth,* Revised Edition (San Francisco: Harper & Row, 1988), 113-115.
[4] Ibid, 59.
[5] M. Robert Mulholland, Jr., *Invitation to a Journey: A Road Map for Spiritual Formation* (Downer's Grove, IL: InterVarsity Press, 1993), 128-129.
[6] Romans 8:13.
[7] Benedict J. Groeschel, *Spiritual Passages: The Psychology of Spiritual Development* (New York: The Crossroad Publishing Company, 1983), 81.
[8] M. Robert Mulholland, Jr., *Invitation to a Journey: A Road Map for Spiritual Formation* (Downer's Grove, Il : InterVarsity Press, 1993), 80-81, 94.
[9] Bernie Siegel and Jennifer Sander, *Faith, Hope & Healing: Inspiring Lessons Learned from People Living with Cancer* (Hoboken, NJ: John Wiley & Sons, Inc., 2009), 220.
[10] William R. Miller and Janet C' de Baca, *Quantum Change: When Epiphanies and*

Sudden Insights Transform Ordinary Lives (New York: The Guilford Press, 2001), 141.

[11] Gerald G. May, *Addiction & Grace: Love and Spirituality in the Healing of Addictions* (New York: Harper Collins Publishers, 1988), 147.

[12] Ibid, 147-149.

[13] Isaiah 40:31.

[14] Philippians 1:6 (The Living Bible)

[15] 1 Peter 4:1-3, 5:10.

Chapter 37

Chapter 38

[1] The Fourth Noble Truth of Buddhism prescribes this type of lifestyle in the form of the Eightfold Path which consists of: 1) right views, 2) right intent, 3) right speech, 4) right conduct, 5) right livelihood, 6) right effort, 7) right mindfulness, and 8) right concentration.

[2] The renowned Vietnamese monk, Thich Nhat Hanh describes his application of the principle of mindful consuming: "Aware of the suffering caused by un-mindful consumption, I vow to cultivate good health, both physical and mental, for myself, my family, and my society by practicing mindful eating, drinking, and consuming. I vow to ingest only items that preserve peace, well-being, and joy in my body, in my consciousness, and in the collective body and consciousness of my family and society. I am determined not to use alcohol or any other intoxicant or to ingest foods or other items that contain toxins, such as certain TV programs, magazines, books, films, and conversations. I am aware that to damage my body or my consciousness with these poisons is to betray my ancestors, my parents, my society, and future generations. . . ." Thich Nhat Hanh, *Living Buddha, Living Christ* (New York: Riverhead Books, 1995), 105.

[3] Thich Nhat Hanh's approach may seem a bit extreme, especially to us westerners who don't want to miss a thing and therefore live by the motto "if it feels good, do it." But, nevertheless a healthier lifestyle of moderation and balance, per the dictates of your conscience and convictions, should be cultivated. Buddha himself advocated "the principle of the Middle Way between the extremes of asceticism, on the one hand, and indulgence on the other. It is the concept of the rationed life, in which the body is given what it needs to function optimally but no more." Huston Smith, *The World's Religions: Our Great Wisdom Traditions* (San Francisco: HarperCollins, 1991), 85.

[4] With regards to the prohibition of alcoholic beverages, "it is reported that an early Russian Czar, faced with the decision as to whether to choose Christianity, Islam, or Buddhism for his people, rejected the latter two because both included

this . . . proscription." Ibid, 108.

[5] One of the things I find refreshing about Jesus is that he appeared to have a healthy attitude towards the good things of this earth; he was no ascetic. The first public miracle he performed, as recorded in the Gospel of John, was turning the water into wine at a marriage feast so the merriment could continue! Referring to himself, Jesus once said "The Son of Man came eating and drinking, and they say, 'Here is a glutton and a drunkard, a friend of tax collectors and 'sinners.'" (Matthew 11:20) Now, I don't believe Jesus was a glutton or a drunkard, nor do I believe that he condoned cheating or immorality, but I do suspect that he enjoyed people, in fact he loved people; and sharing good food and good wine, most likely in moderation, was a means of connecting with them on a human level. I also suspect that, just as he was never controlled by people, he was not controlled by his appetites for food or drink.

[6] The Hindus teach that one of the ways to achieve union with God is through psychophysical exercises – what they refer to as 'raja yoga.' Huston Smith, *The World's Religions: Our Great Wisdom Traditions* (San Francisco: HarperCollins, 1991), 41.

[7] 1 Timothy 4:7-8.

[8] 2 Corinthians 4:16-18.

[9] John 10:10.

[10] The Taoists also speak of the need to 'repair' life, and to 'restore' the flow of ch'i or vital energy into our lives.

[11] Ephesians 3:16-17.

[12] In the Quran 48:4, God (i.e. Allah) is portrayed as actively working to strengthen believers: "It is He who from on high has bestowed inner peace upon the hearts of the believers so that . . . they might grow yet more firm in their faith." Zehra Ansari, "Islamic Psychology" in *Religious Theories of Personality and Psychotherapy: East Meets West,* ed., R. Paul Olson (New York: Hayworth Press, 2002), 349.

[13] The Sufi mystic, Ibn Arabi has described this spiritual process well, "A very solid cup has to be prepared to hold the increasingly burning wine of gnosis, and this solid cup can only be created in us by a desire to purify ourselves of every habit, disordered appetite, and fantasy that keeps us slaves to ourselves." Andrew Harvey and Eryk Hanut, *Perfume of the Desert: Inspiration from Sufi Wisdom* (Wheaton IL: Quest Books Theosophical Publishing House, 1999), 34.

[14] Paul DeBlassie III, *Deep Prayer: Healing for the Hurting* Soul (New York: The Crossroad Publishing House, 1990), 17.

[15] Tim Stafford, "The Squeeze" in *Victory over Temptation*, ed., Bruce H. Wilkinson (Eugene Oregon: Harvest House Publishers, 1998), 104-105.

[16] Richard Foster, *Life with God: Reading the Bible for Spiritual Transformation* (New York: Harper One, 2008), 9.

[17] Hinduism teaches that oneness with God can be achieved in four different ways: via the paths of knowledge, love, work, or psychophysical exercise. These paths are referred to as yogas. According to Huston Smith, "the word *yoga* derives from the same root as does the English word yoke." Huston Smith, *The World's Religions: Our Great Wisdom Traditions* (San Francisco: HarperCollins, 1991), 27.

[18] John 14:6.

[19] Hebrews 3:1.

[20] Hebrews 5:8-9.

Chapter 39

[1] Gerald G. May, *Addiction & Grace: Love and Spirituality in the Healing of Addictions* (New York: Harper Collins Publishers, 1988), 136.

[2] Richard J. Foster, *Celebration of Discipline: The Path to Spiritual Growth,* Revised Edition (San Francisco: Harper & Row, 1988), 8.

[3] Nate Larkin, *Samson and the Pirate Monks: Calling Men to Authentic Brotherhood* (Nashville: Thomas Nelson, Inc., 2006), 127.

[4] Leanne Payne, *The Healing Presence* (Westchester, IL: Crossway Books, 1989), 52.

[5] Ibid, 61.

[6] It is interesting to note that Taoist philosopher Chang Tzu wrote "Straighten up your body, unify your vision, and the harmony of Heaven will come to you. Call in your knowledge, unify your bearing, and the spirits will come to dwell with you. Virtue will be your beauty, the Way will be your home. . . ." Joseph A Loya, Wan-Li Ho, and Chang-Shin Jih, *The Tao of Jesus: An Experiment in Inter-Traditional Understanding* (New York/Mahwah NJ: Paulist Press, 1998), 123.

[7] Dale A. Matthews, *The Faith Factor: Proof of the Healing Power of* Prayer (New York: Viking Penguin, Penguin Putnam, 1998), 131-132.

[8] Ibid, 10.

[9] Frank Moore, *Breaking Free from Sin's Grip: Holiness Defined for a New Generation* (Kansas City: Beacon Hill Press, 2001), 91.

[10] M. Robert Mulholland, Jr., *Invitation to a Journey: A Road Map for Spiritual Formation* (Downer's Grove, IL: InterVarsity Press, 1993), 38.

[11] Ibid, 136.

[12] Terry H. Wardle, *The Transforming Path: A Christ-Centered Approach to Spiritual Formation* (Abilene TX: Leafwood Publishers, 2003), 21.

Chapter 40

[1] Gerald G. May, *Addiction & Grace: Love and Spirituality in the Healing of Addictions* (New York: Harper Collins Publishers, 1988), 105.

[2] Ibid, 17.

[3] Huston Smith, *The World's Religions: Our Great Wisdom Traditions* (San Francisco: HarperCollins, 1991), 211.

[4] Herbert Benson, *Timeless Healing: the Power and Biology of* Belief (New York: Scribner, 1996), 213.

[5] Benedict J. Groeschel, *Spiritual Passages: The Psychology of Spiritual Development* (New York: The Crossroad Publishing Company, 1983), 139.

[6] Richard J. Foster, *Celebration of Discipline: The Path to Spiritual Growth,* Revised Edition (San Francisco: Harper & Row, 1988), 96.

[7] Stephen Post and Jill Neimark, *Why Good Things Happen to Good People* (New York: Broadway Books, 2007), 40.

[8] Brian D. McLaren, *A Search for What is Real: Finding Faith* (Grand Rapids: Zondervan, 1999), 60.

[9] Taoists suggest that "quietness is needed to hear the whisper of the Tao." Lynne Hagen, "Taoism and Psychology" in *Religious Theories of Personality and Psychotherapy: East Meets West,* ed., R. Paul Olson (New York: Hayworth Press, 2002), 182.

[10] Charles Spurgeon, "An Antidote to Satan's Devices" in *Victory over Temptation*, ed., Bruce H. Wilkinson (Eugene Oregon: Harvest House Publishers, 1998), 165.

[11] There is a little story I remember reading once in which a cruel frog tries to scare some little fishes, by telling them they are in great danger – they will die without water. The little fishes start fretting and looking everywhere for this elusive and valuable substance. They don't realize they are already swimming in it. Agnes Sanford, *The Healing Light* (New York: Ballantine Books, 1972), 61-62.

[12] Acts 17:28.

[13] Joey Green, *The Zen of Oz: Ten Spiritual Lessons from Over the Rainbow* (Los Angeles: Renaissance Books, 1998), 44.

[14] Leanne Payne, *The Healing Presence* (Westchester, IL: Crossway Books, 1989), 178.

[15] Terry Wardle, *Healing Care Healing Prayer: Helping the Broken Find Wholeness in Christ* (Abilene TX: Leafwood Publishers, 2001), 102.

[16] Wes D Tracy, E Dee Freeborn, Janine Tartaglia, Morris A Weigelt, *The Upward Call: Spiritual Formation and the Holy Life* (Kansas City MS: Beacon Hill Press of Kansas City, 1994), 98.

[17] 2 Corinthians 6:16.

[18] Wes Tracy, Gary Cockerill, Donald Demaray, Steve Harper, *Reflecting God* (Kansas City MS: Beacon Hill Press of Kansas City, 2000), 100.

Chapter 41

[1] EEG studies of yoga meditation have revealed "no response in the yogis brain to external stimuli during meditation. In effect, concentration practices produce a state of relaxation by shutting out all distracting or anxiety arousing perceptions

and thoughts." Scott Kamilar, "A Buddhist Psychology" in *Religious Theories of Personality and Psychotherapy*, ed., R. Paul Olson (New York: Hayworth Press, 2002), 111.

2 Herbert Benson, *Timeless Healing: the Power and Biology of* Belief (New York: Scribner, 1996), 134.

3 Ibid, 135.

4 Patients they measured in Boston experienced an average 10 to 17 percent drop; and a monk in Sikkim experienced a 64 percent drop. Ibid, 166.

5 Benson describes a trip that he and his team took to visit some monasteries in Ladakh on the eastern fringe of the Tibetan plateau: "There, monks covered only by thin wool shawls and wearing only sandals on their feet spent the night . . . at 19,000 feet in zero and subzero temperatures. They were comfortably sustained by heat generated by their practice of g Tum-mo yoga, 'fierce woman,' or heat yoga. Practitioners elicit the relaxation response and then visualize themselves as having an inner channel passing from the center of their skulls through their torsos through which a heat drawn from the universe can travel, burning away defilements and improper thinking. In the same way a fierce woman protects her young, this heat burns away defilements to achieve purity." Ibid, 164.

6 Richard J. Foster, *Celebration of Discipline: The Path to Spiritual Growth,* Revised Edition (San Francisco: Harper & Row, 1988), 15.

7 Ibid, 20.

8 Ibid, 15.

9 Genesis 24:63.

10 We read that "The Lord would speak to Moses face to face, as a man speaks with his friend." (Exodus 33:11)

11 Psalm 63:6.

12 Henry David Thoreau wrote: "If I am to be a thoroughfare, I prefer that it be of the mountain brooks, the Parnassian streams, and not the town sewers. There is inspiration, that gossip which comes to the ear of the attentive mind from the courts of heaven. There is the profane and stale revelation of the barroom and the police court. The same ear is fitted to receive both communications. . . . We should treat our minds, that is, ourselves, as innocent and ingenuous children, whose guardians we are, and be careful what objects and what subjects we thrust on their attention. Read not the Times. Read the Eternities." Benjamin Hoff, *The Te of Piglet* (New York: Penguin Books USA Inc, 1992), 64-65.

13 Rhonda Byrne recommends making a list of 'secret shifters', which she defines as "things that can change your feelings in a snap. It might be beautiful memories, future events, funny moments, nature, a person you love, your favorite music." She goes on to suggest, "Then if you find yourself angry or frustrated or not feeling good, turn to your secret shifters list and focus on one of them . . . It only takes a minute or two of changing focus to shift yourself and shift

your frequency." Rhonda Byrne, *The Secret* (New York: Aria Books, 2006), 37.

[14] Phil Jackson, *Sacred Hoops: Spiritual Lessons of a Hardwood Warrior* (New York: Hyperion, 1995), 120.

[15] Ibid, 169.

[16] David G. Benner, *Psychotherapy and the Spiritual* Quest (Grand Rapids: Baker Book House Company, 1988), 88.

Chapter 42

[1] Matthew 5:8.

[2] Chang-Tzu offered similar counsel to his Chinese audience: "Seek . . . to keep your mind undivided. Dissolve all ideas into the Tao." Joseph A Loya, Wan-Li Ho, and Chang-Shin Jih, *The Tao of Jesus: An Experiment in Inter-Traditional Understanding* (New York/Mahwah NJ: Paulist Press, 1998), 156.

[3] 1 Peter 4:7.

[4] Larry Dossey, *Prayer is Good Medicine: How to Reap the Healing Benefits of Prayer* (San Francisco: HarperCollins Publishers, 1996), 104-105.

[5] 1 Thessalonians 5:17; Ephesians 6:18.

[6] Thomas Merton, quoted in Larry Dossey, *Prayer is Good Medicine: How to Reap the Healing Benefits of Prayer* (San Francisco: HarperCollins Publishers, 1996), 83.

[7] Taoist, Te-ch'ing, who lived from 1546-1623 A.D., wrote "Those who cultivate the Tao should first focus their minds. When the mind doesn't stray, it becomes calm. When the mind becomes calm, the breath becomes balanced. When the breath becomes balanced, essence becomes stable, spirit becomes serene, and our true nature is restored. Once we know how to breathe, we know how to endure. And once we know how to endure, we know our true nature. If we don't know our true nature but only know how to nourish our body and lengthen our lives, we end up harming our body and destroying our lives. A restless mind disturbs breath. When the breath is disturbed, the essence weakens. And when the essence weakens, the body withers." Joseph A Loya, Wan-Li Ho, and Chang-Shin Jih, *The Tao of Jesus: An Experiment in Inter-Traditional Understanding* (New York/Mahwah NJ: Paulist Press, 1998), 157.

[8] Wayne E. Oates, *Temptation: A Biblical and Psychological Approach* (Louisville KY: Westminster/John Knox Press, 1991), 72.

[9] Genesis 2:7.

[10] Calvin Miller, quoted in Terry Wardle, *Healing Care Healing Prayer: Helping the Broken Find Wholeness in Christ* (Abilene TX: Leafwood Publishers, 2001), 90.

[11] Matthew 11:28.

[12] Philippians 4:6-7.

[13] I love the following story told by Larry Dossey: "Abraham Lincoln had a rich prayer life and is regarded as one of our most spiritual presidents. In his early years he had intimations that meaningful work lay ahead for him but that he

would have to refine his skills if he was to fulfill his destiny. In his frontier environment, however, few tools or opportunities for professional development were available, and Lincoln feared that his hope would never be fulfilled. One day a stranger came by with a barrel full of odds and ends and old newspapers, and he offered to sell the lot to Lincoln for a dollar. Realizing the man was needy, Lincoln, with his characteristic kindness, gave him a dollar, although he had no idea how the barrel's contents would be of any use. When he later cleared out the barrel, he found among the junk an almost complete edition of Blackstone's 'Commentaries.' These books helped Lincoln become a lawyer and eventually enter politics." Reflecting upon this story, Dossey writes "The reverence and kindness Lincoln felt for others, which are often the fruits of prayer, created an opening for a life-changing event that otherwise might not have happened. Lincoln did not get zapped during prayer with a sudden revelation of his life's work. Humble ingredients – a barrel of junk, a stranger down on his luck, a dollar, and Lincoln's innate compassion – combined unspectacularly to help shape the destiny of a nation and affect millions of lives." Larry Dossey, *Prayer is Good Medicine: How to Reap the Healing Benefits of Prayer* (San Francisco: HarperCollins Publishers, 1996), 189-190.

[14] Romans 8:26-27.

[15] Wes Tracy, Gary Cockerill, Donald Demaray, Steve Harper, *Reflecting God* (Kansas City MS: Beacon Hill Press of Kansas City, 2000), 100.

[16] Mark 4:30-32.

[17] Phyllis Tickle, quoted in Tony Jones, *The Sacred Way: Spiritual Practices for Everyday* Life (Grand Rapids: Zondervan, 2005), 122.

[18] Gordon Mursell, quoted in Tony Jones, *The Sacred Way: Spiritual Practices for Everyday* Life (Grand Rapids: Zondervan, 2005), 131.

Chapter 43
[1] Henri Nowen, quoted in Tony Jones, *The Sacred Way: Spiritual Practices for Everyday* Life (Grand Rapids: Zondervan, 2005), 199.

[2] Romans 12:1.

[3] Pierre Tielhard De Chardin, quoted in Philip Yancey, *Rumors of Another World: What on Earth are We Missing?* (Grand Rapids: Zondervan Publishing House, 2003), 71.

[4] Richard J. Foster, *Celebration of Discipline: The Path to Spiritual Growth,* Revised Edition (San Francisco: Harper & Row, 1988), 13.

[5] Brian McLaren calls for "restoring a sacred normalcy to the rhythms of life." He suggests what we need is "a fusion of the sacred and the secular . . . an everyday sacredness." Brian McLaren, *Finding Our Way Again: The Return of the Ancient Practices* (Nashville: Thomas Nelson, 2008), 4-5.

[6] Marc Chagall, quoted in Herbert Benson, *Timeless Healing: the Power and*

Biology of Belief (New York: Scribner, 1996), 191.

[7] Emily Dickinson, quoted in Bernie Siegel and Jennifer Sander, *Faith, Hope & Healing: Inspiring Lessons Learned from People Living with Cancer* (Hoboken, NJ: John Wiley & Sons, Inc., 2009), 2-3.

[8] Ibid, 219.

[9] Stephen Post and Jill Neimark, *Why Good Things Happen to Good People* (New York: Broadway Books, 2007), 108.

[11] The Islamic tradition also emphasizes the importance of gratitude - that a 'lack of thankfulness' is the root of the human dilemma. "The Arabic word 'infidel' is actually shaded more towards 'one who lacks thankfulness' than one who disbelieves." [The thankfulness referred to here is that of acknowledging life as a gift from the Creator.] Huston Smith, *The World's Religions: Our Great Wisdom Traditions* (San Francisco: HarperCollins, 1991), 239.

[12] 1 Thessalonians 5:16-19.

[13] Peter Marshall and David Manuel, *The Light and the Glory* (Old Tappan NJ:Fleming H. Revell Company, 1977), 136.

[14] Abraham Maslow, quoted in Stephen Post and Jill Neimark, *Why Good Things Happen to Good People* (New York: Broadway Books, 2007), 28.

[15] Ibid, 246.

[16] Albert Schweitzer, quoted in Stephen Post and Jill Neimark, *Why Good Things Happen to Good People* (New York: Broadway Books, 2007), 35.

[17] Ibid, 10.

[18] Ibid, 31.

[19] Ibid, 31.

[20] Ibid, 34.

[21] Matthew 5:23-25.

[22] Stephen Post and Jill Neimark, *Why Good Things Happen to Good People* (New York: Broadway Books, 2007), 88-89.

[23] In the Buddhist tradition, the first experience of enlightenment is often associated with an outburst of laughter. The Buddha himself is often portrayed as laughing." Ibid, 144.

[24] Harry Emerson Fosdick, quoted in Stephen Post and Jill Neimark, *Why Good Things Happen to Good People* (New York: Broadway Books, 2007), 144.

[25] Ibid, 131

[26] Bernie Siegel and Jennifer Sander, *Faith, Hope & Healing: Inspiring Lessons Learned from People Living with Cancer* (Hoboken, NJ: John Wiley & Sons, Inc., 2009), 219.

[27] I have always liked the Hindu gesture of greeting referred to as 'Namaste', which consists of placing one's palms together with fingers facing up while bowing slightly before the other person. It signifies one's acknowledgement of

the divinity within the other person. Although I don't personally believe that we are all little 'gods,' I do believe we are created in God's image and have the capacity to be filled with the Divine Spirit.

[28] Catherine of Sienna, quoted in Paul DeBlassie III, *Deep Prayer: Healing for the Hurting* Soul (New York: The Crossroad Publishing House, 1990), 138.

[29] Stephen Post and Jill Neimark, *Why Good Things Happen to Good People* (New York: Broadway Books, 2007), 151.

[30] Lamentations 3:22-23.

[31] 2 Corinthians 1:3-4.

[32] Post and Neimark also state that "Pilot studies with Buddhist monks show that regular compassionate meditation may permanently change brain patterns leading to greater happiness." They point out that "of course, monks don't simply meditate on loving-kindness – they offer their lives in service to others in many ways." Stephen Post and Jill Neimark, *Why Good Things Happen to Good People* (New York: Broadway Books, 2007), 180, 187.

[33] Paul DeBlassie III, *Deep Prayer: Healing for the Hurting* Soul (New York: The Crossroad Publishing House, 1990), 6.

Chapter 44

[1] Matthew Fox, quoted in Wes D Tracy, E Dee Freeborn, Janine Tartaglia, Morris A Weigelt, *The Upward Call: Spiritual Formation and the Holy Life* (Kansas City MS: Beacon Hill Press of Kansas City, 1994), 204.

[2] The Dalai Lama has said, "If you engage in some service to others, give at least a short moment of happiness to others, including animals . . . then you get deep satisfaction. You get fulfillment of your existence." Stephen Post and Jill Neimark, *Why Good Things Happen to Good People* (New York: Broadway Books, 2007), 188.

[3] The Dalai Lama is also quoted as having said, "My religion is very simple. My religion is kindness." Larry Dossey, *Prayer is Good Medicine: How to Reap the Healing Benefits of Prayer* (San Francisco: HarperCollins Publishers, 1996), 198.

[4] Bernie Siegel and Jennifer Sander, *Faith, Hope & Healing: Inspiring Lessons Learned from People Living with Cancer* (Hoboken, NJ: John Wiley & Sons, Inc., 2009), 219.

[5] Galatians 5:13.

[6] Matthew 20:26-28.

[7] Richard Foster, quoted in Wes D Tracy, E Dee Freeborn, Janine Tartaglia, Morris A Weigelt, *The Upward Call: Spiritual Formation and the Holy Life* (Kansas City MS: Beacon Hill Press of Kansas City, 1994), 208.

[8] Ibid, 208.

[9] Colossians 3:23.

[10] Oswald Chambers, quoted in Wes D Tracy, E Dee Freeborn, Janine Tartaglia,

Morris A Weigelt, *The Upward Call: Spiritual Formation and the Holy Life* (Kansas City MS: Beacon Hill Press of Kansas City, 1994), 213.

[11] Wikipedia, Cycling 'domestique' - Definition

[12] Dale A. Matthews, *The Faith Factor: Proof of the Healing Power of* Prayer (New York: Viking Penguin, Penguin Putnam, 1998), 199.

[13] Ibid, 200.

[14] Ibid, 28.

[15] James 5:16.

[16] Larry Dossey, *Prayer is Good Medicine: How to Reap the Healing Benefits of Prayer* (San Francisco: HarperCollins Publishers, 1996), 106-107.

[17] Henri Nouwen, quoted in Bob Benson Sr. and Michael W Benson in *Disciplines for the Inner Life* (Nashville TN: Generoux Nelson, 1989), 105.

[18] Larry Dossey, *Prayer is Good Medicine: How to Reap the Healing Benefits of Prayer* (San Francisco: HarperCollins Publishers, 1996), 188.

[19] Ibid, 189.

[20] Ibid, 145.

[21] John Polkinghorne, quoted in Larry Dossey, *Prayer is Good Medicine: How to Reap the Healing Benefits of Prayer* (San Francisco: HarperCollins Publishers, 1996), 145-146

[22] Ibid, 146.

Chapter 45

[1] Chief Dan George of the Coast Salish, quoted in *The Wisdom of the Native Americans,* ed., Kent Nerburn (Novato CA: New World Library, 1999), 29-30.

[2] Ernest Kurtz and Katherine Ketcham, *The Spirituality of Imperfection: Storytelling and the Search for Meaning* (New York: Bantam Books, 1992), 230.

[3] Singer/songwriter, Sting echoes this in his lament "Some may say I'm a lost man in a lost world."

[4] Larry Crabb, quoted in Terry Wardle, *Healing Care Healing Prayer: Helping the Broken Find Wholeness in Christ* (Abilene TX: Leafwood Publishers, 2001), 71-72.

[5] Bernie Siegel and Jennifer Sander, *Faith, Hope & Healing: Inspiring Lessons Learned from People Living with Cancer* (Hoboken, NJ: John Wiley & Sons, Inc., 2009), 212.

[6] Dale A. Matthews, *The Faith Factor: Proof of the Healing Power of* Prayer (New York: Viking Penguin, Penguin Putnam, 1998), 250.

[7] Leanne Payne, *The Healing Presence* (Westchester, IL: Crossway Books, 1989), 52.

[8] An anonymous Shoshone Native American, quoted in *The Wisdom of the Native Americans,* ed., Kent Nerburn (Novato CA: New World Library, 1999), 31.

[9] Benedict J. Groeschel, *Spiritual Passages: The Psychology of Spiritual*

Development (New York: The Crossroad Publishing Company, 1983), 152.

[10] I Corinthians 10:13.

[11] James 5:16.

[12] Henri Nowen, quoted in Terry Wardle, *Healing Care Healing Prayer: Helping the Broken Find Wholeness in Christ* (Abilene TX: Leafwood Publishers, 2001), 40.

[13] The 6th-Century Saint Brigit of Ireland advised people to forgo eating until they had found a soul friend, because in her opinion "anyone without a soul friend is like a body without a head." Wes D Tracy, E Dee Freeborn, Janine Tartaglia, Morris A Weigelt, *The Upward Call: Spiritual Formation and the Holy Life* (Kansas City MS: Beacon Hill Press of Kansas City, 1994), 169.

[14] The eighteenth-century preacher John Wesley wrote "It is a blessed thing to have fellow travelers to the New Jerusalem. If you do not find any you must make them, for none can travel this road alone." Ibid, 137.

[15] Justifying the need for this type of friendship, Wesley wrote "The Lord has given us to each other, that we may strengthen each other's hands." Ibid, 148.

[16] Luciano de Crescenzo, quoted in Wes Tracy, Gary Cockerill, Donald Demaray, Steve Harper, *Reflecting God* (Kansas City MS: Beacon Hill Press of Kansas City, 2000), 127.

[17] Wes D Tracy, E Dee Freeborn, Janine Tartaglia, Morris A Weigelt, *The Upward Call: Spiritual Formation and the Holy Life* (Kansas City MS: Beacon Hill Press of Kansas City, 1994), 135.

[18] Philip Yancey, *What Good is God? In Search of a Faith that Matters* (New York: FaithWords –Hachette Book Group, 2010), 250-252.

[19] Hebrews 3:12-14.

[20] Wes D Tracy, E Dee Freeborn, Janine Tartaglia, Morris A Weigelt, *The Upward Call: Spiritual Formation and the Holy Life* (Kansas City MS: Beacon Hill Press of Kansas City, 1994), 146.

[21] Benedict J. Groeschel, *Spiritual Passages: The Psychology of Spiritual Development* (New York: The Crossroad Publishing Company, 1983), 49-50.

[22] Hebrews 10:24-25.

[23] St. Vincent de Paul used to say "Love the poor and your life will be filled with sunlight." Benedict J. Groeschel, *Spiritual Passages: The Psychology of Spiritual Development* (New York: The Crossroad Publishing Company, 1983), 50.

[24] Stephen Post and Jill Neimark, *Why Good Things Happen to Good People* (New York: Broadway Books, 2007), 131.

[25] Colossians 3:15-16.

[26] It is the 'secret' of which the Muslim, Sultan Valad spoke so eloquently about: "Through the passion of the fire of love in the furnace of absolute sincerity. How else can you free yourself from the veils of your existence and become drunk on God? Yes, you must be born twice, once from your mother; And the second time from yourself. You have passed already through the first birth, now strive to

attain the second so you can know the secret of Union. Dedicate your soul to the path of reality so you can receive the help and teaching of God." Andrew Harvey and Eryk Hanut, *Perfume of the Desert: Inspiration from Sufi Wisdom* (Wheaton IL: Quest Books Theosophical Publishing House, 1999), 39-40.

Chapter 46
[1] Benedict J. Groeschel, *Spiritual Passages: The Psychology of Spiritual Development* (New York: The Crossroad Publishing Company, 1983), 165.
[2] 1 Peter 2:25.
[3] Psalm 23 (The Message).
[4] The Judeo-Christian tradition is not the only one that uses the metaphor of the tree for the spiritual life. For example, a primary goal of Taoism is to arrive at a state of being known as *Wu wei* , which is to become sensitive to both one's own inner nature and to the natural rhythms of the universe (i.e. natural world). "Wu wei is embodied in the allegory of the mighty oak and willow tree. When covered with heavy snow, the rigid oak branches crack under the weight of the snow. The willow branch, however, yields to the snow's weight lowering itself and allowing the snow to fall off. The willow is not flaccid, but flexible, resourceful, and resilient. It bends with the forces of nature and allows its branches to remain whole and unbroken." Lynne Hagen, "Taoism and Psychology" in *Religious Theories of Personality and Psychotherapy: East Meets West,* ed., R. Paul Olson (New York: Hayworth Press, 2002), 152.
[5] Lynne Hagen writes "The purpose of Taoist therapy is to assist clients in being comfortable with their genuine self so that they feel free to 'sprout, blossom, and yield fruit as they dance in the breeze of life.'" The goal of becoming a Sage in the Taoist tradition is to find emotional and spiritual balance. Ibid, 174.
[6] Psalm 1.
[7] Galatians 5:22-23.
[8] Wes Tracy, Gary Cockerill, Donald Demaray, Steve Harper, *Reflecting God* (Kansas City MS: Beacon Hill Press of Kansas City, 2000), 135.
[9] Leanne Payne, *The Healing Presence* (Westchester, IL: Crossway Books, 1989), 217.
[10] Oswald Chambers, quoted in Wes Tracy, Gary Cockerill, Donald Demaray, Steve Harper, *Reflecting God* (Kansas City MS: Beacon Hill Press of Kansas City, 2000), 87.
[11] M. Robert Mulholland, Jr., *Invitation to a Journey: A Road Map for Spiritual Formation* (Downer's Grove, IL: InterVarsity Press, 1993), 98.
[12] Gregory of Nyssa, quoted in Leanne Payne, *The Healing Presence* (Westchester, IL: Crossway Books, 1989), 37.
[13] Benedict J. Groeschel, *Spiritual Passages: The Psychology of Spiritual Development* (New York: The Crossroad Publishing Company, 1983), 164.

---

¹⁴ Ibid, 173

¹⁵ Trappist monk, Thomas Merton wrote "I have only one desire . . . to disappear into God, to be submerged in His peace, to be lost in the secret of His face." Paul DeBlassie III, *Deep Prayer: Healing for the Hurting* Soul (New York: The Crossroad Publishing House, 1990), 105.

¹⁶ Richard J. Foster, *Celebration of Discipline: The Path to Spiritual Growth,* Revised Edition (San Francisco: Harper & Row, 1988), 79.

¹⁷ Ibid, 80

¹⁸ Quaker scholar and author, Thomas Kelly encouraged people to live out of the "Divine Center."

¹⁹ Richard J. Foster, *Celebration of Discipline: The Path to Spiritual Growth,* Revised Edition (San Francisco: Harper & Row, 1988), 79.

Chapter 47

¹ Benedict J. Groeschel, *Spiritual Passages: The Psychology of Spiritual Development* (New York: The Crossroad Publishing Company, 1983), 43.

² Yuichiro Miura, quoted in Ernest Kurtz and Katherine Ketcham, *The Spirituality of Imperfection: Storytelling and the Search for Meaning* (New York: Bantam Books, 1992), 155.

³ Once the Buddha reached the state of nirvana, and had broken free from suffering, rather than simply continuing to remain in a state of meditative bliss he chose to devote the rest of his earthly life to helping others along the spiritual path to freedom. He exemplified the concept of *Bodhisattva* – one who puts off one's own liberation to relieve the suffering of others. The *Sage* of the Taoist tradition "is ever hopeful and this hope gives strength to persevere despite pain and suffering. The Sage openly shares this belief in hope openly and feely with others, in a manner reminiscent of the Bodhisattva's concern for others in the Buddhist tradition." Lynne Hagen, "Taoism and Psychology" in *Religious Theories of Personality and Psychotherapy: East Meets West,* ed., R. Paul Olson (New York: Hayworth Press, 2002), 165.

⁴ A Muslim author of the eighth century, Abu Sai'id wrote that being a *Perfect Sufi* does not mean being "an ecstatic devotee lost in contemplation of Oneness, nor a saintly recluse shunning all commerce with mankind; but the true saint goes in and out amongst the people and eats and sleeps with them and buys and sells in the market and takes part in social intercourse and never forgets God for a single moment." Andrew Harvey and Eryk Hanut, *Perfume of the Desert: Inspiration from Sufi Wisdom* (Wheaton IL: Quest Books Theosophical Publishing House, 1999), 140.

⁵ An interesting and relevant Sufi story is as follows: "A man walking through the forest saw a fox that had lost its legs, and he wondered how it lived. Then he saw a tiger come up with game in its mouth. The tiger ate its fill and left the rest of

the meat for the fox. The next day God fed the fox by means of the same tiger. The man began to wonder at God's greatness and said to himself, 'I too shall just rest in a corner with full trust in the Lord and he will provide me with all I need.' He did this for many days but nothing happened, and he was almost at death's door when he heard a voice say, 'O you who are in the path of error, open your eyes to the truth! Stop imitating the disabled fox and follow the example of the tiger.'" Ernest Kurtz and Katherine Ketcham, *The Spirituality of Imperfection: Storytelling and the Search for Meaning* (New York: Bantam Books, 1992), 93.

[6] The *Warrior* of Native American culture is altruistic and spiritual. In the Lakota tradition "A warrior didn't try to stand out from his fellow band members; he strove to act bravely and honorably, to help the group in whatever way he could to accomplish its mission. If glory befell him, he was obligated to give away his most prize possessions to relatives, friends, the poor, and the aged. As a result, the leaders of the tribe were often its poorest members." Phil Jackson, *Sacred Hoops: Spiritual Lessons of a Hardwood Warrior* (New York: Hyperion, 1995), 109.

[7] Elaine E. Hartsman, "Jewish Anthropology: The Stuff Between," in *Religious Theories of Personality and Psychotherapy*, ed., R. Paul Olson (New York: Hayworth Press, 2002), 224.

[8] Gerald G. May, *The Dark Night of the Soul: A Psychiatrist Explores the Connection Between Darkness and Spiritual Growth* (New York: Harper Collins Publishers, Inc., 2004), 49.

[9] Matthew Fox, quoted in Wes D Tracy, E Dee Freeborn, Janine Tartaglia, Morris A Weigelt, *The Upward Call: Spiritual Formation and the Holy Life* (Kansas City MS: Beacon Hill Press of Kansas City, 1994), 224.

[10] In the Buddhist tradition, the practice of personal spiritual disciplines gives birth to compassion, which in turn gives birth to celebration. According to Chogyam Trungpa, a Tibetan Buddhist meditation master: "We must begin our practice by walking the narrow path of simplicity, the Hinayana path, before we can walk upon the open highway of compassionate action, the Mahayana path. And only after our highway journey is well on its way need we concern ourselves about how to dance in the fields – the Vajrayana or tantric teachings." Scott Kamilar, "A Buddhist Psychology" in *Religious Theories of Personality and Psychotherapy*, ed., R. Paul Olson (New York: Hayworth Press, 2002), 88.

[11] Taoist philosopher Lao Tzu posed a rhetorical question: "How can one liberate the many?" In reply he said "By first liberating his own being. He does this not by elevating himself, but by lowering himself. He lowers himself to that which is simple and modest and truthful, and by integrating it into himself, he becomes a master of simplicity, modesty, truth." Joseph A Loya, Wan-Li Ho, and Chang-Shin Jih, *The Tao of Jesus: An Experiment in Inter-Traditional Understanding* (New York/Mahwah NJ: Paulist Press, 1998), 118.

[12] Ernest Kurtz and Katherine Ketcham, *The Spirituality of Imperfection:*

Storytelling and the Search for Meaning (New York: Bantam Books, 1992), 96-97.

[13] Frederick Buechner, quoted in Wes Tracy, Gary Cockerill, Donald Demaray, Steve Harper, *Reflecting God* (Kansas City MS: Beacon Hill Press of Kansas City, 2000), 143.

[14] Richard J. Foster, *Celebration of Discipline: The Path to Spiritual Growth,* Revised Edition (San Francisco: Harper & Row, 1988), 190-191.

[15] Wes Tracy, Gary Cockerill, Donald Demaray, Steve Harper, *Reflecting God* (Kansas City MS: Beacon Hill Press of Kansas City, 2000), 160.

[16] Gerald G. May, *Addiction & Grace: Love and Spirituality in the Healing of Addictions* (New York: Harper Collins Publishers, 1988), 90.

[17] Proverbs 16:18.

[18] Galatians 6:1.

[19] 1 Corinthians 10:12.

[20] 1 Corinthians 9:26-27.

Chapter 48

[1] Richard J. Foster, *Celebration of Discipline: The Path to Spiritual Growth,* Revised Edition (San Francisco: Harper & Row, 1988), 193.

[2] Ibid, 201.

[3] Ibid, 191.

[4] Ibid, 190.

[5] John 15:10-16.

[6] John Wesley, quoted in Wes Tracy, Gary Cockerill, Donald Demaray, Steve Harper, *Reflecting God* (Kansas City MS: Beacon Hill Press of Kansas City, 2000), 87.

[7] Catherine of Genoa, quoted in Benedict J. Groeschel, *Spiritual Passages: The Psychology of Spiritual Development* (New York: The Crossroad Publishing Company, 1983), 79.

[8] Gerald G. May, *Addiction & Grace: Love and Spirituality in the Healing of Addictions* (New York: Harper Collins Publishers, 1988), 216.

[9] Rabi'a of Bosra, an eighth-century Muslim nun, portrays this type of love for God rather poignantly in the form of a prayer: "O God, whatsoever thou has apportioned to me of worldly things, do thou give that to my enemies; and whatsoever thou has apportioned to me in the world to come, give that to thy friends; for thou suffices me. O God, if I worship thee for fear of Hell, burn me in Hell, and if I worship thee in hope of Paradise, exclude me from Paradise; but if I worship thee for thy own sake, grudge me not thy everlasting beauty." Benedict J. Groeschel, *Spiritual Passages: The Psychology of Spiritual Development* (New York: The Crossroad Publishing Company, 1983), 15.

[10] Leanne Payne, *The Healing Presence* (Westchester, IL: Crossway Books, 1989), 181.

[11] Benedict J. Groeschel, *Spiritual Passages: The Psychology of Spiritual Development* (New York: The Crossroad Publishing Company, 1983), 191.
[12] Therese of Lisieux, quoted in Paul DeBlassie III, *Deep Prayer: Healing for the Hurting* Soul (New York: The Crossroad Publishing House, 1990), 105.
[13] Ernest Kurtz and Katherine Ketcham, *The Spirituality of Imperfection: Storytelling and the Search for Meaning* (New York: Bantam Books, 1992), 49.
[14] Lao-tzu wrote in the Tao Te Ching, "Be content with what you have; Rejoice in the way things are. When you realize there is nothing lacking, the whole world belongs to you." Joey Green, *The Zen of Oz: Ten Spiritual Lessons from Over the Rainbow* (Los Angeles: Renaissance Books, 1998), 131.
[15] Lao-tzu also stated that "to know harmony is to be in accord with the eternal Tao." Joseph A Loya, Wan-Li Ho, and Chang-Shin Jih, *The Tao of Jesus: An Experiment in Inter-Traditional Understanding* (New York/Mahwah NJ: Paulist Press, 1998), 156.
[16] Writing from a Taoist perspective, Huston Smith gives the following advice "Let anxiety be dispelled and harmony between the mind and its cosmic source will come unsought." Huston Smith, *The World's Religions: Our Great Wisdom Traditions* (San Francisco: HarperCollins, 1991), 203.
[17] The Native American Black Elk wrote "Peace . . . comes within the souls of men when they realize their relationship, their oneness with the Universe and all its powers, and when they realize that at the center of the Universe dwells the Great Spirit, and that center is really everywhere. It is within each of us." Phil Jackson, *Sacred Hoops: Spiritual Lessons of a Hardwood Warrior* (New York: Hyperion, 1995), 109.
[18] The highest stage in the three-stage theory of spiritual development, postulated by the Muslim Al Gahzali, is called *nafs Mutmainnah* – the satisfied soul. A satisfied soul is said to be "in a state of bliss, contentment, and peace. The soul is at peace because it knows that in spite of its failures in this world it will return to God." Zehra Ansari, "Islamic Psychology" in *Religious Theories of Personality and Psychotherapy: East Meets West,* ed., R. Paul Olson (New York: Hayworth Press, 2002), 341.
[19] Agnes Sanford, *The Healing Light* (New York: Ballantine Books, 1972), 61.
[20] Paul DeBlassie III, *Deep Prayer: Healing for the Hurting* Soul (New York: The Crossroad Publishing House, 1990), 82-83.

Chapter 49
[1] Benedict J. Groeschel, *Spiritual Passages: The Psychology of Spiritual Development* (New York: The Crossroad Publishing Company, 1983), 43.
[2] Galatians 5:25.
[3] Doug Pagitt and Tony Jones (editors), *An Emergent Manifesto of Hope* (Grand Rapids, MI: Baker Books, 2007), 241.

---

4 Ernest Kurtz and Katherine Ketcham, *The Spirituality of Imperfection: Storytelling and the Search for Meaning* (New York: Bantam Books, 1992), 131.
5 Benedict J. Groeschel, *Spiritual Passages: The Psychology of Spiritual Development* (New York: The Crossroad Publishing Company, 1983), 160.
6 M. Robert Mulholland, Jr., *Invitation to a Journey: A Road Map for Spiritual Formation* (Downer's Grove, IL: InterVarsity Press, 1993), 79-80.
7 Gerald G. May, *The Dark Night of the Soul: A Psychiatrist Explores the Connection Between Darkness and Spiritual Growth* (New York: Harper Collins Publishers, Inc., 2004), 187.
8 Henry Miller, quoted in Ernest Kurtz and Katherine Ketcham, *The Spirituality of Imperfection: Storytelling and the Search for Meaning* (New York: Bantam Books, 1992), 138.
9 In the words of T.S. Eliot "We shall not cease from exploration; and the end of all our exploring will be to arrive where we started, and know the place for the first time." T.S. Eliot, quoted in Ernest Kurtz and Katherine Ketcham, *The Spirituality of Imperfection: Storytelling and the Search for Meaning* (New York: Bantam Books, 1992), 138.
10 The Taoists speak of recovering a state of innocence and purity referred to as "the uncarved block."
11 Asha Mukherjee, "Hindu Psychology and the *Bhagavad Gita*" in *Religious Theories of Personality and Psychotherapy: East Meets West*, ed., R. Paul Olson (New York: Hayworth Press, 2002), 70.
12 Elaine E. Hartsman, "Jewish Anthropology: The Stuff Between," in *Religious Theories of Personality and Psychotherapy*, ed., R. Paul Olson (New York: Hayworth Press, 2002), 231.
13 Paul Tournier, *The Healing of Persons* (New York: Harper & Row Publishers, 1965), xx.
14 Gerald G. May, *Addiction & Grace: Love and Spirituality in the Healing of Addictions* (New York: Harper Collins Publishers, 1988), 180.
15 Wes Tracy, Gary Cockerill, Donald Demaray, Steve Harper, *Reflecting God* (Kansas City MS: Beacon Hill Press of Kansas City, 2000), 78.
16 Ibid, 78.
17 Malachi 4:2-3.

CPSIA information can be obtained at www.ICGtesting.com
Printed in the USA
LVOW101605080413

328163LV00016B/994/P